o JL 18
∧ JL 30 Y1

2

D1548215

CELTIC STUDIES

Essays in memory of Angus Matheson

Angus Matheson, 1912–1962

Angus Matheson was born in Borve, Harris, on 1st July, 1912, the younger son of Malcolm Matheson and Mary Murray, both natives of Lewis. When he was three years old the family moved to Sollas, North Uist, and it was in this Gaelic-speaking community that he spent his early years. He was educated at the local school and afterwards at Tarbert, Harris, and Inverness Royal Academy. At Edinburgh University he had a distinguished record in all his classes, and graduated with first class honours in Celtic in 1934. Having won the McCaig Scholarship in Celtic by competitive examination, he continued his studies for a year with Osborn Bergin and J. Lloyd-Jones in Dublin, followed by a second year in Bonn with Rudolf Thurneysen. Returning to his Alma Mater, he was assistant to W. J. Watson in the department of Celtic from 1936 to 1938, when he was appointed McCallum-Fleming Lecturer in Celtic in Glasgow University. On the outbreak of war he was seconded to the monitoring service of the B.B.C., with special responsibility for listening-in to propaganda broadcast from Germany in Irish. During the later stages of the war he was on army service with the Intelligence Corps. Because of his knowledge of German much of his work was concerned with the decipherment of enemy signals in code. He saw service in France and Belgium following the invasion of Europe in 1944, and the end of the war found him on his way to India. Soon after taking up duties once more at Glasgow University he was promoted Senior Lecturer, and when the chair of Celtic was founded in 1956 he became its first incumbent. He married Christina Macraild, with issue a son and a daughter. He died on 2nd November, 1962.

A portrait of Angus Matheson

CELTIC STUDIES

Essays in memory of

ANGUS MATHESON

1912—1962

Edited by

James Carney and David Greene

NEW YORK

BARNES & NOBLE, INC.

First published in Great Britain
by Routledge & Kegan Paul Ltd.

Published in the United States of America 1968
by Barnes & Noble, Inc., New York, N.Y.

© The Gaelic Society of Glasgow 1968

Printed in Great Britain

CONTENTS

CONTENTS

Ach-an Dà Theàrnaidh

Do'n Ollamh Aonghus Mac Mhathain

Tha an soirbheas o Lochlann
A nochd am bàrr sléibhe
Air na bearraidhean Aillseach,
    Far na chaisgeadh an léir-chreach;
Far na stadadh na Tuathaich
    Ged a bhuail iad an Eòrpa;
Far robh Fearchar 's am Mathan,
    Fir gu tilleadh na tòrachd.

Ged tha 'n Tuathach 's an Gàidheal
    Ri spàirn 'na mo chuislean,
'S e plosgadh na cainnte
    Chuireas ainm air an t-sruthadh;
Ged thug mi o m' shìnnsre
    Leth mo dhìlsean o'n Tuathach,
'S i a' Ghàidhlig thug briathran
    Do fhiaradh mo dhualchais.

Tha am foghlum a' drùdhadh
    O dhùthchas 's o dhualchas:
Gun do choisrig a' Ghàidhlig
    Fearann àlainn l' a buadhan.
Làmh fhuilteach a' Mhathain
    Ann an altan na cànain . . .
Sin aon rud a thuigear
    Aig Ach-an-Dà-Theàrnaidh.

An còrr cha do thuig mi,
    'S cha thuig mi gu bràth e:
Dé chuir Fearchar 's am Mathan
    'S gach fear gus an àraich;
Ma tha 'n Tuathach 's an Gàidheal
    An suaimhneas 'nam chnàmhan,
Dé a b'fhiach fear seach fear dhiùbh
    Ach mar mheasar a chànan?

Bha na leanabain Sgitheanach
Air an spealtadh le pìcean
Gus am bruidhnteadh a' Ghàidhlig
Ann am bailtean Clàr Sgìthe:
Gum biodh Asgallach, Neacallach,
Suaineach is Leòdach
Cho labhar 'nar cànain
Ri Cloinn Mhathain 's Cloinn Dòmhnaill.

Tha na bearraidhean geàrrte
Ann am maise an ioghnaidh,
'S tha Ach-an-Dà-Theàrnaidh
Air a dheiltreadh thar smaointean
Le leathadan gorma
'S le bhadan de choille,
'S tha gaisgich Chloinn Mhathain
An Cille-Chomhghain 'nan doille.

Ach cuid dhiùbh air fògradh
N'as fhaide na 'n clachan
Far bheil ginealan Aillseach
'Nan daimh fo'n an talamh:
Cuid thug sgrìob thar an eòlais
Air rathad fada as giorra
Gus am faigheadh iad tòrradh
Air Sliabh gòrach an t-Siorraim.

Ma thug iadsan a' choiseachd
Bho Ach-an-Dà-Theàrnaidh
Gu amaideas Sheumais
Chur thar burraidheachd Sheòrais,
'S ann a b'fhaoin dhaibh an t-astar
Thug gu faiche a' bhàis iad . . .
Their cuid eile gun d'fhalbh iad
Air sgàth na h-Albann 's na Gàidhlig.

SOMHAIRLE MAC GHILLEATHAIN

PUBLICATIONS OF

PROFESSOR ANGUS MATHESON

BOOKS

1954 *Carmina Gadelica: Hymns and Incantations* . . . Orally collected in the Highlands and Islands of Scotland by Alexander Carmichael. Vol. V. Edinburgh. (Editor.)

1960 *More West Highland Tales:* Transcribed and translated from the original Gaelic MSS. [in the Collection of John Francis Campbell of Islay] by J. G. Mackay. Vol. II. Edinburgh and London. (Joint Editor.)

Carmina Gadelica, vol. VI, Indexes. (In preparation.)

Bishop Carswell's Liturgy. (Co-editor.) (In preparation.)

CONTRIBUTIONS TO PERIODICALS

1939 'A Traditional Account of the Appin Murder.' *Transactions of the Gaelic Society of Inverness,* vol. XXXV, pp. 343–404. Inverness.

1940 'Macc-shlabra.' *Éigse,* vol. II, pp. 45–6. Dublin.

1946 'A Ughdar so Fearchar mac Phádraig Grannd.' *Ibid.,* vol. V, pp. 156–7.

1946 'A Proposed Emendation in Táin Bó Fraích.' *Ibid.,* p. 157.

1948 'Some Notes on the Morrisons.' *Ibid.,* vol. VI, pp. 56–8.

1948 'Varia [Lexicographical Notes].' *Ibid.,* pp. 59–69.

1948 'W. J. Watson [Obituary].' *Ibid.,* pp. 70–1.

1950 'Sgoltadh a' bhradain fhìor-uisg' ort.' *Ibid.,* pp. 180–1.

1950 'The Woman who chose her Brother.' *Ibid.,* p. 181.

1950 'Some Proverbs and Proverbial Expressions from Lewis.' *The Journal of Celtic Studies,* vol. I, pp. 105–15. Temple University, Baltimore.

1951 'Some Textual Notes on the Poems of Alexander MacDonald.' *Éigse,* vol. VI, pp. 265–9.

1951 'Sgoltadh a' bhradain fhìor-uisg' ort.' *Ibid.,* p. 270.

1951 'Bishop Carswell and Bardic Poetry.' *Ossian,* pp. 30–1. Inverness.

1952 'Air Chùl an t-Saoghail.' *Gairm,* vol. I, pp. 67–70. Stirling.

1953 'Gleanings from the Dornie Manuscripts.' *Transactions of the Gaelic Society of Inverness,* vol. XLI, pp. 310–81. Inverness.

1954 'Aos Dàna.' *Gairm,* vol. II, pp. 343–7; vol. III, pp. 33–6, 124–9.

1956 'Some Words from Gaelic Folktales.' *Éigse,* vol. VIII, pp. 247–58.

1956 'Miscellanea.' *Ibid.,* pp. 259–60.

1957 'The Department of Celtic in the University of Glasgow.' *Ossian,* pp. 23–6. Glasgow.

1958 'Traditions of Alasdair mac Colla.' *Transactions of the Gaelic Society of Glasgow*, vol. V, pp. 9–93. Stirling.

1958 'Documents connected with the Trial of Sir James MacDonald of Islay.' *Ibid.*, pp. 207–22.

1958 'Scottish Gaelic Language and Literature.' *Everyman's Encyclopaedia*, vol. XI, pp. 182–5. Fourth edition. London.

[1959] 'Tàladh Choinnich Oig.' *Ossian*, pp. 18–19. Stornoway.

1960 'Review of *The Highlands* by Calum I. Maclean.' (London, Batsford, 1959.) *The Scottish Historical Review*, vol. XXXIX, pp. 137–9.

1963 'Review of *Monro's Western Isles of Scotland and Genealogies of the Clans* 1549 by R. W. Munro.' (Edinburgh, Oliver & Boyd, 1961.) *Ibid.*, vol. XLII, pp. 48–51.

1963/4 'Poems from a Manuscript of Cathal Mac Muireadhaigh.' *Éigse*, vol. X, pp. 270–8; vol. XI, pp. 1–17.

1965 'Bishop Carswell.' *Transactions of the Gaelic Society of Inverness*, vol. XLII, pp. 182–205. Stirling.

JOHN BANNERMAN

The Dál Riata and Northern Ireland in the sixth and seventh centuries

Whether the Dál Riata had settled in Scotland before the advent of Fergus Mór mac Eirc *c.* 500 is open to argument, but there is little doubt that in his person the Dalriadic dynasty removed from Ireland to Scotland. The question which we will attempt to answer in this paper is for how long and by what means the two sections of the Dál Riata, the one in Scotland and the other in Ireland, remained united under the rule of Fergus Mór's descendants.

There is no indication that Fergus Mór relinquished his authority over his Irish territories when he left for Scotland. The genealogy of the Irish domiciled royal family of the Dál Riata comes to an end with Fergus Mór; or rather there is no named king of Dál Riata, other than those who became kings of Dál Riata in Scotland, for many years after Fergus Mór flourished.[1] But the first positive evidence for the assumption that Fergus Mór and his immediate successors continued to rule Dál Riata in Ireland is the Convention of Druim Cett.[2] This assembly was convened in 575[3] to discuss the future status of the Irish Dál Riata in relation, on the one hand, to Aed, son of Ainmire (d. 598), leader of the Northern Uí Néill, the most powerful people in the north of Ireland at that time, and, on the other, to Aedán mac Gabráin, king of Dál Riata in Scotland (d. *c.* 608).[4] According to the accounts of the proceedings which have come down to us there is no question but that Aedán was also considered to be king of the Irish Dál Riata. The Convention of Druim Cett itself more or less confirmed the Scottish dynasty in this position, for it was finally decided that, although the right to the armed forces of Dál Riata in Ireland should go in future to Aed, son of Ainmire, as overlord of Northern Ireland, Aedán should continue to levy taxes and tributes,[5] which meant that effective government of the territory

I

was to remain in the hands of Aedán and his successors for as long as they could prove capable of retaining it.

Dál Riata in Ireland formed part of the historical province of Ulster which corresponded more or less to the present-day counties of Antrim and Down.[6] The Dál Riata, established along the Antrim coast, shared the province with two other peoples, namely, the Dál Fiatach, often called the Ulaid,[7] on the coast of Down, and the Dál nAraide or Cruithne[8] in the interior. The province of Ulster or Ulaid, as distinct from the people Ulaid, was ruled in turn by the kings of the Dál Fiatach and of the Dál nAraide, no doubt depending on which was the more powerful at the time. Thus, the list of the kings of Ulster entitled *Ríg Ulad* in the *Book of Leinster* (LL)[9] shows that approximately fifteen kings of the Dál Fiatach[10] were thought to have held this position during the period *c.* 500–*c.* 800 as compared with nine or ten of the Dál nAraide. There is much evidence in the annals of enmity between these two peoples, probably arising, in part at least, from the rival claims of their leaders to authority over the whole province. It is chiefly within this framework that the known history of the Dál Riata in Ireland should be seen to fit.

The first reference to a king of the province of Ulster in connection with the Dál Riata is to Báetán mac Cairill of the Dál Fiatach who died in 581 AU.[11] He is named as one of the seven leaders of the Dál Fiatach who were also kings of Ireland in a passage in LL[12] which goes on to state: *giallais Aedán mac Gabráin dó i rRoss na Ríg i Semniu,* 'Aedán, son of Gabrán, submitted to him in Ros-na-ríg in Semne' (Island Magee). It is unlikely that this event took place before 574 the year in which Aedán became king of Dál Riata, for not until then would his submission to Báetán be noteworthy or even likely. Indeed, the Convention of Druim Cett in 575 may also have preceded it, for the importance of Báetán, at least in Northern Ireland, implicit in the claim that he was king of Ireland, is difficult to reconcile with the role of Aed, son of Ainmire, at the Convention. Aed, as leader of the Uí Néill for whom the title king or high-king of Ireland was usually reserved,[13] demanded certain rights from Dál Riata in Ireland, a part of Báetán's own province of Ulster. Báetán's claim to be king of Ireland is repeated elsewhere[14] and it is possible that he usurped Aed's position of authority in the north for a time, but presumably not until after the Convention of Druim Cett, which would explain why there is no mention of him in the accounts of this event.

No doubt it was for his Irish territories that Aedán made submission to Báetán and it may be that he was forced to hand over part or all of the tribute due to him from the Irish Dál Riata, in which he had been confirmed at the Convention of Druim Cett.[15] Certainly such a move on Báetán's part on becoming the major power in Northern Ireland is a likely one.[16]

Finding the Dál Riata in opposition to the Dál Fiatach at this time, we might look for evidence of an alliance or, at the least, friendly relations between them and the third people of Ulster, the Dál nAraide. This is certainly the position in the first half of the seventh century but there is the possibility that it began much earlier. Thus, Adomnán tells us that Aed Dub mac Suibne, king of the Dál nAraide, who died in 588, spent part of his life among the Scottish Dál Riata as a cleric.[17] It may be that he was forced to take refuge in Scotland as a result of killing Diarmait, son of Cerball, of the Southern Uí Néill in 565. Adomnán does not correlate the two events in this way but he does say that Aed Dub had already killed Diarmait by the time he arrived in Scotland.[18] We are told further that he eventually returned to Ireland and in the *Ríg Ulad* we find (omitting Daig mac Cairill)[19] that he succeeded Báetán mac Cairill as king of Ulster.[20]

The opening of the seventh century saw the first recorded clash between the Dál nAraide and the Dál Fiatach, the first of many such, no doubt frequently arising from the aspirations of one or other of their leaders to be overlord of all Ulster. Thus, in 602, according to AU, they fought the battle of Cul Coil:

> Bellum Cule coil in quo Fiachna mac Demain fuigit. Fiachna mac Baetan victor erat.[21]

Fiachna mac Báetáin[22] of the Dál nAraide became king of Ulster in succession to Aed Dub, while Fiachna mac Demmáin, a nephew of Báetán mac Cairill, was king of the Dál Fiatach.

Fiachna mac Báetáin figures again in the Old Irish story entitled *Compert Mongáin*,[23] 'Birth of Mongán',[24] as an ally of Aedán mac Gabráin in a campaign *fri Saxanu*, 'against the Saxons'. Did Fiachna lead or send a force to Degsastan in 603?[25] At any rate, this is the first hint we possess in point of time to a military alliance between the Dál nAraide and the Dál Riata.

In 626 AU Fiachna mac Báetáin was killed by Fiachna mac Demmáin at the battle of Lethet Midind.

Bellum Leithet midind in quo cecidit Fiachna Lurgan. Fiachna mac Demmain victor erat.[26]

Another of the Mongán stories called *Compert Mongáin agus Serc Duibe Lacha do Mongán*,[27] 'The Birth of Mongán and Dublacha's[28] Love for Mongán', preserves the tradition of the death of Fiachna mac Báetáin at the hands of Fiachna mac Demmáin and goes on to say that the latter: *do ghabh ríghi n-Ulad*,[29] 'seized the kingship of Ulster'. That he became king of Ulster in succession to Fiachna mac Báetáin is corroborated by *Ríg Ulad*.[30] Since Fiachna mac Báetáin, the former ally of the Dál Riata, was killed by the common enemy the Dál Fiatach, we might expect to find the Dál Riata taking up arms against the Dál Fiatach, and this is in fact what happened, for in the very next year we read in AT[31] of the defeat and death of Fiachna mac Demmáin by Connad Cerr, son of Eocho Bude,[32] king of the Dál Riata.

Cath Aird Corainn in [quo] Dáil Ríada victores erant, in quo cecidit Fiachna mac Demain la Connadh Cerr ríg Dalríada.

A.Clon. go so far as to state that the battle was fought to avenge the slaying of Fiachna mac Báetáin.

AT tell us that Connad Cerr was killed in his turn at the battle of Fid Eoin, fought in 629 according to AU, along with his brother Failbe and Rígullán mac Conaing, another grandson of Aedán mac Gabráin.[33]

Cath Fedha Eoin in quo Mael caith mac Scandail, rex Cruithniu, victor erat. Dal Riada cecidit. Condadh Cerr rí Dal Riada cecidit, 7 Dicull mac Eachach rí ceneoil Cruithne cecidit, et nepotes Aedan ceciderunt, id est Rigullan mac Conaing 7 Failbe mac Eachach. . . .

At first sight it would seem that the alliance of the Dál Riata and the Dál nAraide had broken down, for Connad Cerr's opponent was Máelcáich, a king of the Dál nAraide[34] and a grandson[35] of Fiachna mac Báetáin. However, Connad Cerr's Irish ally in the battle, Dícuill, son of Eochaid, was also of the Dál nAraide according to AT.[36] It looks as if the Dál Riata were taking part in an internal struggle perhaps with the intention of safeguarding their own interests in Ireland.

What seems to be the final episode in this account of the united Dál Riata in Irish politics of the period is the battle of Magh

Rath fought according to AU in 637.[37] AT have this to say of the battle:

Cath Muighe Rath ria nDomnoll mac Aeda 7 ria macaibh Aeda Sláine . . . in quo cecidit Congal Caech rí Ulad et Faelchu cum multis nobilibus, in quo cecidit Suibne mac Colmáin Cuar.

Domnall, son of Aed, was a descendant of Niall Noígiallach through his son Conall Gulbán and therefore of the Northern Uí Néill. The sons of Aed Sláine were also descended from Niall Noígiallach through another son Conall Crimthann. The leader of the opposition was Congal Cáech of the Dál nAraide and a brother of Máelcáich. According to the king-list *Ríg Ulad*,[38] Congal Cáech succeeded Fiachna mac Demmáin of the Dál Fiatach as king of Ulster.

Cummíne, abbot of Iona (657–669), tells us that Colum Cille foretold disaster for Aedán's descendants should they attack Colum Cille's relations in Ireland and he goes on to say:

Hoc autem vaticinium temporibus nostrís conpletum est in bello Roth, Domnallo Brecco nepot[e] Aidani sine causa vastante provinciam Domnail nepotis Ainmuireg.[39]

Relying on this account alone, one would have to assume that Domnall Brecc was the chief adversary of Domnall, son of Aed. However, as we have seen, Congal Cáech heads the list of his opponents in AT, while there is no mention of the participation of Domnall Brecc or indeed of the Dál Riata. And although we cannot doubt that the Dál Riata were involved, this, together with the evidence provided by the stories in the *Yellow Book of Lecan* which deal with the battle, namely, *Fledh Dúin na nGédh*[40] and the two independent versions of *Cath Muige Rath*,[41] make it quite clear that Congal Cáech was the moving spirit of the opposition to Domnall, son of Aed. Indeed, these stories specifically state that it was Congal Cáech who was responsible for the presence of the Dál Riata at Magh Rath, for he is made to send to them for help in his coming trial of strength with the Uí Néill.[42]

The outcome of the battle was an overwhelming defeat for Congal Cáech's forces. Congal Cáech was slain and, although Domnall Brecc, if he was in fact present,[43] escaped with his life, his influence and that of the Scottish Dál Riata in Northern Ireland were at an end, judging by the complete absence of further reference to their participation as a people in Irish affairs.[44] Between the time of Fergus Mór mac Eirc

(d. *c.* 500) and the battle of Magh Rath (637 AU), Dál Riata is not mentioned in the annals, as far as one can judge, in other than a demonstrable Scottish context. That is to say, there are apparently no recorded instances of the Irish Dál Riata acting independently of their compatriots in Scotland. Thereafter there are a number of references to the Dál Riata in Ireland as distinct from the Dál Riata in Scotland.[45] It seems likely that from this time the Scottish and Irish Dál Riatas began to go their separate ways and that the Scottish dynasty forfeited all claims to territory in Ireland.[46]

Even if we did not have evidence of this kind from the annals, a glance at the troubled times in the Scottish Dál Riata of this period would lead us to suspect that they were too weakened to be able to hold on to their Irish possessions. Thus, all four battles noted in the annals, in which the Dál Riata participated during the reign of Domnall Brecc, were defeats, that is, in AU *c.* 634,[47] 637, 638 and 642. Furthermore, we have the independent testimony of Cummíne who, writing some time during his occupation of the abbacy of Iona (657–669) about the battle of Magh Rath, says of the Dál Riata:

> Et a die illa usque hodie adhuc in proclivo sunt ab extraneís: quod suspiria doloris pectori incutit.[48]

Finally, from about this time it may be possible to trace in the annals a royal family, apparently located in the Irish Dál Riata. The earliest recorded member of this family may be a certain Fereth, son of Totholán, who died in 653 AU. The death is noted in 700 of Fiannamail of the fourth generation[49] who is actually called king of Dál Riata in AU.[50]

As a postscript, testifying to the complete breakdown in the second half of the seventh century of the pattern of alliance between the Dál Riata under their Scottish kings and the Dál nAraide and of their shared hostility toward the Dál Fiatach, we may note an entry in AU in 691 which records an attack by the Dál Riata, presumably of Ireland, on the Dál nAraide and the Dál Fiatach.[51]

> Dalriati populati sunt Cruthniu 7 Ultu.

NOTES

1 See note by Professor John MacNeill, *Buile Suibhne*, ed. J. G. O'Keeffe, ITS, 12. xxii, n. 2, but see below, p. 11, for the rise of an Irish based royal family.

2 The Preface to the *Amra Choluim Chille* contains the earliest detailed account of the proceedings. The earliest extant version of the Preface is apparently that found in the eleventh-century *Lebor na Huidre*, ed. R. I. Best and O. Bergin, pp. 11–15. The Preface is generally thought to derive from the second half of the tenth century, J. F. Kenney, *The Sources for the Early History of Ireland*, p. 427.

3 *Annals of Ulster* (AU) ed. W. M. Hennessy. All references and quoted entries from AU were checked with a photostat copy of MS. A. Cf. also *Annals of Clonmacnoise* (A.Clon), ed. D. Murphy, and *Annals from the Book of Leinster* (ALL), ed. R. I. Best, O. Bergin and M. A. O'Brien, 1. 95.

4 See J. Bannerman, 'The Convention of Druim Cett', SGS, 11. 114–32.

5 *Lebor na Huidre*, ed. R. I. Best and O. Bergin, p. 14.

6 T. F. O'Rahilly, *Early Irish History and Mythology*, p. 223.

7 *Ibid.*, p. 346.

8 *Ibid.*, p. 344.

9 Ed. R. I. Best, O. Bergin and M. A. O'Brien, 1. 192f. LL belongs to the second half of the twelfth century, *ibid.*, pp. xv–xvii. See also the poem entitled *Clann Ollaman Uaisle Emna* (ed. F. J. Byrne, SH, 4. 54–94) and composed *c.* 1165 (*ibid.*, p. 59).

10 Omit Daig mac Cairill, eighth on the list, *ibid.*, p. 83.

11 His obit in AU 587 is clearly a subsequent addition.

12 Ed. M. A. O'Brien, *Corpus Genealogiarum Hiberniae*, 1. 406 (330ab).

13 The high-kingship seems to have had no historical basis, but was later thought to have been held by the more powerful kings in Ireland, usually the leader of the Uí Néill dynasties, see D. A. Binchy, 'Fair of Tailtiu and Feast of Tara', *Ériu*, 18. 113–38.

14 *Rawl. B.* 502, ed. M. A. O'Brien, *Corpus Genealogiarum Hiberniae*, p. 124 (137a5, 11).

15 Aedán may even have paid tribute for his territories in Scotland, if we are to believe the claims of the genealogists that Báetán was king of Alba (*Corpus Genealogiarum Hiberniae*, pp. 275, 406). Cf. also an obscurely worded poem in *Senchus Síl hIr* (ed. M. E. Dobbs, ZCP, 13. 322) which seems to tell of tribute received by Báetán from Scotland.

16 O'Rahilly (*Early Irish History and Mythology*, pp. 237, 503f.) suggests that Aedán's victory in the battle of Manau in 582 or 583 AU was won on the Isle of Man and represents a further development in the hostilities between the Dál Fiatach and the Dál Riata. However, *Manau*, genitive *Manonn* or *Manand* as in AU, could equally well be the British territory of that name in southern Scotland, a view most recently stated by A. O. and M. O. Anderson in their edition of Adomnán's *Vita Columbae*, p. 43f.

17 *Ibid.*, I. c. 36.

18 According to the story entitled *Aided Diarmada* (ed. S. H. O'Grady, *Silva Gadelica*, 1. 80), Diarmait banished Aed Dub to Scotland on hearing a prophecy foretelling the circumstances of his own death.

19 See above, n. 10.

20 LL, p. 192f.

21 Cf. also *Annals of Tigernach* (AT), ed. W. Stokes, RC, 17. 120–263, *Chronicon Scotorum* (CS), ed. W. M. Hennessy, and *Annals of Innisfallen* (AI), ed. S. MacAirt.

22 Sometimes called Fiachna Lurgan, see AU 625, 626, and *Ríg Dáil Araide*, LL, p. 196.

23 Ed. K. Meyer and A. Nutt, *The Voyage of Bran*, 1. 42–3.

24 There is an obscure reference in AT to Mongán, son of Fiachna mac Báetáin, in Kintyre; cf. also AU, CS and *Annals of the Kingdom of Ireland by the Four Masters* (FM), ed. J. O'Donovan. Aedán, son of Mongán, son of Sárán (*Corpus Genealogiarum Hiberniae*, p. 324), is called king of Dál Riata in his obit in 616 AU. In MS. A of AU *araide* has been written over *Riatai*. Perhaps in the first instance Aedán was confused with his namesake Aedán mac Gabráin, king of the Dál Riata (d. *c.* 608), while *Araide* and *Riata* are in any case sometimes written in error for one another.

25 For the circumstances and date of this battle, see Bede's *Historia Ecclesiastica*, ed. C. Plummer, *Baedae Opera Historia*, I. c. 34. Evidence that Aedán did have Irish allies in the battle of Degsastan is implied in AT which state that the brother of Aethelfrith, king of the Northumbrians, was killed by a certain Máelumai mac Báetáin. Máelumai's obit is entered in AU in 610 and the *Laud Genealogies* (ed. K. Meyer, ZCP, 8. 293) show him to be descended from Eogan, son of Niall Noígiallach, and therefore of the Northern Uí Néill.

26 Cf. also AT, CS, *Ríg Ulad* (LL, p. 193), and *Clann Ollaman Uaisle Emna* (SH, 4. 64, v. 18).

27 Ed. K. Meyer and A. Nutt, *The Voyage of Bran*, 1. 58–70.

28 Sometime during Fiachna mac Báetáin's lifetime it is just possible that there was an attempt to resolve the Dál Fiatach-Dál nAraide conflict, for Dub-lacha a daughter of Fiachna mac Demmáin is said to have been the wife of Mongán, son of Fiachna mac Báetáin, in the *Senchus Dáil Fhiatach* (*Corpus Genealogiarum Hiberniae*, p. 409 330d) and also in the above story, p. 61. Furthermore the *Senchus Dáil Fhiatach* (*ibid.*, p. 409 330d) goes on to show that a certain Cumne or Cummíne Fhinn, apparently a sister of Fiachna mac Báetáin, was married to Fiachna mac Demmáin.

29 p. 61.

30 LL, p. 193.

31 Cf. also AU, CS, FM, *The Synchronisms of Fland Mainistrech* (ed. W. F. Skene in *Chronicles of the Picts and Scots*, p. 19), *Ríg Ulad* (LL, p. 193), and *Clann Ollaman Uaisle Emna* (SH, 4. 64, v. 19).

32 For this relationship, see my edition of *Senchus Fer nAlban* and commentary shortly to appear in *Celtica*.

33 Cf. also CS and A.Clon.

34 Presumably a sub-king, since his brother Congal Cáech, who precedes him as king of the Dál nAraide in the LL king-list (p. 195), was still alive and still leader of the Dál nAraide as we shall see.

35 *Senchus Síl hÍr*, ed. M. E. Dobbs, ZCP, 14. 111.

36 There is a Diucaill mac Echdach, apparently of the Dál nAraide, mentioned along with Aedán mac Mongáin (d. 616) and Fiachna mac Báetáin (d. 626) in *Rawl. B. 502.*, ed M. A. O'Brien, *Corpus Genealogiarum Hiberniae*, p. 155 (143b).

37 AT place it twelve years before 651, the year in which Aedán, bishop of Lindisfarne, died according to Bede (*Historia Ecclesiastica*, III. c. 17), that is, in 639, as do AI. Other records of this battle occur in CS, A.Clon., FM, ALL, *Ríg Ulad* (LL, p. 193), and *Clann Ollaman Uaisle Emna* (SH, 4. 64, v. 20).

38 LL, p. 193.

39 Adomnán's *Vita Columbae*, III. c. 5. Cummíne was the author of a book, no longer extant, on the *virtutes* of Colum Cille. This quotation is present in a passage taken from Cummíne's book and inserted in MS. A of Adomnán's *Vita*, probably by Dorbene who died in 713 AU (A. O. and M. O. Anderson, pp. 103–5; see also G. Bruning, 'Adomnans Vita Columbae und ihre Ableitungen', ZCP, 11. 260, n. 1).

40 *The Banquet of Dun na n-Gedh and the Battle of Magh Rath*, J. O'Donovan, pp. 2–86. In its present form it dates to the eleventh century, M. Dillon, *The Cycles of the Kings*, p. 57.

41 The earlier version (ed. C. Marstrander, 'A New Version of the Battle of Mag Rath', *Ériu*, 5. 232–46) possibly dates from the early tenth century, M. Dillon, *The Cycles of the Kings*, p. 65. The later version, dating to *c*. 1300 (*ibid.*, p. 65), is edited by J. O'Donovan, *The Banquet of Dun na n-Gedh and the Battle of Magh Rath*, pp. 90–320.

42 The earlier version of *Cath Muige Rath* (ed. C. Marstrander, *Ériu*, 5. 242) implies that, though Domnall Brecc sent an army to Magh Rath, he himself remained at home. Finally, we should note that in *Fledh Dúin na nGédh* (p. 44) Congal Cáech is said to be a grandson of Eocho Bude, Domnall Brecc's father, a relationship which, if true, falls neatly into the continuing pattern of alliance between the Dál nAraide and the Dál Riata in this period.

43 See above, n. 42.

44 Not until 733 AT do we find a record of the Scottish Dál Riata as a fighting force in Ireland, and even then they were apparently not acting on their own behalf but at the behest and under the command of Flaithbertach, king of the Northern Uí Néill.

45 In AU 691, 700, 731, etc.

46 A. O. Anderson (*Adomnan's Life of Columba*, p. 48) is of the opinion that Cummíne's statement of the loss by the Scottish dynasty of *eorum sceptrum regni huius de manibus suis* (III. c. 5) after the battle of Magh Rath refers to the Irish Dál Riata in particular. But Professor Jackson in his review of the Anderson's edition of the *Vita* (EHR, 78. 319) shows that the Scottish Dál Riata was intended.

47 This entry stands eight years before the misplaced obit of Domnall Brecc in 686 AU and AT.

48 Adomnán's *Vita Columbae*, III. c. 5.

49 See A. O. Anderson, *Early Sources of Scottish History*, 1. 190, for the family tree but omit Cuanda d. 677, Conall Cáel d. 681 and Conaing d. 701, all of whom AU show to be connected with Scotland. Anderson included these people because he was of the opinion that Fiannamail was king of the Scottish Dál Riata as well as of the Irish and therefore that Fiannamail and his family were of Scottish origin. He reaffirms this conclusion in his *Adomnan's Life of Columba*, pp. 49 and 56. However, the sixth-, seventh- and early eighth-century genealogies of the Scottish Dál Riata as preserved for us in the *Senchus Fer nAlban* (ed. J. Bannerman, *Celtica*, 7. 142–62) and the *Genelaig Albanensium* (see my forthcoming edition in appendix to above) have no place for Fiannamail or his immediate ancestors. Nor does his name appear in any of the versions of the king-list of the Scottish Dál Riata (see A. O. Anderson, *Early Sources of Scottish History*, 1. cxxixff.), while it should at least be noted that both he and Eochu, son of Domangart, the reigning king of the Scottish Dál Riata seem to figure among the guarantors of *Cáin Adomnáin* (ed. K. Meyer, *Anecdota Oxoniensia*, p. 21) promulgated in 697 AU. A certain Indrechtach, apparently Fiannamail's son, is also located in Ireland fighting in a battle between the Dál Riata and the Dál nAraide in 741 according to AU. The name Indrechtach appears in the list of the kings of the Dál nAraide in LL (p. 195) at about this time. If this is indeed Indrechtach, son of Fiannamail, his name may have been entered in the king-list because he gained suzerainty over the Dál nAraide or simply because of the confusion liable to arise between the people names Dál Riata and Dál nAraide (see above, n. 24, and below, n. 50). Whatever the reason, the evidence, such as it is, connects him with Ireland rather than Scotland.

50 In AT Dál nAraide is substituted for Dál Riata.

51 Perhaps we should add that the extremely derogatory remarks about Aed Dub, king of the Dál nAraide (d. 588), would probably not have found a place in Adomnán's *Vita Columbae* (I. c. 36), compiled sometime between 688 and 704, if relations between the Dál Riata and the Dál nAraide were as before.

CARL HJ. BORGSTRÖM

Notes on Gaelic grammar

The following notes are based mainly on the dialect of Barra in the Outer Hebrides, as recorded by the author in *Norsk Tidsskrift for Sprogvidenskap*, VIII, Oslo, 1935, and again in *The Dialects of the Outer Hebrides*, Oslo, 1940. Some examples have been taken from other sources. The grammatical phenomena in question are common to all Hebridian dialects and also, I believe, to nearly all other Gaelic-speaking areas, although their formal expression varies to some extent.

Like the other Neo-Celtic languages, Scottish Gaelic shows highly complicated mutations of consonants and of vowels. In root morphemes of nouns, adjectives and verbs, initial consonants are subject to one type of mutation, viz. lenition: *cat—dà chat*; prefixation of a nasal consonant is also a common grammatical process: *cat—an cat*, phonemically /(ə) Nkahd/. Final consonants of root morphemes are subject to another type of mutation, viz. palatalization: *an cat—a' chait, na cait*; this is often accompanied by, or even replaced by, vocalic mutation: *an ceann—na cinn*.

Initial and final mutations often have different grammatical functions, but sometimes they combine, or may replace one another, in order to characterize the same grammatical forms, e.g. cases of nouns after the article: *an cat—leis a' chat* (dative) = *a' chas—leis a' chois*.[1] Terminations generally have functions similar to those of the final mutations: *cat—cait* (plur.) = *cas—cas-an*.

In verbs, final mutation (palatalization) is relatively unimportant, but initial mutation and terminations function much as in nouns. The proclitic syllable *do*, written as a separate word, is better regarded as a prefix characterizing the dependent mode[2] of the preterite, e.g. fut. *cuiridh—cha chuir* = pret. *chuir—cha do chuir*. Also the so-called relative particle *a* /ə/, before a vowel *a dh'* /əɣ-/, as in *'nuair a dh'fhal-bhas tu* 'when you leave', is a prefix characterizing the relative mode of all tenses.

But this complicated morphological apparatus is to some extent redundant, because many grammatical forms are entirely subordinate to other means of expression, such as prepositions, conjunctions, particles and word order. This applies to the cases of nouns: the nominative, the genitive and the dative,[3] and to the modes of verbs: the independent, the relative and the dependent. Many nouns, e.g. (*an*) *latha*, (*an*) *duine*, do not formally distinguish the cases, and the conditional of verbs has only a rudimentary and precarious distinction of modes. Such unchangeable forms are used exactly like characterized forms, because the surroundings practically always determine the choice of case and mode. It is very rarely possible to substitute one case for another, or one mode for another, in unchanged surroundings. An example, made up by the author of this paper, might be: *phreab each am ballach* 'a horse kicked the boy' vs. *phreab each a' bhallaich* 'the boy's horse kicked, or pranced'; if the unchangeable *an duine* is put instead of *am ballach* and *a' bhallaich*, the sentence becomes ambiguous. The intricate morphology of cases and modes is only an intellectual play without much informative value.

A closer examination reveals even more surprising and unusual properties of this play. As will be demonstrated in some detail below, the syntax of cases is, in certain respects, parallel to the syntax of modes, the nominative functioning like the independent mode, the genitive like the relative, and the dative like the dependent mode. One might in fact speak of 'verbal cases' instead of 'modes'.

The crucial point is the relation of cases and modes to antecedent morphs (words, particles) in the sentence. It is important to note that the definite article, a possessive pronoun, or a numeral, all of which precede the noun (*an ceann, mo cheann, dà cheann, an dà cheann*) are not antecedents determining the choice of case, but parts of noun phrases which are in a given case.

A noun or noun phrase in the nom. can be uttered by itself for the sake of naming or drawing attention to something or as answer to a question. In a sentence it can be preceded by various parts of speech; as subject it stands directly after the verb, as object it comes after the subject pronoun or noun, or after an adverb or conjugated preposition (*chuir i uaithe a' bhucaid* 'she threw away the bucket'). It can be preceded by the conjunctions *agus, ach, no (na)* 'or', *na* 'than'. The prepositions *eadar* and *gun* govern the nom. (*eadar an t-Oban agus Barraidh* 'between Oban and Barra'; *latha gun ghrian* 'a day without sunshine'). A few other ways of using the nom. will be mentioned below.

A verb in the indep. can be used by itself in answers. In a sentence it usually occupies the first place, but it may be preceded by subordinate clauses, by certain adverbs, complements, etc. (*am màireach air sia uairean bidh waggon a dol sìos* 'to-morrow at six o'clock a waggon will go down'), or by the conjunctions *agus, ach, no* (*na, air neo*) 'or'.

A noun in the gen. is always governed by some antecedent, which may be: (*a*) a noun (*biadh a' choin* 'the dog's food'); (*b*) a verbal noun governing its object in the gen. (*thà a' bhò 'g ithe an fheòir* 'the cow is eating the grass'); if the noun is indefinite, it may be in the gen. or in the nom. (*'g ithe feòir* or *feur* 'eating grass'); (*c*) a compound preposition, e.g. *air son* 'for the sake of', *an aghaidh* 'against', and a few simple ones like *fad* 'during', *bharr* 'out of, from'; (*d*) the adjective *làn* (*làn fala* 'full of blood'). Two nouns in the gen. can be co-ordinated by *agus* or *no* without repetition of the antecedent (*bha iad a' caitheamh na cuirme 's na cuideachd* 'they were enjoying the feast and the company').

A verb in the rel. is governed by some antecedent, which may be: (*a*) a noun (*biadh a dh'itheas an cù* 'food that the dog will eat'); the noun is determined by the relative clause much in the same way as it is by another noun in the gen.; (*b*) certain conjunctions: *'nuair* 'when', *mà* 'if', *mar* 'as', *agus, 's* 'as' (after an adjective preceded by *cho*), *na* 'than' (after an adjective in the comparative); (*c*) interrogatives (*cò thuigeas sin?* 'who can understand that?'); (*d*) any words that are emphasized by being put in front of the verb and preceded by *'s e* or *'s ann* (*'s ann am màireach a thilleas e* 'it is tomorrow he will return'). Two verbs in the rel. can be co-ordinated by *agus* or *no* without repetition of the antecedent (*'nuair a thàinig esan dhachaidh 's a shuidh iad mu'n bhòrd* 'when he came home and they sat down at the table').

A noun in the dat. is always governed by a preposition. Of the fifteen prepositions that can be conjugated, all except *chun* and *eadar* govern a noun in the dat. An exception is that a noun followed by another noun in the gen. with article must remain in the nom. (*sheas mi air cas a' ghille* 'I trod on the lad's foot' vs. *sheas mi air a chois* 'I trod on his foot'). When two or more co-ordinated nouns are governed in the dat. by a preposition, the latter is repeated before each noun. Thus a noun or noun-phrase in the dat. is always directly preceded by a preposition, and not by *agus, ach* or *no*. (This explains why *eadar* 'between' governs the nom.; the second noun after this preposition must be preceded by *agus*, cf. the example above.)

A verb in the dep. is always governed by a proclitic particle, conjunction, etc. The most important ones are: *an* (interrogative particle), *cha, nach, gu'n, mu'n* 'before', *mura* 'unless', and the relative particle *an*, which is in turn preceded either by *cà, c'àite* 'where?' or by a preposition, e.g. *dha'n, ris an* 'to whom, to which' (*an t-àite ris an can iad Bréibhig* 'the place to which they say (which is called) B.'). When two or more co-ordinated verbs are governed in the dep., the particle or conjunction is repeated before each verb. Thus the dep. is always directly preceded by a governing particle or conjunction, and not by *agus, ach* or *no*.

The interrogative particle is heard as a prefixed nasal before initial vowels and stops: *'n ith thu?, 'n cuir thu?*, etc., but before other consonants it is usually absent: *fàg thu?*, etc. In such cases we may say there is a zero allomorph, implying that the dep. is even here governed by (an allomorph of) the particle.

Let us now sum up. The nom. and the indep. do not presuppose any antecedents, they can form an utterance by themselves. The gen. and the rel. presuppose antecedents which are often nouns or have a certain affinity to nouns; the antecedent need not be repeated in co-ordinated constructions. The dat. and the dep. presuppose immediately preceding antecedents which are not nouns, adjectives or verbs.

The parallelism between cases and modes breaks down on a few points. The nom. functions as an unmarked case which replaces the gen. or the dat. under certain conditions: indefinite nom. for gen. after verbal nouns (*'g ithe feur*), nom. for dat. before another noun in the gen. (*air cas a' ghille*), and after the prepositions *gun* and *eadar*. The indep., on the other hand, never replaces the other modes, it never occurs after a governing antecedent.

An interesting but difficult question that must be raised in this connection, is that of word boundaries. It was suggested above that *do* in the dep. preterite and *a* in rel. forms should be regarded as prefixes rather than as separate words, because they serve as markers of grammatical forms on a par with terminations and mutations. Unfortunately there is no generally accepted definition of 'word' or procedure for finding word boundaries, nor can we be sure that one definition or one procedure would apply to all languages. The principle underlying the present usage in writing Irish and Gaelic may be stated in phonological terms: stressed syllables are, with few exceptions, treated as word initial. But Munster Irish has a divergent stress pattern and does not conform to this rule. The principle may also be stated in morphological terms: root morphemes are, with some exceptions, treated as word initial. There is also a type of word with two stressed syllables, e.g. *seann-duine, droch-latha, mì-chàilmhear* 'disagreeable'; some of the initial morphemes of these so-called compounds are not roots but derivational prefixes, e.g. *droch-* and *mì-*.

According to these principles one writes *cha do chuir* and not *cha dochuir* or *cha do-chuir*.

But if the possibility or impossibility of intercalating morphs in a sequence is a valid morphological criterion, as I believe it is, it will be right to treat *chadochuir* as one word, since nothing can be intercalated without breaking the grammatical connection between the three morphs. The same applies to *nachdochuir, gu'ndochuir, risancan*, etc. Hence also *chachuir, nachcuir*, etc., are single words, since only the prefix *do* can be intercalated. But conjunctions governing the rel. will be separate words, e.g. *mà chuireas*, because one can intercalate another verb without repeating the conjunction: *mà leigeas tu - - agus achuireas tu - -*.

Similarly the article should be treated as a prefix to nouns: *antathair, nacait*, etc. Numerals can be intercalated here, but they function as prefixes, *dà-latha* like *droch-latha*, and the article is then a prefix to these word units, *andà-latha* like *androch-latha*. (So far as I know, one does not say e.g. **ochd no naoi taighean* but *a h-ochd no (a) naoi de thaighean* 'eight or nine houses'; the adjectival cardinal numbers are used only as prefixes with a directly following noun.) The possessive pronouns are prefixes too: *mocheann, (tha thu) gamthuigsinn* 'understanding me'. Prepositions with the dat., which cannot be separated from the following noun except by prefixes, are themselves prefixes: *leisanduine, airmodhà-chois* 'on my two feet'. It will be seen that this way of drawing word boundaries agrees fairly well with the practice more or less consistently followed in Old and Middle Irish MSS.

If the above turns out to be a correct, though admittedly incomplete, theory of word boundaries in Gaelic, it will entail changes in many statements of traditional Gaelic grammar. Instead of the dative case, there will be some thirteen cases, each one characterized by a prefix: *aig-, air-, le-* or *leis-*, etc.; the forms which are traditionally labelled 'dative case forms', e.g. *c(h)ois* or *a' chat*, will be combinatory allomorphs required by the prefixes. The nom. and the gen. will remain as they are, since their antecedents must be regarded as separate words. The dependent mode will be subjected to the same treatment; it will split into a number of modes with prefixes: *an-*, *cha-*, *nach-*, *gu'n-*, etc., and the forms *-chuir*, *-dochuir*, etc., will acquire the status of combinatory allomorphs. The indep. and the rel. will remain unchanged.

One can, however, discern a certain stratification within these complex word forms because some morphs belong more intimately together than others. The definite article agrees with its noun in case and number and forms part of the sequences (termed 'noun phrases' above) which are governed by the prepositional prefixes. The verbal prefixes *do* (dep. preterite) and *a* (rel.) are likewise parts of the forms governed by conjunctional prefixes or other antecedents. The article, *do* and *a* always stand next to the root morpheme or compound stem, and they occasionally have zero allomorphs, e.g. *chachuala* 'did not hear', *chanfhaca* 'did not see', *(an)latha* 'the day'. These prefixes, then, seem to form an inner core of the word units together with root morphemes and terminations. The prepositional and conjunctional prefixes, on the other hand, form an outer layer which is less intimately connected with the rest. Within the system outlined here, the parallelism between cases and modes applies to the nom. and the indep., to the gen. and the rel., and to the inner cores of the remaining cases and modes.

Whether a Gaelic grammar based on these principles would be simpler and more consistent than the traditional ones, is of course uncertain until an attempt has been made to write one. A Gaelic text with word boundaries as described above will perhaps be difficult to read unless the stress is marked; the placement of stress will be at least potentially distinctive in such highly complex word forms.

A detailed examination of how the cases and modes are used in Old and Modern Irish lies outside the scope of this paper. In O. Ir. the parallelism seems to be so restricted as to be almost non-existent. The accusative of nouns does not correspond to anything in the morphology of verbs. The use of conjunct terminations in compound verbs (*berid* 'he carries' vs. *asbeir* 'he says') finds no parallel in the morphology of nouns. In Mod. Ir., only some irregular verbs have conjunct (dependent) forms, e.g. *chonnaic* 'saw' vs. *ní fhaca* 'did not see'; in all other verbs one can at most distinguish between a relative and a non-relative mode. With this restriction, however, the cases and modes function much as they do in Scottish Gaelic.

With regard to word boundaries, I believe that the theoretical considerations presented in this paper also apply, with certain changes in details, to Old, Middle and Modern Irish. The practice of scribes referred to above is an argument in favour of this view. R. Thurneysen says: 'In general all words which are grouped round a single chief stress and have a close syntactic connection with each other are written as one in the manuscripts. Thus conjunctions and pronouns affixed to them are written with the following verb, the article and attached possessives with the following noun, the copula with the following predicate, prepositions and affixed pronouns or article with the following verb or noun, enclitics with the preceding stressed word, etc'.[4] The phonological part of this rule ('grouped round a single chief stress') is probably less important than the grammatical one ('a close syntactic connection'). However, a more detailed examination of the practice followed by the scribes would be needed before one could venture a definite statement.

Excursus on word boundaries. The following principle seems to hold good for many languages: any sequence of morphs which is a word has a certain morphemic structure, and intercalation of morphs into such a sequence is subject to strict limitations which mostly imply that the new sequence should also be one word with the same structure as the original one.

For a more detailed discussion some preliminary notions are needed. Morphs are the smallest meaningful parts of utterances. A morpheme is a type of morph with a common range of meaning and sometimes comprising alternating allomorphs; e.g. *cas*, *chas*, *cois* are members of one morpheme. Morphemes are either lexical or grammatical (hereafter abbreviated L and g respectively). L-s can in some utterances have an indefinite number of substitutes; g-s have only a limited number of substitutes. After morpheme classes have been defined, L-s may be defined as morphemes belonging to classes with unlimited membership (nouns, adjectives, verbs), and g-s as belonging to classes with limited membership. The chief g classes in Gaelic are: pronouns, numerals, prepositions, preverbal particles, derivational morphemes (prefixed or suffixed), morphemes of case and number, of tense, mood and mode, and the unique verb *is*, *bu*.

The most frequent structure of word units is g . . Lg . ., i.e. one L preceded and/or followed by one or more g-s, with the proviso that nothing can be intercalated that would change this structure. The proviso implies that g . . Lg . . is a word if nothing can be intercalated, or only one or more g-s. Thus *nataighean so* 'these houses' consists of two words; there is no word boundary between *na* and *taighean* where only g-s such as *trì* or *droch* can be inserted; but there is a word boundary between *taighean* and *so* where L-s (adjectives) can occur.[5] *Chadobhuail mi amballach* 'I did not strike the boy' consists of three words; in *cha-do-bhuail* nothing can be inserted; the permutation to *chadobhuail amballach mi* is equivalent to insertion of *amballach* (gL) between *-bhuail* and *mi*; between *mi* and *amballach* one can insert e.g. *ancù no* 'the dog or'.

The above rule is almost sufficient for a language like Gaelic where compounds of two or more L-s are very rare. But if e.g. *leth* 'half' is taken to be a L in all its occurrences, then *leth-duine* 'twin', *leth-bhliadhna* 'six months', etc., are compounds. In that case *an leth-duine* differs from *anduine* by the intercalated L, in violation of our rule.

Such cases are taken care of by defining a c o m p o u n d (hereafter C) as a sequence of L-s which has the same general distribution (including inflection) as the single morpheme members of a given class, *in casu* the noun class; *leth-duine* is a noun with the same distribution and inflectional properties as *duine*, *mac*, etc.; hence it is one word. Our formula for word units will now be g . . L/Cg . ., i.e. a C can take the place of a single L. It follows that insertion of a L into a structure g . . Lg . . is permissible if, and only if, the result is a structure g . . Cg . . .

A word may consist of a single morph: L (*duine*) or g (*mi, so, agus, ach*), or of two or three g-s (*or-m, or-t*; '*s-mi* 'it is I'; *or-m-sa*).

Attributive adjectives present a difficulty. Consider the following paradigm: *a'chaileag bheag* 'the little girl', gen. *nacaileige bige,* 'dat.' *leisa'chaileig bhig.* We have said that the form *-chaileig* is a combinatory allomorph occurring after prepositional prefixes in the same word unit, whereas the adjectival form *bhig*, which agrees with *-chaileig*, appears as a separate word. To remove this inconsistency, we may let attributive adjectives form one word unit with the preceding noun: *a'chaileag-bheag, nacaileigebige, leisa'chaileigbhig.* This has also the advantage that practically all projected mutations (cf. note 1) will now occur in word medial position. The only morphs that can be intercalated between a noun and an attributive adjective, are other adjectives; *agus* is not used between co-ordinated adjectives in the positive. If this solution is adopted, the enclitic pronouns *so* 'this', *sin* 'that', *ud* 'yon' and the particles *sa, san, ne* (*molàmhsa* '*my* hand') will also form one word with the morphs preceding them: *a'chaileagso* 'this girl' and *a'chaileagbheagso* 'this little girl'.

The formula for *a'chaileagbheag, nacaileigebige*, etc., may be written gLLg, where *g* is a morph which is wholly or partly expressed by mutations, and which is repeated or discontinuous. In *nacaileigebige* the *g* 'genitive singular (feminine)' is expressed in the article, in the initial unmutated *c-*, the final palatalized *-g* and the termination *-e* of the noun, and in the unmutated *b-*, the palatalized *-g* and the termination *-e* of the adjective. To our previous rules for word units we now add this: A sequence of two or more L-s is one word if the sequence contains a discontinuous *g* and only other Lg-s may be intercalated, so that the structure LL . . *g* remains unaltered. We shall then have *caileagbheag* and *duinemór* as single word units, but *anduine 'smotha* 'the biggest man' as two word units, since superlatives contain no discontinuous *g*, they do not agree in number, case and gender with the noun. By the same token predicative adjectives are separate words, e.g. *tha a'chaileag beag*.

The possibility of regarding LLg, a noun with an attributive adjective, as a word unit, is peculiar to Gaelic (and probably Irish); a similar rule would not be workable in Norwegian, German or Latin. On the basis of these rules for word division Gaelic would have to be classified as a (mildly) polysynthetic language.[6]

NOTES

1 For a classification of Celtic initial mutations see Magne Oftedal: *A Morphemic Evaluation of the Celtic Initial Mutations*, Lochlann II (Oslo, 1962), pp. 94ff. In Oftedal's terminology, the mutation in *an cat—leis a' chat* is projected from the article. Since the article is in the same case (and number) as the noun, the mutations projected from it are marks of case-forms. On the other hand, mutations projected from possessives, e.g. *a cheann* 'his head', *a chinn* 'of his head', are independent of cases. Mutations which are not projected from preceding morphs, Oftedal calls incorporated mutations, e.g. lenition in the gen. plur. without article (*chon, dhaoine*), and in the independent conditional and preterite (*chuireadh, chuir*). As the examples show, incorporated mutations in Gaelic go together with final mutations (*chon* vs. nom. plur. *coin*) or terminations (*chuir-eadh* vs. *cuir-idh* and *chuir-O*).

2 The term 'mode' (not to be confounded with 'mood') is adopted here to designate the category of verbal forms which comprises the independent (or absolute) mode, e.g. *cuiridh*, the relative mode, e.g. *a chuireas*, and the dependent (or conjunct) mode, e.g. *(cha, nach, etc.) c(h)uir*.

3 The vocative is left out of the account as not forming an integrated part of syntactic constructions.

4 *A Grammar of Old Irish*, p. 24. See also G. Dottin, *Manuel d'irlandais moyen*, I, pp. 29ff. on word division in Middle Irish MSS.

5 The conclusion with regard to enclitics like *so* will be modified below.

6 The rules concerning the structure g. .L/Cg. . and the restrictions on intercalation were worked out by me (in a slightly different form) for Norwegian and other languages in my handbook *Innføring i sprogvidenskap* (Oslo, 1958) pp. 63ff. Cf. also my remarks in *Word* 10 (1954) p. 157, Footnote 4. Joseph H. Greenberg's procedure for determining word units, *Essays in Linguistics*, New York 1957, and *IJAL* 26 (1960), pp. 191ff., also makes use of insertion as a criterion, but differs from mine in other respects.

Alf Sommerfelt has informed me that he is going to publish a paper entitled *Word Limits in the Dialect of Torr* in Lochlann III. From a conversation with Professor Sommerfelt I gather that his conclusions are similar to mine, and I wish to state that neither of us had any knowledge of the other's work before the papers were completed.

(Owing to the delayed publication of the present paper, Professor Sommerfelt's article has now been in print for some years already: Lochlann III appeared in 1965.)

JAMES CARNEY

Two poems from Acallam na Senórach

A very common literary form in Irish is the tale which is a mixture of prose and verse, the prose being used for narrative, the verse for emotional statements by the characters involved. Well-known examples of this are the story of Liadan and Cuirithir and Scéla Cano maic Gartnáin. Often, as in the case of the famous Caillech Béirre poem, or the supposed love-poem *It é saigte gona suain* put—but quite wrongly as it seems to me[1]—into the mouth of Guaire's daughter Créd, the poem is preceded by a brief prose introduction, purporting to state the occasion on which the poem was uttered. There is, I think, a general tendency to assume that in cases such as the two last-mentioned the poem once formed part of a saga of which the brief prose introduction is a remnant. With regard to the relationship of poem and prose (whether saga or brief introductory passage) I would like to state the following conclusion: We cannot always assume that prose and verse were a unity from the beginning, although this, of course, may often be so.

But there are many other possibilities: a redactor may compose poems, and insert them in an older prose tale; a saga writer may take a series of old poems and write a saga around them; a late 'editor' may add an introductory passage to an early poem, purporting to state the circumstances under which it was originally composed. In cases such as the last mentioned the 'editor' will inevitably draw much of his information from the poem itself; he is making a learned comment, which like all learned comments, must be treated with critical suspicion. In the case of the two poems already mentioned, the Caillech Béirre poem and *It é saigte gona suain*, we must, I am convinced, reach our conclusions as to the meaning and intent of each poem strictly from the text itself. The two sagas I have mentioned, Liadan and Cuirithir and Scéla Cano maic Gartnáin, present problems of great complexity and cannot be dealt with in the present brief article. It must suffice to say that in these two cases it is dangerous to assume that poetry and prose were a unity from the beginning. The poetry, I would say (particularly in the case of Liadan and Cuirithir) is the creation of a superior mind, and the prose-writer sometimes erred in his re-creation of the circumstances under which a given poem was uttered. This, however, is a matter which awaits precise investigation.

In the present article detailed comment will be made on two poems and their prose settings: (1) *Géisidh cuan* and (2) *Turas acam Día hAíne.*[2]

1. *Géisid cúan*

We must first look at the saga-setting of this poem and that other which is associated with it *Turus acam Día hAíne.*

Finn and his warrior band are on the way to fight the battle of Ventry when they meet Cael ua Nemnainn who is journeying south to woo Créide, daughter of Cairbre, king of Ciarraige Luachra. Finn points out to him that she is a very cunning woman and has gathered in her dwelling most of the treasures of Ireland; furthermore that she expected anybody experienced in the craft of poetry to bring her a poem praising her goblets, her horns, her cups, her vats, her vessels and her great royal dwelling. Cael said that he had such a poem ready, which he had got from his foster-mother, Muirenn, daughter of In Derg. Cael then accompanied the warrior band to Créide's dwelling at Loch Cuire. They were met by Créide, surrounded by three bands of fifty maidens. When she found out that Cael came seeking her hand she asked if he had the poem ready for her. Cael then rose and recited *Turus acam Día hAíne.*

The wedding feast took place there and then. Everybody was happy, except for anxiety over the fact that foreigners had landed at Ventry and a battle was imminent. Finally, after a wedding-feast lasting for seven days, the warrior-band, accompanied by Cael and Créide, set out for Ventry. Créide endowed the band richly with stock, and during the course of the battle she fed the warriors and nursed their sick and wounded. On the last day of the battle Cael was drowned. Here we may translate: 'And there were other animals that had equal life with Cael. And the wave carried him out when he had been drowned. And the maiden and the good men of the fianna went after him. And he was brought by them to the southern strand, south of Ventry, so that ever afterwards that strand was called the Strand of

Cael and the Grave of Cael. The maiden came then and lay by his side, and gave vent to lamentation and great sorrow. "Why," she asked, "should I not die of sorrow for my husband since the wandering wild beasts are dying of sorrow for him?" And Créide said "*Géisid cúan.* ...." And the maiden lay beside Cael and died of sorrow for him.'

There is no original relationship between the prose and the verse. Sometime about A.D. 1100 in south Kerry, a man of some importance called Cael son of Crimthann was drowned. A poet who had been closely associated with him wrote a lament in which he referred to him as *in laech ro laiged lim* (§ 5), 'the warrior who used to lie with me'; he also says: *is ed rom-mer mét a aéb.*[3] The language and the feeling of the poem were such that a saga-writer could quite easily take it and work it into a story framework where it appeared to be an emotional statement by a woman on her dead husband or lover.[4] But the inter-weaving of the old poetry and the newly created prose was not done very skilfully. The prose tale is set in the Irish pagan period. Yet the poet has said of Cael that he lies tonight *is cros úasa chinn*, 'with a cross above his head' (§ 5). Irish poets were never given to this type of anachronism. They were quite conscious of the fact that the cross was an exclusively Christian symbol, and in referring to pagan burial are careful to use such a phrase as *tócbad a lia ós a lecht*, 'his memorial stone was raised over his grave'. This suggests that the poem has a Christian, and not a pagan background.

In Bardic poetry the pathetic fallacy is a commonplace: the hero is dead and all nature mourns. *Géisid cúan* is an excellent example of this: the sea mourns the dead hero. There is then something that is not quite the pathetic fallacy, but a logical extension of it. The poet's sorrow is to be compared with that of the heron when the fox of Dá Lí seeks her young, with that of the stag of Druim dá Léis when its mate, the doe of Druim Sílenn, has died.[5]

It is then clear that in the poem we have a quite conventional and ordinary use of the pathetic fallacy such as one might find in any bardic lament. But in the prose tale all the animals mourn for Cael, and there is no hint that they have their own individual sorrows. At this point the tale descends to a folk idea, that of the external soul: certain wild beasts were 'of equal life' with Cael (*comsaegal acu re Cael*). The implication here is that these beasts were born on the same day, shared a soul with him, and hence died on the same day.[6] With the introduction of this idea we are obviously in touch with a more popular type of thinking than that which lies behind the poem.

There is no phrase or idea in the poem that is inconsistent with its being a conventional bardic elegy. Cael is identified as the son of Crimthann, and the oblique reference to his mother (*mac na mná o Dhoire dá Dos*), is quite conventional.[7] In bardic poetry there is a common conceit that the poet is the patron's lover. To discuss this with anything approaching completeness would require a special essay. Here it must suffice to quote some instances to show that there is no difficulty in regarding the reference to *in laech ro laiged lim* as an instance of this common conceit.[8]

Sometime within the period 1293–1309 Seaán Ó Clumháin wrote a poem seeking to be reconciled with Aodh Ó Conchobhair whom he had struck with his first. In the course of this poem he says:

> *Ná bíom ní as fhaide, a fholt fionn,*
> *gan luighe ar aon ar aonphioll;*
> *'s ná bíom, a bhile Suca,*
> *gan fhíon d'ibhe a haonchupa.*

> *Mé t'fhear grádha, a ghéag Eachtgha,*
> *fa mé riamh t'fhear éinleabtha,*
> *mé fear do ghualann gile,*
> *a nuabharr geal Gáiridhe.*[9]

'Let us not be any longer, you of the fair hair, without lying on a single couch, and let us not be, scion of the Suck, without drinking wine from the same goblet.

I am the man who loves you, branch of Aughty, I was always the man who shared your bed, I am the man of (= who has the right to be beside) your bright shoulder, fresh bright chief of Gáiridhe.'

In the fifteenth century a poet, Lughaidh Ó Dálaigh, goes to Trim to seek the grave of his dead patron, Féilim Ó Raghallaigh. He represents himself as composing his elegy as he looks at the grave. During the course of this lengthy poem he wishes to die, and to lie in the same grave as Ó Raghallaigh. He says:

> *Bíom mar do bhámur roimhe*
> *fán leaba, a fhlaith Bóroimhe:*
> *leabaidh chaol nír chumang linn*
> *d'fhulang ar-aon, a Fheidhlim.*[10]

'Lord of Bóroimhe, let us be in the bed as we were before: we did not think a narrow bed too narrow for us two, Feidhlim.'

It is precisely this conceit that underlies the well-known seventeenth-century poem *Féuch féin an obair-si, a Aodh*. If, as I think, the same conceit underlies *It é saigte gona suain*, which is a very early composition, possibly seventh-century in its original form, we have to do with a habit of thought that can be documented in Ireland for fully a thousand years. Thus we see that the language and thought of *Géisidh cúan* are completely consistent with its being the work of a professional poet, speaking of a dead patron. That *Géisidh cúan* is the work of a professional poet is strongly supported by the fact that the poem with which it is associated in the *Acallam*, that is, *Turus acam Día hAíne*, demands a similar explanation.

2. *Turus acam Día hAíne*

The circumstances in which this poem was made to be uttered in the saga have been detailed above. The poem was used by the author of the *Acallam* in exactly the same way that he has used *Géisid cúan*. In fact it is a bardic letter written by a poet of about A.D. 1100 to a woman called Créd, expressing his intention of visiting her house for about a week (*ceithre lá is leithshechtain*), beginning on Friday (§§ 1–2). The visit is quite clearly in the future, and the poet expresses the hope that she will not put him off, but will make him welcome; the better she treats him in the matter of hospitality, the more will her fame endure in the praise-poetry that he will compose for her (§§ 15–16). It is a regular bardic bargain, and there is not the slightest hint of love.

Murphy, in his treatment of this poem, fails to appreciate its nature, precisely because he regards the prose and poetry as an original unity, and hence the verse must be interpreted in the light of its saga setting. It may be useful at this point to illustrate how different general conceptions of the nature of a poem can be reflected in the translation of a particular verse. The following is the first stanza as translated by Murphy:

Turus acam Día hAíne
(gé dech, isam fíraíge)
co tech Créide (ní sním suail)
re hucht in tsléibe an-airtúaid.

'I travel in great anxiety on a Friday (though I do so I am a true guest) to Créide's house which lies north-east of the mountain, facing it.'[11]

Murphy, by his whole 'Otherworld' approach to this poem, is precluded from giving any Christian interpretation to the reference to Friday (*Día hAíne*), a word which to the poet meant 'Day of Fast', and had an immediate Christian connotation. He forces the phrase *ní sním suail* in the third line to refer back to Friday in the first, 'I travel in great anxiety on a Friday'. Bringing this phrase back, as he does, takes the whole stanza into the realm of primitive superstition, and this idea is elaborated in a note (p. 231): 'In quatrain 1 there seems to be a reference to some superstition connected with Friday. Friday is looked on today in Ireland and Gaelic Scotland as an unlucky day for beginning things.' This note is at variance with the facts. In Ireland, as is well known, it is considered lucky to move into a new house on Friday.[12]

If we admit that the poem was composed in a Christian context there is no difficulty. The poet is simply stating that, having made such an exhausting journey, he expects to be treated with lavish hospitality despite the fact that it is a fast day.

It may be remarked here that the poem stands in need of re-editing, for, in the process of edition, secondary readings have been adopted by the editor, and words and phrases essential to proper understanding have been excluded. This can be clearly shown by an examination of those lines where the name *Créide* is found in either the dative or accusative.

It has become quite clear in recent years that the name Créd underwent declensional change in the course of the Middle Irish period. The earlier usage was nom. *Créd*, gen. *Créide*, dat., acc. *Créid*.[13] Later *Créide* is generalized for all cases. When we examine the variant readings of this poem we find something very significant with regard to lines in which this name is found in the nominative, accusative, or dative. In every such line one set of variants accommodates a monosyllabic form (*Créd*, *Créid*) the other a disyllabic (*Créide*). From the declensional history of the word it is quite clear that the variant readings which will admit a monosyllable are correct, and those which demand a disyllable are secondary, the result of re-writing. It may also be remarked that the correct *Créd* or *Créid* is frequently supported by that version of the *Acallam* edited by Nessa Ní Shéaghdha, which was not used by the editor in establishing his text.

I give here the lines in question, first as given in Murphy's text, then as they will be read when we accept the correct monosyllabic form of the name. I also quote Nessa Ní Shéaghdha's text, where it preserves the shorter form:

1.   *co Créide i Cíchaib Anann* (§ 2)
        co Créid dán crích Cnoc Anann.[14]

2.   *ac Créide finn foltbuide* (§ 4)
        ac Créid álainn foltbuide.[15]

3.   *Mad áil do Chréide (ro-clos)* (§ 5)
        Mad ail do Chréid Chnuic na Cross.[16]

4.   *do Chréide dá ngairenn caí* (§ 15)
        do Chréid dá ngairenn in caí.[17]

5.   *Mad áil la hingin Cairbre* (§ 16)
        Mad áil do Chréid d'fhuil Cairbre.[18]

6.   *Ruc Créide a Tulchaib Trí mBenn* (§ 22)
        Ruc Créid a Tulchaib Trí mBenn.[19]

7.   *co Créide cruthaig i fus* (§ 23)
        co Créid o Shruthair i fus.[20]

The method of edition, as has already been said above, has served to conceal some very important facts concerning this poem. We may sum up what can reasonably be said of it.

The poet lives in a place called Sruthar, which must lie south-west of the Paps Mountains. He decides to visit a wealthy lady called Créd. He sends her a letter in verse, informing her of his intention, expressing the hope that he will be well treated. He gives a flattering description of her dwelling, with deliberate reminiscences of descriptions of Otherworld dwellings found in such texts as *Serglige Con Culainn*. Créd in the prose of the Acallam is described as the daughter of Cairbre, king of Ciarraige Luachra. But the text of the poem makes it very doubtful that her father's name was Cairbre: it is much more likely that Cairbre was the name of a remote ancestor. She lived in the Paps Mountains (*Cnoc Anann = Cíche Anann*), near Loch Cuire. The precise spot is called *Cnoc na cCros*. Here we have, indeed, another indication that the poem must be understood in a Christian setting, and we may compare the remarks made above on the phrase *is cros úasa chinn* in *Géisid cúan*.

In this article I have considered two particular instances of poems which, to be properly understood, must be separated from their prose contexts. There are, I have no doubt, many other such in Irish literature. There is another obvious instance in the *Acallam*, the poem *Na hocht caire colnaide*,[21] which I would regard as a religious production of the eleventh century. Thus we learn something about the method of composition of this great *Rahmenerzählung*: the author took poems from older manuscript sources and put them in a context with which they had originally nothing to do. This, indeed, raises the question as to whether a certain amount of the poetic Dindshenchas material in the Acallam is to be separated from its prose context, a matter which it is not possible to discuss at the moment.

A special article could be written on *It é saigte gona súain*, but here a few comments must suffice. In the opinion of the present writer the poem is spoken, not by a woman, but by Gúaire's court poet. The subject of the poem, Dínertach of the Uí Fidgeinte, is to be regarded as still living at the time of composition.[22] The circumstances are, I would say, as follows: Dínertach has visited Gúaire's court, and returned to his own country. Gúaire's poet sends him a poem that commemorates his visit and regrets his departure. We must, indeed, consider the possibility that, in its original form, the poem was a genuine seventh-century production. If I am right in this matter it is the earliest example of the 'lover-poet' conceit that we see in *Géisid cúan*.

Attention may be called to two other examples of the incorporation of old poems in later saga-settings. Metrical and, perhaps, aesthetic criteria suggest that the poem *A Bé Find in ragha lium* had originally nothing to do with the saga of Tochmarc Etaíne. The author took an old poem, or rather, perhaps, excerpted some stanzas from a composition of the type of *Immram Brain*: he wrote a poor introductory stanza and added an equally poor closing stanza: thus of the seven stanzas, five have no original connection with the saga. The second example is from Caithréim Cellaig: the first three stanzas of *Is mochen a maiten bán*,[23] 'Welcome, fair morning', are best taken as a comparatively early poem (about A.D. 1000?) in which a monk welcomes the coming of dawn to his cell: the author of the saga forced it into a new context and made it the basis of a lengthy poem which he was to put into the mouth of his hero, Cellach.

NOTES

1 My views on this poem are given briefly above, p. 29.

2 The references will be to Murphy's edition of the poems *Early Irish Lyrics*, pp. 140–50. In both cases, and in other similar ones, I am forced to differ from Murphy. These differences seem to rest ultimately on our general approach to early Irish literature, a matter, perhaps, of a difference of emphasis, rather than of diametric opposition. I would agree with Murphy that there is, generally speaking, an oral background to early Irish literature. But from the earliest period there is always the possibility that a given tale is a new literary creation, with only a minimal basis in oral tradition. Even in cases where a tale has an oral basis, in the transference of the tale from the oral to the manuscript level, there may be such changes and additions that the first writer must be considered to a certain degree an author. Murphy makes less allowance for the strictly literary element in any given tale than do I.

3 Murphy translates: 'the greatness of his beauties set my wits astray'. But the meaning may rather be: 'What has driven me to (sorrowful) distraction is (the remembrance of) the measure of his gracious qualities.'

4 It could, of course, be maintained that the poem was in fact composed by a woman on the death of her husband or lover, Cael, son of Crimthann, about A.D. 1100. It is, however, much more likely to be a professional poem; the use of the language of love by a poet for a patron, as will be shown below, is quite conventional.

5 The thrush in Druim Caín and the blackbird in Leitir Laíg are probably to be taken as mourning for Cael, since no specific sorrow of theirs is mentioned. Murphy reads *dá lí* and translates 'of two colours'. But we should quite clearly read *Dá Lí* (as does Dr. Knott, in her edition in *Irish Syllabic Poetry*). The poet is using place-names for pathetic effect, and finds those with the numeral *dá* particularly apt. (*Rinn Dá Bhárc, Loch Dá Chonn, Druim Dá Thrén, Druim Dá Léis, Daire Dá Dos*). I would suggest that the poet's intention in using place-names with *dá* may carry a poetic implication that things are properly in pairs, and that with Cael's death a unity between him and the poet has been broken.

6 Compare the idea of a 'stone of equal life' (*cloch comshaeguil*) for a discussion of which see my *Studies in Irish Literature and History*, pp. 204–8.

7 Compare *Cuileán na ríoghna ó Ros Cré*, Poems on the O'Reillys (Carney) line 2965. I can quote, but only from memory, a similar line: *mac na mná ó ríoghLunnain*.

8 Since the above was first written I have dealt with this conceit in *The Irish Bardic Poet*, Dolmen Press, 1967.

9 Dioghluim Dána (Mac Cionnaith), p. 270.

10 Poems on the O'Reillys (Carney), line 3878.

11 I would translate: 'I make a journey on Friday (though I do so I am a true guest) to the house of Créide—no little stress—towards the mountain lying in the north-east.'

12 Mr. Seán Ó Súilleabháin of the Irish Folklore Commission tells me that Friday is considered lucky for beginning things (ploughing, etc.). Monday is the 'unlucky' day.

13 Also, sometimes, *Craoidhe*. For discussion of the name see *Poems on the Butlers* (Carney), p. 102, *Poems on the O'Reillys* (Carney), p. 293, *Scéla Cano meic Gartnáin* (Binchy), p. 26.

14 *go Créidhe dan críoch Anann* (Ní Sh.). Here the scribe has obviously dropped *cnoc* before *Anann*.

15 This stanza is omitted (Ní Sh.).

16 *Mad áil do Chréidh Chnuic na cCros* (Ní Sh.).

17 *do Chreidhe da ngoir in chaoi* (Ní Sh.).

18 This line is essentially as in the Ní Shéaghdha text. Murphy's variant texts have *claind Cairbre*, *c*lann Cairbre.

19 There is no variant here, since elision between the last vowel of *Créide* and the following vowel made it unnecessary to rewrite the line. Here again, however, the Ní Shéaghdha text supports the monosyllabic reading: *rucc Crédh a tulchoibh trí m[b]eann*.

20 The last two lines have been completely re-written in the Ní Shéaghdha version: *abradh riom Créidhe co ngus/'mo cion, a Chaoil, dot thurus'*.

21 SG, p. 160.

22   *Cráidid mo chride cainech,*
         a Chríst cáid, a ḟoraided
'His grievous death, holy Christ, torments my kindly heart' (Murphy, EIL, p. 88). I find it hard to accept *cainech* 'kindly': *a ḟoraided*, 'his violent death', is too far from the manuscript reading: *i ḟorroídhedh*.

23 Dr. Mulchrone's edition (1933), p. 13.

Dreams in early European literature

It is a mark of our modern civilization that dreams have disappeared from the world of literature. We no longer take them seriously as a part of our consciousness. We rarely trouble to record, or even to remember them, still less to cultivate them deliberately. The cultivation is a lost technique, the interpretation a lost art. The world of dreams, together with most aspects of our supernatural consciousness, is a lost world to the modern age.

With this sharply defined distinction between dream and reality we have lost the world of vision and of supernatural appearances and experiences generally. When, however, we look into early Celtic and Norse literature, and also into that of Greece and Rome, we are constantly in a state of uncertainty as to whether the supernatural experience is a dream, or a vision; whether the experience occurs, that is to say, to the subject subjectively, in his sleep, or as an objective reality.

The supernatural experiences in early Celtic and Norse literature fall into two classes—those in which a supernatural being appears to a mortal and those in which mortals make supernatural journeys to the land of the dead. Such stories are often indistinguishable from dreams, as the two types of experience tend to merge into one another. But the two classes of experience—the ghostly and the dreams—are nevertheless distinct fundamentally.

In losing our personal interest in dreams a valuable literary motif has disappeared. The Greeks and Romans recognized its value at all times, and made extensive use of it. But by the time they reached the threshold of the Dark Ages—by the late fourth century—their treatment of dreams had become in general realistic, and it is interesting to notice how topical the subjects have become.

The Gaulish poet, Ausonius, was evidently a tremendous dreamer. He has an interesting passage in his poem *Ephemeris*, 'the Daily Round',

33

in which he enumerates all the principal types of dreams and nightmares to which he is habitually subject—'Now I see myself applauding as one of a triumphal throng; again I am dragged through the streets, a disarmed Alan prisoner of war. And now I gaze upon the temples of the gods, their sacred portals and golden palaces; or seem to recline at a feast upon a couch of Garron (Tyrian) purple, and presently sit feasting at the table of some steamy eating-house.'[1]

The whole passage is especially interesting for its modern tone. In spite of the setting in a Roman world, the kind of experiences which the poet has in sleep bears the same relationship to those of his normal life as our own dreams tend to do. And they are just as random, just as chaotic.

Even when the scene is laid in Heaven the dream of the late Roman is topical and realistic in character, and modelled on, though not necessarily reproducing, an actual experience. St. Jerome,[2] haunted by a feeling of guilt arising from his unquenchable love of the Classics, records an experience in a dream or ecstasy that he is being flagellated before the tribunal of the judge who reproaches him for his love of the ancient pagan writers: 'You are not a Christian, you are a Ciceronian.'

This we should call a topical dream, the direct result of St. Jerome's sensitive conscience. It is noticeable, however, that the imagery of the literary record has nothing in common with a spiritual experience in a Christian Heaven. It is closely modelled on a secular court presided over by a judge, the prisoner receiving his stripes as punishment in his presence.[3]

St. Patrick, in the small compass of his extant writings, records no less than three dreams. The first relates to the period of his captivity in Ireland in his youth. He dreams[4] that a ship is riding at anchor in a certain port, far away, perhaps two hundred miles, and a voice is saying to him: 'Lo thy ship is ready.' He obeys the implications of the dream and finds the ship, and sails away as he has been directed. This we should call a prophetic dream, perhaps a touch of Celtic second-sight.

The second experience[5]—he does not actually call it a dream—is a pure nightmare in the literal sense; for while he was wandering— perhaps in Gaul—after a sea voyage of three days he dreamed that a heavy weight 'like a huge rock' fell upon him which he ascribes to Satan, and he awoke crying: 'Helias, helias!' Why does he record it? It appears to be quite unmotivated.

34

Finally, after his return to his kindred in Britain, St. Patrick has his famous dream[6] of the messenger from Ireland, the letter-carrier Victoricus who was carrying a bundle of letters. One was addressed to the 'sanctus puer', and was signed on the cover by the writers, the 'voice of the Irish', and as he read it it seemed as if he were listening to the people of Ireland inviting him to come over and visit them again. Later tradition transformed Victor into an angel bringing to the saint a summons from his old companions to come and convert them;[7] but this is remote from St. Patrick's words. The picture which he gives is simply that of a letter-carrier, a postman arriving with the mail from Ireland, and handing to the saint a letter of invitation to revisit old friends.

This dream is, however, followed on other nights by dreams in which he believes himself to have been in communion with Christ; but he seems to state clearly that he is quite uncertain whether the experiences are subjective or objective.[8] Indeed, as in the case of so many other visionaries, it is not always clear whether the saint regarded his experience as a dream or a vision. It is doubtful if he would have been interested in the distinction, or have regarded it as a valid one. Those who are familiar with the contemporary letters of the period will realize how realistic St. Patrick's dream is in his own account, and how free from mysticism. The scene is exactly analogous to the annual arrival of the letter-carrier Victor at the household of St. Paulinus in the Campagna, bringing the mail from his friends in Gaul, and more particularly from Sulpicius Severus.[9] It is a curious coincidence that even the postman's name is the same. One is tempted to ask if it is an appropriate nickname for postmen in a period when many obstacles must have been overcome before the mail could be safely delivered. What I want to emphasize here, however, is the realism of St. Patrick's dream of Victor and its casual nature. St. Patrick may have regarded the experience as an injunction, and he certainly went to Ireland in response to it; but the actual dream as he records it is simply a casual invitation.

So far there is nothing in any of these dreams which, given the circumstances, would call for comment if they were related today, except perhaps St. Patrick's 'second-sight' dream, and even this would not be strange in the Highlands. For the rest they are casual, realistic, directly traceable to the circumstances which gave rise to them, and completely modern. There is on record, however, a supernatural vision of quite a different kind which is attributed to St. Martin of Tours,[10] whose death is believed to have taken place *c*. 397. The saint is told by the people that at a certain spot martyrs had been buried and the place was in consequence held to be holy. The saint is unwilling to discourage the people, but doubtful of the facts, as there was no clear tradition of the martyrdom and so he is anxious to ascertain the truth, and he takes measures to find out.

What are these measures? He goes and stands upright on the tomb and prays God to make known the name and merits of the dead man. Then a hideous and fearful spectre rises beside him, the occupant of the tomb, and confesses himself a brigand who had been executed for his former crimes. The bystanders hear his voice without perceiving anything. The saint, in fact, is making deliberate use of a technique for ascertaining an unknown fact hidden from his conscious self. He seeks a supernatural vision or experience. He goes to work deliberately to get it. He goes to the tomb, and the truth which he is seeking is revealed to him. Its authenticity is subsequently tested and proved by excavation. It will be noted that no actual sleep is mentioned. But sleeping on the tomb of the dead is a well-recognized piece of technique, both in the Ancient World and in the Medieval Church, as a means of inducing a supernatural vision. I shall refer to this more fully later. It should be mentioned here, however, that a number of other dreams and visions are ascribed to St. Martin in the *Life*,[11] and that here, as often elsewhere, it is difficult, and at times impossible, to distinguish between dreams and visions. Very frequently both words are used of the same experience.

Before leaving the subject of dreams in the literature of the fifth century I must mention St. Augustine, who pays great attention to the subject.[12] The dream of his mother,[13] which he relates in full, is well known—of the 'very beautiful young man' who came towards her 'with a cheerful countenance', and prophesied to her in somewhat cryptic terms of the conversion of her son.

Many of his less edifying dreams he ascribes to the devil; but he has one of particular interest which he reports and clearly believes:

> Another told how one night before he slept an old acquaintance of his, a philosopher, came to him and expounded certain Platonisms unto him, which he would not expound to him before. So after-

wards he asked him why he did it there which he would not do in his own house when he was entreated?

'I did it not', quoth the other, 'indeed I dreamed that I did it.' And so that which the one dreamed the other in a fantastical appearance beheld: these now were related by such as I think would not lie, for had anyone told them, they would not have been to be believed.[14]

Now Ausonius, St. Jerome, St. Augustine, even St. Patrick, belonged to the world of Roman culture. Their outlook is modern, and if they had lived today they would not have seemed strange to us— not nearly so strange as the saints of the Middle Ages. But St. Martin is different. His procedure would seem very strange to a modern archaeologist. He belonged to the Greek, not the Roman world, to Pannonia on the Danube, and the monasticism which he introduced was as yet unknown in the West, though already established in the Greek Church. There was much of Oriental mysticism in it, and his treatment of the tomb of the dead as an oracle belongs in origin to the Greek World.

When we turn to the literatures of northern Europe, of Celtic and Teutonic lands, we find that the deliberate cultivation of dreams is very widely practised. Perhaps it would not be too much to say that the majority of the dreams to which prominence is given as a literary motif are voluntary and deliberate, brought on by the practice of a technique, and for a definite, often a practical purpose. They have a practical end in view, and by a deliberate procedure they put the dreamer in direct contact with the supernatural world from which he is seeking guidance, or with which he desires contact. The dreams tend to become part of the equipment of the spiritual specialist. In both Celtic and Teutonic literature, as in the Latin dreams related above, the distinction between a subjective dream and an objective or projected vision is very often obliterated, and no categorical distinction exists between the form which the experience assumes. Dreams and visions, in fact, cannot be distinguished by their own features unless we are told which they happen to be. But very often we are told, and it is chiefly the definite dreams that I propose to consider here.

Our evidence is fullest and clearest for Norse literature,[15] and so I will give first place to it. But the evidence from Celtic lands is hardly less extensive, especially from the rich literature of early Ireland.

Wales and Scotland have also something to contribute. Moreover the consistency of the literature of dreams in all these Celtic countries is impressive—consistency not only with one another but also with early Scandinavian literature. Together they offer an overwhelming array of evidence in regard to the deliberate inducement of dreams; the procedure and technique employed; the definite purpose aimed at; the nature of the supernatural experience, and the practical results. The most striking features which these dreams share in common, however, are (1) that they generally relate to the underworld, or the dead; and (2) that they are for the most part shared with the rest of the community. This will become clear as we proceed. Accidental dreams play no important part in either Celtic or Teutonic literature, with the possible exception of the dreams of a mother before the birth of her child.

In the literatures of northern Europe we find the habit of dreaming generally bound up with special supernatural gifts or experiences and often the mark of a spiritual specialist. Dreams form, in fact, the ritual framework and points of climax in his spiritual functioning. They commonly occur (1) early in life, e.g. frequently at the age of 10, often in circumstances which indicate a spiritual initiation; (2) at great crises, indicating events of importance, and carrying injunctions; (3) in regulated dissociation, and as hired spiritual aid, always paid for. This is consistent with what we read of the initial stages of a shaman's call in other continents, such as Africa, where the coming of a shaman's power is said to announce itself—e.g. among the Nuba—by 'fear dreams or attacks', followed by controlled dissociation, and this again by prophetic dreams of a kind, we are told, which ordinary people do not have. Among the Zulu also frequent and prolonged dreams are said to herald the approach of the shaman's 'call'.

It is characteristic of the dreams of northern Europe—Norse and Irish alike—that although they are part of the paraphernalia of the spiritual specialist they do not seem to belong to the religion or mythology of the accepted pantheon, though they are perhaps associated with certain gods of a pantheon acting in a purely private capacity. The Icelander Snorri, our chief authority on early Norse mythology, who wrote early in the thirteenth century, does not include dreams among the prominent activities of the gods in *Ásgarthr*. We do not hear of dreams in the Irish saga on 'The Second Battle of Moytura',[16] where the pantheon of Irish gods is assembled to fight their overseas invaders, the half monstrous *Fomori*. In Norse we hear of dreams in connection with Thor, but only in his association with grave-mounds. In Irish we have a very prominent dream related of the god Óengus;[17] but again he dwells in a funeral mound.

In both literatures the dream, when associated with gods, is directly connected with the world of the dead, sometimes with dead ancestors. It is no part of a nature religion, or of a religion of the sky god in any form, or of monotheism. It springs from powers under the earth, whether dead ancestors or chthonic deities, and it is a part of what the Siberians would refer to as 'Black Shamanism'. In the great majority of cases the spiritual forces encountered in dreams are hostile in aspect and potentiality, even though their ministration and visitation may have a beneficial potentiality. The dreamer as intermediary and spiritual specialist must see to it that this desirable result is brought about, and his value is correspondingly a high one to the community.

It is a striking fact that in the literature of northern Europe women are seldom spoken of as dreaming except about the fate of their sons. Where the literatures are so extensive as in early Norse and Celtic it is hazardous to make negative statements; but I cannot recall records of women's dreams relating primarily to themselves, or to their husbands, or to national events, and though their supernatural and prophetic visions are recorded, such as that of the prophetess Fedelm to Queen Medb in the Irish saga of the *Táin Bó Cuailnge*,[18] these visions are not said to occur in sleep. In one of the most interesting Norse stories of a prophetic woman—the 'Little *völva*' in *Thorfins Saga Karlsefnis* (cap. 3),[19]—so far from the inspiration being derived from sleep it is stimulated by magic songs, and the *völva* declares that it is essential for her séance that certain songs known as *varthlokkur* should be sung. Yet it is a curious fact that we sometimes read in the Norse sagas that just before beginning to prophesy, the prophetess yawns.[20] Dr. Lindgren[21] noticed the same habit of yawning immediately preceding a performance by the Tungus Shamanka Olga and Sieroszewski describes a Yakut shaman's performance beginning with a great yawn.[22] Why do we read so little of women's dreams in a literature in which women figure prominently?

In early Norse literature instances occur of professional women (*seithkonur spákonur, völur*) who go about with a suite of attendants and organize prophetic séances at feasts in houses of great men for money. In *Örvar-Odds Saga* (cap. 2) we are told of a *völva*, who is also called a *seith-kona*, who was accustomed to attend feasts for the purpose of prophesying men's fates, and that she was attended by a suite of fifteen men and fifteen maidens.[23] In Scandinavia their appearance is only associated with the very earliest times and they are sometimes said to be Lappish.[24]

In Norway, as in other parts of the world, the prophetic gift was hereditary. In the tenth century the Norse prophet Thorleifr Spaki, 'Thorleifr the seer', deliberately exercised the supernatural dreaming faculty inherited from his ancestor, also called Thorleifr Spaki, who was the official seer of King Halfdan the Black of Vestfold in Norway, father of King Harold the Fair-haired. We also find this inherited prophetic faculty very strong in the early royal family of Norway. It is possibly for this reason that King Halfdan the Black complained to his seer Thorleifr Spaki I when he could not dream.

On the other hand his own brother, Óláfr Geirstathálfr, had highly developed supernatural gifts. He dreamed one day that a great plague was coming, and it is interesting testimony to the strength of the belief attached to the warning that he is stated to have built a great barrow in which he and his followers were to be interred when the plague killed them. And so it all came about. Later Óláfr appeared in a dream to the foster-brother of the great grandson of Óláfr's nephew, Harold the Fair-haired, bidding him break into the barrow and take his insignia to the son born to Harold Grenski, great-grandson of Harold the Fair-haired who was Óláfr's nephew. And again everything happened just as the dream had foretold.

The technique for inducing a prophetic dream is highly developed. We have early recipes from Celtic countries. The text of an interesting Irish one, known as *Imbas forosnai*, 'Inspiration which enlightens', occurs in a ninth-century text known as *Cormac's Glossary*.[25] A later Welsh one is referred to incidentally by Giraldus Cambrensis (*c.* 1147–*c.* 1223) in connection with a class of 'inspired' speakers known as *awenyddion*.[26] From the Irish recipe we gather that the seer who seeks supernatural knowledge induces a sleep, during which he is carefully watched by his companions lest he should awaken or be disturbed. So also the *awenyddion*. When the dreamer awakens he relates to those around who have been assisting him all that he has seen and heard in his sleep. He is, in fact, treated as an oracle.

Both Celtic and Norse stories contain many incidental references to the methods by which a prophetic sleep was superinduced. We read in a medieval Welsh story of the hero Rhonabwy sleeping on a yellow calf-skin[27] which had this inevitable result of producing a vision. We may compare the procedure of the Yakut shaman of northern Siberia who lies on a white mare's skin as a preliminary to his performance,[28] possibly as a substitute for the heavenward journey of the Mongol shaman on his hobby-horse. In Norse we find Old Kveldúlfr, the grandfather of Egill Skallagrímsson, who is said in *Egils Saga* to have been in the habit of wrapping his head in his mantle and remaining silent during the evenings in order to acquire supernatural knowledge. At such times he is said to have been *hamramr*. That is to say his soul wandered abroad in strange transformations, generally in the form of some animal. In Norse such supernatural experiences are not rare.[29] They are more often related of those whose spirit leaves them to travel abroad than of those possessed by an alien spirit.[30]

In Early Norse literature the favourite method of inducing a supernatural experience was sleeping on a barrow (a chamber tomb of the dead), or in its immediate neighbourhood. Early Welsh literature also recognizes the practice. The barrows of the dead were regarded as sanctuaries, and to sleep at them was to acquire revelation of the supernatural. The dream motif is a typical opening to Norse stories of supernatural visits and visitations generally, and these are, of course, especially liable to happen to people in the neighbourhood of a barrow, even accidentally.

According to the admirably preserved traditions of the early history of Norway dreams were earnestly cultivated by the royal family, the ancestors of King Harold the Fair-haired. We have seen that his father, Halfdan the Black, is said to have been much put about because he never had dreams, and he made complaint of this to Thorleifr Spaki, his sage, or, as we might say, his right-hand adviser in matters supernatural—Thorleifr Spaki, the 'Seer' or the 'wise' with the sense of supernatural wisdom. Thorleifr advised him to go to sleep in a *svínaboeli*, 'a pig-sty', 'as he himself always did when he sought dreams', and the procedure was always efficacious. The king accordingly complied, and after that, we are told, dreams were never lacking to him. There can, I think, be little doubt that the *svínaboeli*, the 'pig-sty', is a poetical periphrasis for a barrow or tomb of the dead, the dwelling generally associated in mythology with the god Freyr, whose symbol is a swine or boar. The process followed by Thorleifr and the king is simply the incubation which played so large a part in the late classical world, especially the late Greek world. It is interesting to find a descendant of Thorleifr Spaki in a later generation following a precisely similar procedure, for we are told that when his jealous rival wanted to put out his eye, he found him lying on a barrow 'as his custom was'.[31] The reference to the eye is undoubtedly to Thorleifr's prophetic eye, his professional power of seeing the supernatural.

The purpose of the dreams varied. In Welsh and Irish in the formulae cited above the dreamer seems to have been used by his clients as an oracle, doubtless to ascertain hidden facts which they desire to know. We are not always told what the dreams are about but their object is revelation by supernatural means. In Norse the most interesting and the commonest reason for inducing a supernatural sleep by the technique of lying on a barrow is to acquire inspiration, especially poetic inspiration. This is strange and not readily explicable; but the instances are both numerous and striking.[32]

Icelandic prose sagas offer two particularly interesting instances of the deliberate cultivation of dreams as a source of supernatural inspiration. The first[33] relates to a shepherd Hallbjörn who was ambitious to become a poet. He was in the habit of spending the night on the barrow of a dead poet, on whom he was anxious to compose a panegyric; but the muse was coy, and he could never progress beyond the first line: 'Here lies a poet.' One night, falling asleep after his usual failure, he saw the barrow open, and the occupant appeared and said to him:

'There you lie, Hallbjörn, struggling to compose a panegyric on me which is beyond your powers. One of two things will happen, either you will surpass everyone in this art which you will acquire from me—and this is the most probable alternative; or else you need not struggle any longer with it. I am going to recite a verse to you now, and if you acquire it, and remember it when you awake, you will become a great poet and compose panegyrics for many chiefs, and become highly accomplished in this art.'

Then he recited a panegyric on himself which Hallbjörn remembered when he awoke, and he became a great panegyric poet. In short he acquired his gift of poetry by a deliberate procedure, a dream perseveringly acquired on the barrow of a dead poet.

The belief that a dream on a barrow will win the gift of speech or eloquence from its occupant is corroborated in another Icelandic saga from the same manuscript, the well-known *Flateyjarbók*, relating to a certain Thorsteinn Uxafótr, whose mother is said to be dumb.[34] While Thorsteinn and a companion are passing through a deep valley they are overtaken by night and see a tall barrow before them. Thorsteinn tells his companion that he has decided to pass the night on it, and forbids him to waken him whatever his behaviour. Then as he sleeps he contorts his body strangely, and on awakening relates how, in his sleep, he saw the occupant of the barrow come out and tell him that his brother, Oddr, who is buried in the barrow with him, possesses gold which will give the power of speech. Thorsteinn enters and overcomes Oddr and acquires the gold, and when he awakens he finds the gold beside him. When he places it under his mother's tongue she gains the power of speech—or, more probably (poetic) eloquence. Fundamentally the story of the deliberate inculcation of the dream with the purpose of acquiring poetry or eloquence by sleeping on the barrow of a poet, or one possessed of the power to bestow the gift of poetry, is the same in both stories.

The form of technique which consists of repairing to a barrow to get in touch with the supernatural is widely known in Celtic literature also, and here the association with a chthonic cult is demonstrable. Perhaps the most obvious instance is the *Aislinge Óengusso*, the 'Dream of Óengus', already referred to, which relates to a dream of Óengus mac Óc, the god whose home was traditionally stated to be in the great barrow of Brug na Bóinne or New Grange on the river Boyne. Óengus was therefore one of the chthonic deities of Ireland. His dream is unlike the Norse dreams discussed above in that it relates to a female, for the god dreamed that a beautiful woman appeared to him in his sleep, for love of whom he fell sick and pined. In the Norse Helgi poems of the *Older Edda*, however, it is a *valkyrie* who appears to Helgi Hjörvarthsson as he is seated on a barrow. Again it is a *valkyrie* who enters the barrow to pass a night with Helgi Hundingsbani, and we have, in fact, a whole class of Norse literature associating *valkyries* with the barrows of the dead. The Norse parallels with the Irish story are, in fact, very common.

In Welsh literature also dreams are deliberately induced by a recognized technique. In the story of Pwyll, prince of Dyfed (Pembrokeshire), Pwyll seats himself on a mound and at once has a supernatural vision. The mound is either a barrow or a similar structure such as the *gorsedd* at Narberth.[35] At once Pwyll sees a supernatural lady riding by whom he is constrained to follow to her home in the super-natural regions. The story resembles those of the Irish hero Connla the Fair and of the Norse hero Helgi Thórisson, both of whom are lured away from home by supernatural women. There is, however, one great difference. Connla never returns, and Helgi only for a very brief space. Pwyll, however, eventually returns to the world of men, and the story has a happy ending. But these may well be medieval features in the Welsh story, like the detail of the *gorsedd* at Narberth, actually a Norman motte and not really a barrow which, however, it closely resembles. The story as we have it was recorded in medieval times. But we have several other dream stories in our slender library of medieval Welsh tales, such as the famous 'Dream of Maxen Wledig' —the Emperor Maximus—as well as the 'Dream of Rhonabwy'.[36]

Perhaps the closest Celtic parallel to our Norse dream stories, and certainly the most interesting, is the story of Macbeth as related in the earliest version—that of the Scottish historian Wyntoun (c. 1350–c. 1420). In this early version the prophecy of the three 'weird sisters' to Macbeth takes place—not, as in Shakespeare, on a 'blasted heath'—but in a dream, which comes to him while he is sleeping, during a time when, in his youth, he is dwelling with King Duncan, whom Wyntoun regards as his uncle, his mother's brother. Wyntoun in this differs from Bellenden and Boece who represent the encounter with the 'weird sisters' as a real experience, and as shared by Macbeth and Banquo, the thane of Lochaber, when the two are in the open country, and not in the immediate vicinity of the king. But it is important to remember that Wyntoun flourished about a century before Boece and two centuries before Bellenden. Moreover the milieu and circumstances in which he wrote give good ground for taking his early version as the more authentic tradition. Wyntoun was librarian to the Augustinian Priory on St. Serf's Island in Loch Leven, Fife. The foreshore of the island had been given to the Culdees of St. Serf's by Macbeth and his wife Gruoch, but later the Culdees had been supplanted by the Augustinian friars, and it is undoubtedly to the ill feeling which would naturally result under such circumstances between the two religious bodies that we must ascribe the blackening of Mac-beth's character which appears for the first time in Wyntoun's narrative. All earlier accounts agree in representing him as a pious benefactor of the Church, and no hint of murder or other crime is attributed to him till nearly four hundred years later.[37]

Now Wyntoun is responsible, not only for the transformation of Macbeth into a murderer, and the son of the devil: he is also responsible for the whole of the supernatural machinery which we have come to think of as an integral part of the Macbeth story, and of which the earlier Latin and Saxon authorities—several of them contemporary with Macbeth himself—contain no hint. Where did Wyntoun find them? He might, of course, have heard them from oral tradition, which would linger long in the district which formed a part of his donation to the community on St. Serf's island and of his wife's estate. It is more probable, however, that these local traditions had been written down earlier, and that Wyntoun found them in the long *Historia* or Saga which we know to have been contained in one of the Registers kept in the island. This register contained notes of events relating to the community, as well as other items, and formed a part of the tiny library of some sixteen volumes of which Wyntoun was librarian. The *Historia* formed a large part of the register, and though it is lost we have good reason to believe that it contained the account of Macbeth from which Wyntoun derived his supernatural material.[38] If so, it must have resembled the Irish *baile* stories, the stories relating to the supernatural dreams, visions and experiences of the early Irish kings such as Conn Cétchathach and Cormac MacAirt. The point is of interest as suggesting that Scotland has had an early saga literature closely resembling that of early Ireland. Unfortunately few early written remains are extant. But the Macbeth saga is not the only one. The story of the 'Gett' or conception of Malcolm Canmore by the daughter of the Miller of Forteviot, also narrated by Wyntoun, is another example of the same class of saga, and others might be cited.[39]

It will be seen that a close similarity exists between the Norse and the Celtic dream literature and the similarity is much closer and more fundamental than can be demonstrated in the present brief sketch. The most striking characteristic in both literatures is their almost exclusive concern with the supernatural. Both the milieu and the personnel belong to the spirit world. Almost equally striking is their conventional framework. The same kind of dream tends to recur very frequently. This is, of course, attributable in part to literary convention; but not wholly so, for I have shown elsewhere[40] that a similar uniformity underlies the recitals of the Siberian shamans in a state of dissociation. The late Professor Seligman attributed it to the subconscious working of the human mind along traditional lines, and in this he is probably right.

A third feature shared by the Celtic and Teutonic Groups is their functional character. They serve a purpose, whether as prophecies (e.g. the Scottish Macbeth; the Norse Óláfr Geirstatha-álfr and the Irish Conn Cétchathach); or as revelation (e.g. the Norse Thorleifr Spaki and Hrani; the Irish Cormac; the Welsh *awenyddion*) or as inspiration (e.g. the Norse Thorleifr Jarlsskald, Thorsteinn Uxafótr; and the Irish *Imbas forosnai*). Even concrete objects play their part (Thorsteinn Uxafótr, Cormac, etc.).

It is characteristic of the functional character of these Norse and Celtic dreams that they are deliberately cultivated or induced by an acquired technique. We have seen Halfdan the Black instructed by his sage Thorleifr Spaki as to how to set about it. In Welsh tradition one recognized way to acquire a dream was evidently to sleep on a yellow calf-skin; another to sit on a mound. We have seen that both Giraldus Cambrensis in Wales and Cormac's Glossary from Ireland contain full recipes for inducing supernatural dreams.

The professional dreamer is not always distinct from the visionary, and he commonly shares his distinctive social status. He is *spaki* in Norse, 'wise' with the wisdom of revealed knowledge. In Wales the class are known as *awenyddion*, 'the inspired', the Welsh word *awen* denoting inspiration, especially poetic inspiration. I do not know of an Irish equivalent but the verb *ad-cí* 'he sees' is commonly, if not generally used of supernatural rather than natural vision.

Now it will be seen that all these features which the Celtic and Teutonic stories share are absent from the Latin dreams of the fourth and fifth centuries which I described earlier. These Latin dreams deal with the concrete world of reality. For St. Jerome's, though its actual setting appears to be in Heaven, is, as we have seen, a picture based on an earthly culprit being flogged before a judge. The fourth- and fifth-century types are all very different from one another, being occasional and realistic instead of following a conventional pattern. They are not functional, and serve no social purpose, and so are not artificially induced so far as our evidence goes. Nor are they in any case associated with any particular class of people. They belong to a different world of thought from the Northern group. They claim comparison, like everything else in the period, with the modern world of thought.

What is the origin of the highly elaborated form of dream and dream literature which is characteristic of the Celtic and Teutonic Dark Ages? We have seen that St. Martin is responsible for introducing a form of Christian monasticism and mysticism into Gaul from the East, and that he also has a dream like those of the North in all particulars. This hint points to the eastern Mediterranean, and here we find the nearest analogies, in actual practice, flourishing in Epidauras *c.* 421 B.C. in the Incubation temple sacred to Aesculapius to which people repaired for supernatural cures and revelations at the tombs of the dead.[41]

At such incubation temples[42] the sick were induced by various means to sleep and to dream and so to obtain revelation and oracular responses, and on their awakening the priests interpreted their dreams, and ascertained from them the cause of the illness and the method of cure to be pursued. It is a notable fact that the patient was habitually said to sleep on the skin of some animal, like the hero in the medieval Welsh story of the *Dream of Rhonabwy*. The Romano-British temple at Lydney, with its elaborate series of little cubicles, is thought to have been used as an Incubation temple, and the type of temple is traced to the cult of Aesculapius, the divine physician of late Greek mythology. There can be no doubt that it originated in much earlier times, perhaps at the tombs of dead heroes, or heroes who remain forever alive in the earth or cave, such as Trophonios at Lebadeia in Boeotia. The cult is closely bound up with necromancy. It is Greek in origin, spreading to the Latin World only in comparatively late times. This east Mediterranean cult has doubtless affected the Northern World, partly in the form of a cult, as at Lydney; partly in the form of the stories discussed above.

Perhaps we need not attempt to narrow too closely the origin of this highly developed dream cult. In any case to do so would be outside our sphere; for Classical scholars are still uncertain as to the early stages of the incubation cult, despite the evidence at their disposal. At present we must leave it in their hands. But it would seem highly probable that the elaborate dream literature of our Celtic and Teutonic forefathers, especially in connection with the 'barrows' or bee-hive-shaped tombs of the dead, goes back to the incubation cult of the east Mediterranean world.

NOTES

1 *Ausonius*, edited and translated by H. G. Evelyn White, vol. I (London, 1919), p. 12f.

2 Epistle xxii, 30 (to Eustochium).

3 For a brief discussion as to the fictitious nature of the dream see P. de Labriolle, *History and Literature of Christianity*, translated from the French by H. Wilson (London, 1924), p. 11f., and the references there cited.

4 *Confession*, cap. 17.

5 *Ibid.*, cap. 20.

6 *Ibid.*, cap. 23.

7 Cf. the *Tripartite Life of St. Patrick* (edited and translated by Whitley Stokes, London, 1887), vol. I, p. 28.

8 *Confession*, caps. 24, 25.

9 I have given some account of the Gaulish Victor in my book of *Poetry and Letters in Early Christian Gaul* (London, 1955), pp. 72f. and refs.

10 *Life* by Sulpicius Severus, cap. XI.

11 Cf. e.g. *Life*, cap. III, where the saint, after he has divided his cloak with a beggar, has a vision of Christ 'the following night, during his sleep'. Cf. also *Ibid.*, cap. V. 'He was warned in a dream' to go back to Pannonia to convert his parents and province.

12 *Confessions*, X, xxx.

13 *Ibid.*, III, xi.

14 *The City of God*, XIV, xix (Healey's transl. London (Dent), 1931).

15 For a general account of dreams in Old Norse literature, together with appendices containing texts and translations, see G. D. Kelchner, *Dreams in Old Norse Literature and their Affinities in Folklore* (Cambridge, 1935). Much interesting matter relating to Dreams is also contained in H. R. Ellis, *The Road to Hel* (Cambridge, 1943).

16 Translated into English by Cross and Slover, *Ancient Irish Tales* (New York, 1936), pp. 28ff.

17 *The Dream of Óengus (Aislinge Óenguso)*, edited by the Rev. F. Shaw (Dublin, 1934); translated by K. H. Jackson, *A Celtic Miscellany* (London, 1951), pp. 97ff.

18 Edited by E. Windisch, *Die Altirische Heldensage Táin Bó Cúalnge* (Leipzig, 1905); translated by Joseph Dunn, *The Ancient Irish Epic Tale Táin Bó Cúalnge* (London, 1914), pp. 13ff.

19 The passage is translated by P. B. Du Chaillu, *The Viking Age*, vol. I (London, 1889), p. 397f.

20 E.g. *Hrólfs Saga Kraka*, cap. 3; cf. *Orkneyinga Saga*, cap. 26.

21 See her unpublished Ph.D. Dissertation, no. 732 (Cambridge). 'Notes on the Reindeer Tungus of Manchuria', 1936, ch. IV, p. 197

22 See M. A. Czaplicka, *Aboriginal Siberia* (Oxford, 1914), p. 234.

23 Cf. *Hrólfs Saga Kraka*, cap. 3; *Nornagests Tháttr*, cap. 11. *Orms Tháttr Stórólfssonar*, cap. 5; *Vatnsdæla Saga*, cap. 10. Here, however, no attendants are mentioned. In *Vatnsdæla Saga* the *völva* is said to be Lappish (Finna).

24 Cf. note 23 above.

25 For text, translation and parallel stories and references see my paper on 'Imbas Forosnai' in *Scottish Gaelic Studies*, IV, pp. 97ff.

26 *Ibid.*, pp. 132ff.

27 The motif is common, and a number of instances are cited by Mrs. Ettlinger in an interesting paper in a recent number of *Folklore*.

28 See Czaplicka, *op. cit.*, pp. 234, 238.

29 Cf. e.g. *Landnámabók*, V, 5.

30 On this subject see H. R. Ellis, *The Road to Hel* (Cambridge, 1943), pp. 122ff.

31 *Hallfretharsaga*, cap. 6.

32 I have made a study of the association of poetic inspiration with the barrows of the dead in a paper entitled 'Norse Ghosts', *Folklore*, LVII (1946), pp. 50ff., 106ff.

33 *Flateyjarbók*, I, pp. 207ff.

34 *Ibid.*, pp. 249ff.

35 The story of Pwyll is the first of the series of stories in the medieval Welsh collection known as the *Mabinogion*, of which the most recent and scholarly edition is that of Sir Ifor Williams, *Pedeir Keinc y Mabinogi* (Cardiff, 1930); and translation, that of G. Jones and T. Jones (London, 1949).

36 *Breudwyt Rhonabwy*, edited by Melville Richards (Cardiff, 1948); English translation by G. Jones and T. Jones, *op. cit.*

37 I have made a detailed study of the sources and the growth of the Macbeth story in *Scottish Gaelic Studies*, VI (1949), pp. 189ff.; VII (1951), pp. 1ff.

38 For the evidence and references see my article cited above.

39 For the evidence, see my article cited above.

40 *The Growth of Literature*, vol. III (Cambridge, 1940), p. 204.

41 A number of inscriptions from Epidauros, dating from the late fourth and early third century B.C., record cures from the Aesculapian temple, such as are referred to earlier in the *Plutos* of Aristophanes, produced in 388.

42 For a general account of the procedure in Epidauros and elsewhere in Classical Greece see W. K. C. Guthrie, *The Greeks and their Gods* (London 1950), pp. 248ff.

DAVID GREENE

A satire by Cathal Mac Muireadhaigh

One of the books planned by Angus Matheson was a collection of Scottish bardic verse; it was with this in mind that he edited the poems by Cathal Mac Muireadhaigh contained in RIA MS. E i 3, see *Éigse*, x–xi. It seems, therefore, appropriate to offer, in this memorial volume, another poem by the same author. It is *Sona do cheird, a Chalbhaigh*, found in Cathal's autograph in RIA MS. A v 2, 75 B, and it has been known for many years, since it was partially translated by Osborn Bergin in his lecture on Bardic Poetry (Journal of the Ivernian Soc. 5. 234).

The text presents many difficulties, the most important of which is that in several places it departs from strict metre, which is the more surprising when we consider that Cathal was capable of writing correctly, and that the poem is precisely a satire on a slovenly poet. It is possible to offer emendations in most of these cases, but it seems doubtful whether the editorial methods appropriate to a MS. like the *Book of the Dean of Lismore* should be used when we have the poet's autograph before us. I therefore print the poem as it stands, and offer emendations in the notes, rather than incorporate them in a standardized text.

1   Sona do cheird, a Chalbhaigh,
a ghiolla dhuinn dheghadhbhraigh,
tarrla d'onāir is d'ágh ort
gabhāil re dán gan docracht.

2   Maith an ceird do thogh tusa
d'fagháil muirne is macnusa,
dénamh rann gan chóir ccertuis
a n-am óil is oireachtais.

3   As sona trá tarrla dhuit
gan amus d'foghluim orrdhuirc,
bheith fa lán mogha go mer
le dán dona gan dénamh.

4   ] tagra ar ghnás nó ar ghirre
gan fheitheamh d'iúl fīrinne,
sonas nach] lér libh
's donas gan shén ar shaoithibh.

5   ] daoibh
le conntrachd dána dīamhaoin,
                       ] cháigh
ad mhionn cod [   ] is comhráigh.

6   Dā n-íosda da mhéis do mhuic
créd sin acht obair oirrdhuirc?
Uaibhse dob fherr ar domhan
geall ar uaisle ag th'ealadhuin.

7   Cur do bhriathar bun ōs cionn
fuair siph do choimes choitchionn,
's beith ar uair n-óla go lemh
córa no duan do dhénamh.

8   Gē bhuailfeá fer an tighe
d'im nō d'feoil go haingidhe,
badh cóir sgolāir do rādh ribh,
clódh ar th'onāir nī héidir.

1 Prosperous is your trade, Calbhach, strong lad of good substance; you have had the honour and success of making poetry without hardship.

2 Good is the trade you have chosen to win affection and luxury— the making of incorrect verses at the time of drinking and assembly.

3 Prosperous is your career, to win full respect quickly with a bad misshapen poem, without attempting honourable learning.

4 Without reference to custom or to brevity, without respecting true knowledge . . . while learned men are poor, without luck.

5 . . . with a bold vain imprecation . . . a talked-about object(?).

6 If you were to eat your pig from a platter, what is that but noble work; you would get respect for the nobility of your learning.

7 The ability to mix up your words is yours by common consent; being foolish while drinking is more in your line than making a poem.

8 Though you should throw butter or meat viciously at the host (?) you should still be called a scholar; your honour cannot be impugned.

3 *b* read *orrdhruic*; *c* read *modha*; *d* read *déineamh*.
4 The MS. is damaged here, so that part of 4 and 5 is illegible.
a Restore *gan*. *b* I know no word *lér* (:*shén*), which seems to be required here.
5 *d* Perhaps *mionn comhráidh* is parallel with *mionn súl*, etc.
6 *a* The subj. is required after *dá* (*dá n-itteá*).
d Read *geall ar uaisle th'ealadhan* (:*domhan*).
8 *a* *gé* requires the subj. There is no alliteration in the line: read *ben* for *fer*?
d Read *cládh* (:*rádh*).

9   Níor chuir Dia ad dheoigh do dhochar
anmhuin ris an altachadh
    gan bhúain briuais da gach bord
    a n-uair niuais do nemlorg.

10   Bheith a ccomaidh gach iarla
daoibhsi as rabhadh rímhiadha,
    go cur ghreama muin ar muin
    's do theanga ag bleith re briathraibh.

11   Truagh trā nach derna misi
amas ar iúl th'aisdisi,
    le céill gan chert gan chuma
    's gan techt ar fréimh foghluma.

12   Tréigim dlaoi an dána dhírigh
mar fuair sinn 'sna seinnlínibh,
    's bím ad t'ord go nuaidhe a-nos;
    buaine iná an lorg dar lenas.

13   Leanmhuin ghlūn nginelach cáigh
fios a n-einigh is a n-iomrāidh,
    dob ferr dhúinn dul red trēidhibh
    's cúl do chur rēr gcéidchéimeibh.

14   Maith an tráth dā dhēnamh dhūinn,
dá bhfédmaois, ar n-iúl d'iompūdh,
    's gan sbéis ag duine dar ndán
    d'éis na cruinne do chaochládh.

15   Ceird an Chalbhaigh acht gidh cóir
dul 'na seilbh budh dál dobróin,
    do-gheibh ór is annsa dho
    dhamhsa go mōr as meso.

9 God did not impose on you the hardship of waiting for the grace before you snatched brose from the tables, without asking for news (?)

10 To be in the company of an earl is an omen of high honour for you, till you put one bite on top of another while your tongue is grinding out words.

11 Alas, indeed, that I didn't try to follow your style, with incorrect, formless import, and with no relation to basic learning.

12 Let me forsake the shelter of strict verse, as I found it in the old generations, and let me enter your order in the new fashion—it is more lasting than the path I have followed!

13 To follow the degrees of each man's genealogy, to know their generosity and their fame—it would be better for me to behave like you and turn my back on my early life.

14 It would be a good time for me to change my course, if I could, since nobody takes any interest in my poetry since the world has changed.

15 However right the Calbhach's trade may be, it would be a sad thing to take it up; he gets gold, which is most dear to him—so much the worse for me.

9 The words *briuais* and *niuais*, which rhyme, must both be disyllables. On the analogy of *triubhus* (IGT Decl. § 17) from Eng. *trewes*, I take the first to be the *gs.* of **brias*, **briughas*, from Eng. *brewes* (see NED) 'brose, pottage'; Scottish Gaelic has *bruthaist* (Dwelly) which, as Professor Derick Thomson suggests to me, may have been influenced by *bruth*. If this is right, **niubhas* might mean 'news', but that is very speculative.

10 *a* No alliteration. cd. *bleith* in the final line is left without a rhyme; we could read *go ceilt greama muin ar muin/'s do theanga ag beilt re briathraibh*.

12 *a* Read *dírigh*.

13 *c* Read *dún* (:*cúl*).

14 *a* Read *dún* (:*iompúdh*).

DONALD G. HOWELLS

The Gaelic of Carloway, Isle of Lewis: prepositions with verbal nouns

This contribution describes some features of the dialect of Carloway, on the west side of Lewis, as spoken by my only informant, Miss Catherine Macdonald. I am deeply indebted to Miss Macdonald for her patient help over a long period. My thanks are due also to Miss Agnes Mackay, of Uig, and Mrs. MacIver, of Lochs, both of Lewis, who helped in maintaining the recorded conversations from which my material was in part drawn.

The Verbal Noun Unit

I use this term for the section in capital letters in the four types of sentence following:

A   *Tha e cho math dhomh* FALBH
B   *Chan urrainn dhuit* AM FAGAIL
C (i)   *Faodaidh mi* SIN A DHEANAMH
C(ii)   *Faodaidh mi* DEANAMH SIN

The *a* of type C(i) is not heard before vowels and lenited *f-*.

The initial of most vns. in type A is unmutated, except sometimes after leniting prepositions (see below). But for *dol, tighinn, gràdh—* '*ràdh*' in the literature—one always gets *a dhol, a thighinn, a ghràdh,* the *a* being heard only after final consonants. Other vns., such as *creidse, cluinntinn, faicinn,* are frequently heard aspirated, and with a *gu/nach* clause following: *chòrdadh e rium a chluinntinn gun robh Calum Cameron air an television.* The *c-* of *creidse* is always aspirated in the expression *bheir mi a chreidse air gu* . . . 'I shall make him believe that. . . .'

One never gets type C where the logical object is a simple personal

56

pronoun, as *chan urrainn dhuit iad a fhàgail; but esan a fhàgail is regular, and one finds feumaidh mi mi fhéin a nighe equally with feumaidh mi mo nighe fhéin. Where the 'object' is a noun, type C(ii) is used in perhaps 15 per cent only of the cases recorded, the noun then being nearly always in the nominative rather than in the genitive: am feum i fhéin ceannach an t-aodach aice? This type occurs most frequently after preps: air son faicinn na balaich, though even here air son na balaich a fhaicinn would be more usual. It is frequent also after agus in sentences such as: tha mi a' coimhead air adhart ri a faicinn agus cluinntinn an naidheachd aice. No doubt it is obligatory, too, where the 'object' of the vn. is itself a vn. unit, as in feumaidh e a bhith nach b'urrainn dha affòrdadh leabaidh a cheannach.

The action represented by the vn. either takes place at the same time as that of the main verb or has just been completed or else is about to take place. Thus tha/bha/bithidh mi toilichte sin a dheanamh 'I am/was/shall be pleased to do that/to have done that'. If the action is one that took place before that of the main verb or is to take place in the future, as 'I am pleased that I did that', then, as in the English equivalent, a gu/nach clause is used. For the unambiguous expression of a tense or aspect of the verb, a bhith + ag/air can be introduced: is dòcha gum bheil iad air son a bhith a' snàmh leò fhéin; bu chòir dhuit a bhith air innseadh dha m'a dheidhinn 'you should have told him about it'.

If the verbal concept requires to be negated in any one of the four types, gun is inserted immediately before the vn. unit (with or without aspiration—see below): thubhairt e rium gun suidhe ann.

Sometimes there is a passive meaning, this being most common after feumaidh: feumaidh a h-uile rud bùrn a chur air 'everything needs to be watered'. In type B, the poss. adj. can refer to the subject of the main verb; thus feumaidh an duine a fhreagairt can mean 'the man must be answered'. Here, too, a bhith can be used for clarity: feumaidh barrachd obair a bhith 'ga dheanamh/air a dheanamh 'more work needs to be done'. If the 'object' noun of type C becomes the antecedent of a rel. clause, the form of the vn. is the same as it would be if no rel. clause were involved, i.e., its initial is aspirated: na rudan is urrainn dhomh a dheanamh; cf. na daoine ris am bheil dùil aca a thighinn 'the people they expect to come'. The rel. form of feumaidh an duine a fhreagairt above is an duine a dh'fheumas a fhreagairt, pl. na daoine a dh'fheumas am freagairt.

To express the verb 'have' +logical object, the vn. unit comprises *a bhith* preceded by what can only be described as its subject: *feumaidh sinn tuilleadh còmhradh a bhith againn.* (This could also have been expressed by means of type A: *feumaidh tuilleadh còmhradh a bhith againn*). Cf. negative: *thubhairt e gun eagal air bith a bhith ort.*) In many subordinate phrases, the agent of the action represented by the vn. need not be expressed: *an àite a thighinn air ais, dh'fhuirich mi ann* (but also *an àite dhomh*). In most main clauses, the agent is implied in the first part of the sentence. For instance, in *feumaidh mi, chuimhnich mi (air), cha d'fhuair mi tìde (air), tha mi air,* the agent of the vn. following is identical with the *mi* of the subject; in *leig leam, dh'fhàg e fios agam, bu chòir dhomh,* it is identical with the 'object' of the prep. There is, however, a third category, in which a word has to be specially introduced to express the agent. In most cases of this sort a *gu/nach* clause is chosen instead, and in some it is the only method in use; for instance, where Keating has *do-chualaidh an crann-chor do thuitim ar a mac,* our dialect would have *chuala i gun do thuit . . .,* or *chuala i gun robh an crann-chor air tuiteam.* So with all tenses of this verb. The vn. unit with agent comes most often after preps. Besides *cha bhiodh tu air son gun toirinn na rudan sin leam* one can get *cha bhiodh tu air son mi na rudan sin a thabhairt leam.* Cf. *tha i air bann ùr a dhol oirre* 'it has had a new band put on it'. *a bhith* is the vn. most frequently found in this construction: *b'fheàrr leam esan a bhith ann na mi fhéin; chan eil móran feum mise a bhith a' coimhead air a shon.* The 'have' idioms above can take the place of vn. +'object' in this construction, too, giving us both an agent and a subject: *cha robh i air son esan fios a bhith aige air càil* 'she did not want him to know anything'. To negate the verbal idea in the vn. unit, *gun* appears either before or after the agent word. Note that there is no aspiration of the vn. of type A (apart from the exceptions noted at the outset). Thus: *b'fheàrr leam thusa bruidhinn rithe* 'I should prefer you to talk with her'. Ct. the *do* in the sentence from Keating above. Note also that whereas the simple pronoun 'object' is always in the gen. the simple pron. agent is, of course, in the nom. The agent in this type of sentence is, in my material, more often a pronoun than a noun.

The vn. unit can, where sense and tense permit, perform any of the functions of the noun or of the explicative *gu/nach* clause. The instances in most of the categories below are numerous, and only one or two examples are given.

I Subject of Verb: *thàinig orm* (*falbh*, etc.). Here can be included *chòrdadh e rium* 'it would please me', where a 'preparatory' subject is introduced, as in English, at the point where the actual subject would be if it were a noun. (Cf. the copula below). So also *rinn e dìreach slàinte do mo chridhe a faicinn an sin.*

II Object of Verb: *thubhairt mi ris, thug e orm, rinn mi* (functioning as an auxiliary), *faodaidh mi.* The vn. unit as object of a verb expressed periphrastically can also be placed here, as there is no question of the initial noun or vn. of the unit being in the gen.: *bha i ag iarraidh orm fuireach.* Some of these verbs are separated from their object by a prep., as *dh'fheuch e ri.* Many appear either with or without a prep.: *chuimhnich mi* (*air*), *fhuair mi* (*air*) 'I managed'.

III 'Object' of Preposition: *gun, ach,* as *cha do rinn mi càil ach an sgian a leigeil sìos.* The compound preps., such as *air son, an dèidh, mu dheidhinn,* can go as well into this category, with the simple preps., as into VI below, as neither the vn. of A, C(ii), nor the noun of C(i) ever appears in the gen.

IV Subject of Copula Sentence. The predicate can be simple as in *is urrainn dhomh, b'fheàrr leam,* or complex as in the sentence *chan e èiginn idir a tha ann dhomhsa a dhol ann.* Here, too, can be placed those expressions comprising the verb *tha* + adj. that have largely replaced *is* + predicate: *tha e furasda* (= *is* + pred.), *tha e cho math dhomh* (= *is* + noun/adj. + *dhomh*). The poss. adj. of type B may be anticipated in the subject of *tha,* giving a passive, or retroactive, meaning: *cha bhi iad duilich an cur suas idir* 'they will not be difficult to put up'.

V Predicate of Copula Sentence: *'se lìonadh nan duilleagan* (C(ii))/*na duilleagan a lìonadh* (C(i)) *an aon rud a tha i ag iarraidh.*

VI Adjunct to an abstract noun or an adjective functioning as subject, object or predicate in the first part of the sentence. The relationship between the one and the other is in many cases difficult to define, and I merely note some examples: *tha a thìde agam; tha tìde agam* (*ri*); *cha d'fhuair mi tìde* (*air*/*ri*); *chan eil math dhomh; tha thu math* (*air*); *rinn thu math; tha dùil agam; tha còir agam; cha robh feum dhuit; chan eil dòigh* (*air*); *dh'fhàg e fios agam; thàinig fios orm; tha eagal orm; cha leig thu a leas; tha iad deònach* (*air*); *bithidh mi toilichte; tha cuimhne agam* (*air*); *am b'fhiach i* (*a dhol dh'a h-iarraidh*)? 'was it worth (going to fetch)?'

The autonomy of the vn. unit is in some cases respected, in others violated:

(*a*) Aspiration or non-aspiration of the vn. of types A, C(ii), and of the indefinite noun of C(i) by a preceding prep.: there is no consistency. One gets *thubhairt e rium gun falbh/fhalbh.* So with *roimh,* and with *gun, roimh* before nouns: *gun clach/chlach a leigeil.*

(*b*) The case of the noun of C(i) after a prep.: Compound preps. are followed by the nom. form: *air son an taigh a fhaicinn.* With the simple prep., the indefinite noun is in the nom., the sg. noun after the article is only sporadically in the dative where the dat. form can be distinguished from the nom. The sg. article more often than not aspirates the initial of the following noun, where the prep. forms part of the construction of a verb/noun/adj., and there is fusion of *ri* with the article: *chuimhnich mi air a' bhuntata a chur air; dh'fheuch mi ris a' bhalach a ghlacadh.* But *air am buntata, ri am balach* would also be used here, and even *ris am balach.* The *air* used to form the perfect tenses, however, is followed by the nom. form: *tha mi air am balach a fhaicinn* only.

(*c*) The fusion or non-fusion of the prep. and the pronoun *mi fhéin,* etc. of C(i): there seems to be no consistency: *cha do chuimhnich mi air mi fhéin/orm fhéin a nighe; tha mi a' feuchainn ri mi fhéin/rium fhéin a nighe.*

Following are some of the preps. that are used in more or less specialized ways with the vn. unit, notably to link the verb *tha* + subject with the unit.

air 'after'

1. To form the equivalent of the Eng. past participle. A: *agus mi air tòiseachadh ri deanamh deiseil; tha uisge trom air a bhith ann; air falbh* has the meaning 'away'. C(ii): *nam biodh i air ceannach rud-eiginn eile.* C(i): *b' ail leam gun robh mi air an litir a fhaicinn.* B: *bhithinn air a chur dhachaidh.* With the poss. adj. referring to the subject we have a passive meaning: *is iongantach gun cuir thusa ort e 's e air a dheanamh latha na Sàboinnd; bha leisgeul agad air a fhaighinn.* With *air* + vn. unit brought forward by the copula: *an ann air a cheannach a tha an taigh*

aca? The appropriate poss. adj. is used: *tha na taighean air an togail*, but occasionally one gets *air a fhaighinn*, *air a fhàgail* where one might expect *air am faighinn*, *air a faighinn*, etc. *Call* functions as a vn. in *tha mo bhròg air a call* 'my shoe has been lost', but as an abstract noun in *tha mo bhròg air chall* 'my shoe is lost', where *air* is presumably a relic of leniting *ar*—rarer in Sc. Gael. than in Ir.—as in *air chuairt*, *air thurus*, etc.

2. In subordinate phrases, the agent being introduced by *do*: *air dhomh a bhith a' bruidhinn ris*. *Air* in this construction is used far less often than *an déidh* (usage 2. below), and I have no example without the agent.

an déidh 'after'

1. Used like *air* (1), and with the same meaning, except that *an déidh* perhaps is more emphatic: *bha mi an déidh a dheanamh* 'I *had* done it'. The noun/vn. of the vn. unit following it is in the nom. Passive: *tha e an déidh a chàradh* 'it has been repaired'.

2. In subordinate phrases: *an déidh pòsadh*. The agent is introduced by *do*: *an déidh dhaibh pòsadh*. Its use or non-use is determined in part by the identity of the subject of the main clause.

an àite, an àm

Like *an déidh* (2), *an àite* (*dhomh*) 'instead of', *an àm* (*dhomh*) 'at the time (of)' are used in subordinate phrases.

air son 'for'

1. With the verb *tha* + subject: *am bheil thu air son a dhol dhachaidh?* 'do you want to go home?'

2. In subordinate phrases: *théid mi a null Diardaoin air son an duine a leigeil as teach* 'in order to let the man in'. Passive: *air son* (*a bhith air*) *a chàradh* 'to be repaired'.

3. After adjectives such as *feumail, deiseil, math*, attributive or predicative: *tha e math air son an làr a nighe* or '*se rud math air son an làr a nighe a tha ann* or '*se rud math a tha ann air son an làr a nighe*.

gu/gus

1. 'almost, (just) about to'. Before most vns. of A and C(ii), *gu* is far more usual than *gus*: *tha mi gu bàsachadh leis an fhuachd.* ('Almost' before adjectives and adverbs is expressed by *gu bhith*: *bha e gu bhith uair mas do dh'fhalbh i* 'almost one o'clock'). *gus* is used before *a dhol, a thighinn*, *gu* being exceptional: *tha e gus a dhol tioram* 'it has nearly gone dry'. Before the article or poss. adj. of C(i) or the poss. adj. of B, *gus*: *tha i dìreach gus a màthair a chur gòrach; bha am pian gus mo mharbhadh.* Before the indef. noun of C(i), *gu* or *gus*, *gu* being the more usual.

2. 'going to' with the vns. *bhith* (*gu*), *a dhol, a thighinn* (*gus*). (With other vns., *dol a* + aspiration is used in the sense 'going to'—see below). Examples: *tha e gu bhith agam* 'I am going to have it'; *am bheil sinn gus a dhol sìos?*

3. Occasionally, *gus* (rarely *gu*) performs the function of aspirating *a*, or *air son*, 'to, for the purpose of', nearly always before the article or a poss. adj.: *chaidh mi ann gus am faighinn deiseil* 'to get them ready'.

gun 'without'

1. Negates the verbal idea in a vn. unit, standing immediately before the unit: *thubhairt e rithe gun am bùrn a dhòrtadh; 's fheàrr leam gun fhalbh.* (In some cases, the Eng. translation is 'before': *mur bi i ro fhada gun fhalbh*). With *agus*: *am bu chòir dhomh fear a fhaighinn agus gun éisdeachd ris a' bhodach? gun a bhith* negates the adj. or adverb predicate of the verb *tha*: *tha e gun a bhith ann* 'he is not there'; *tha e gun a bhith gu math* 'he is not well'.

2. It replaces perfect-forming *air* when the equivalent neg. meaning is required: *tha iad fhathast gun na rudan sin a chur air; agus i gun a dùnadh.*

Not all preps. take the vn. unit after them; *ag, ri* and *an* take other constructions.

ag, a' 'engaged in'

After a vowel sound, one hears only [g] and zero respectively. Before a poss. adj., [gha] etc.

1. To form the equivalent of the Eng. present participle: *tha mi a' falbh; bheir e greis a' cur air a chòta.* The pronoun attribute of the vn. precedes the vn. as a poss. adj. The noun attribute follows, always in the nom. when indefinite, either nom. or gen. when definite. (In the sg., gen. is perhaps slightly more usual than nom.; in the pl., the nom. is by far the more frequent). When this noun attribute is brought forward by the copula, the vn. has the same form as it has in the non-rel. construction: *chan e sin idir a tha mi a' ciallachadh.* This prep. causes no mutation, but very rarely *dol* and *tighinn* after it take the forms *dhol, thighinn.* With a poss. adj. referring back to a noun one gets a pass. meaning: *'s ann a tha e 'ga atharrachadh* 'it is being changed'; *tha mi a' cluinntinn soithichean 'gam briseadh.* But this, like other passive formations, occurs infrequently. The poss. adj. usually agrees in gender and number with the noun, but one could also find *'ga bhriseadh* here.

2. *Tòisichidh, leanaidh* are followed by *a(g)* + vn.: *thòisich e a' cantuinn.* (*Tòisichidh* takes other constructions as well—see below).

ri

1. Alternates apparently quite freely with *a(g)* with the meaning 'engaged in', except that where there is a pron. attribute *a(g)* is obligatory: *tha mi 'ga chur*, not **ri a chur.* It causes no mutation of consonants, but one occasionally finds it followed by *dhol, thighinn.* Before vns. with initial vowel it has the form [rig]. In the rel. construction the vn. has the same form: *'se a' Bhliadhna Ùr a bhios sinne ri cumail.*

2. The verb *tòiseachadh* takes this construction as well as the one with *a(g)* above: *thòisich mi ri deanamh sin.* It also takes *air* + vn. unit (and *air* + noun).

3. *ri* + poss. adj. + vn. is used as follows, where Mod. Irish would have *le*, the *a* of the poss. adj. being elided: *chan fhaca e càil ri a dheanamh; bha uiread againn ri a ghràdh le chéile* 'both of us had so much to say'; *chan eil càil aig sin ri a dheanamh ris* 'that has nothing to do with it'. The poss. adj. can agree in gender and number with the noun, but just as often a leniting *ri*, presumably *ri* with a stereotyped 3sg. masc. poss. adj., is found instead: *bithidh leabhraichean agad ri (a) thabhairt leat*, as well as *ri an tabhairt leat.* Aspiration seems to be

the rule with the vns. of normally intransitive verbs: *tha mìltean aca ri (a) choiseachd* 'they have miles to walk'.

Note: *ri* is used in the construction of many verbs: *cuideachadh (duine), tha agam* 'I have (to)', *feuchainn,* but these, of course, are followed by the vn. unit: *bithidh aig a màthair ri sin a phàidheadh* 'her mother will have to pay that'.

an

an + poss. adj. usually replaces the normal *a(g), ri* with *seasamh, suidhe, sìneadh, laighe, cadal* (though *a(g), ri* may be used with these, too): *bha i 'na suidhe; chan eil mi a' creidsinn gum bi e fada 'na sheasamh. Ruith* and *coiseachd,* and possibly one or two others, are sometimes treated in the same way.

Finally, one prep. stands outside this system, in that it is not normally used with the verb *tha,* namely *a* (aspirating), *a dh'* 'to, for the purpose of'. It follows verbs of motion (+ subject), such as *falbhaidh, phónaigidh, ruigidh, gheibh, théid, thig*: *am bheil i a' dol dhachaidh a dh'fhuireach?* 'is she going home to stay?' *chaidh e a dhol dha* 'it has started for him' (of the tape recorder). Also with groups of transitive verb + subject + object, involving motion, such as *bheir e duine, cluinidh e sgeul, cuiridh e duine, gheibh e litir: cuiridh mi a dhol i* 'I shall set it going'. Passive: *chuir mi dh'an gearradh iad* 'I sent them to be cut'. Also, occasionally, in cases of rest after motion, with *fuirichidh, seasaidh* and, where an adverb intervenes, even with *tha: tha i an àirde a shealltuinn am bheil gaoth ann.* The pron. attribute of the vn. precedes the vn. as a poss. adj., and then the prep. has the form *dh': chuir e dh'a iarraidh.* The noun attribute follows the vn., sometimes in the gen., usually in the nom.: *chuir e a dh'iarraidh an dochtuir.* This *a* is a development of *do.* The verbs *sguiridh, stadaidh* have an identical construction, but here the *a* continues *de: cha do sguir e a ghàireachduinn.* Periphrastic constructions with *dol* are used to express future tenses: *bha mi a' dol a choiseachd ann* 'I was going to walk there'. This method is, however, not used with *bhith, dol* and *tighinn, gu/gus* being used instead (see above).

KENNETH JACKSON

The breaking of original long ē
in Scottish Gaelic

The primary field collection undertaken by the Linguistic Survey of
the Gaelic dialects of Scotland on behalf of Edinburgh University is
now complete. Two hundred and five questionnaires of about 1200
items have been filled in, and a basic map of 192 points has been constructed, covering almost the entire area within the traditional 'Highland Line' with the exception of a few border regions (notably most
of Caithness, the Highland parts of Banffshire and Forfarshire, a
border strip within Perthshire, the Highland parts of Stirlingshire and
Dunbartonshire, the island of Bute, and the southern half of Kintyre)
where the language is extinct and local speakers could not be found;
and of regions which are virtually uninhabited, particularly the central
massif of Sutherland, the mountains of Druim Alban from Sutherland
south to western Lochaber, the ridge of the Grampians, and the island
of Rum. The work of analysing, phonemicizing, and synthesizing the
results is being undertaken by Professor Magne Oftedal; and it is
hoped that an atlas, with a phonemic and phonetic analysis, a description of the dialects, and a history of their development, will eventually
be published in collaboration with the present writer. We do not
intend normally to anticipate the findings. certainly not in any extensive
way; but the memorial volume to Angus Matheson so obviously calls
for a note on Gaelic dialects that an exception must be made. The
article which follows concerns the distribution of a familiar dialect
contrast,[1] one which was continually referred to by the late C. M.
Robertson in his invaluable pioneer works on the dialects in the
Transactions of the Gaelic Society of Inverness and the *Celtic Review*,
and is mentioned by most writers on these subjects. It is well known
that Old Irish stressed long *ē* before a non-palatalized consonant
widely becomes diphthongized, or 'broken', in modern Irish and

65

Scottish Gaelic dialect. The matter was discussed briefly by O'Rahilly in his *Irish Dialects Past and Present*,[2] who remarks that in a word like *sgéal* the *sgial* pronunciation is especially characteristic of southern Irish, though it is also found in some words in Ulster; and that in Scotland the 'breaking' is found in only a few words in the southern area but is very common farther north. According to Robertson there are about 110 words in Scottish Gaelic which show this breaking in one region of Scotland or another.[3]

This is the problem now before us. In some regions, a word like Sc. G. *feur* 'grass' (Irish *féar*) is /fɛːr/ with the long *ē* retained and in others it is /fiər/ or /fiar/ with 'breaking'; and moreover, while any given region may have the one treatment with one word it may have the other with another. The questionnaire of the Linguistic Survey has a special section on its page 4 to elicit information on this, though of course it could only be complete if *all* words with Old Irish stressed *ē* before non-palatal consonants had been included, which would have been impossible. Instead, a number of crucial words were chosen from the lists discussed by C. M. Robertson. Not all of these words from the questionnaire have been used in writing the present article, as it turned out in practice that some of them were very widely not known, which would have introduced serious and unnecessary complications into the analysis; and one or two others seem to be more or less 'book-words' not employed in ordinary current speech but heard from literary or ecclesiastical sources and hence liable not to illustrate correctly the true history of local dialect. The words which have been used for present purposes are *a' cheud* 'the first', *deug* 'teen', *beul* 'mouth', *feur* 'grass', *sgreuch* 'screech', *gun deunadh* 'that he would do', *Seumas* 'James', and also *sè* 'six', which has diphthongization very widely in the Gaelic dialects in spite of the fact that the vowel does not stand before a consonant. Of these, *sgreuch* presented something of a problem since some speakers used other words instead, such as *sgiamh* and *sgread*; but this is not at all common, and as it happens it does not make much difference to the results.

Where diphthongization does take place the result may be /iə/, thus falling together with the older *ia* from Archaic Irish *ē* mentioned in the note 2; or /iə/, distinct from it, the latter being /iə/; or the distribution of /iə/ and /iə/ in the case of both sources (which have therefore fallen together) may be allophonic, depending on e.g. whether the diphthong is in contact with a nasal consonant. The present article has a limited scope since it discusses only the degree to which breaking does or does not take place in the various parts of the Highlands, not the exact nature of the diphthong, which would introduce complications needing far greater space and a much more intricate map. It seems simplest, therefore, not to use phonemic symbols, much less phonetic, in reporting the dialect forms, and instead to keep the traditional Gaelic spelling, it being understood that *ia* means 'breaking has taken place' and *eu* (or in the case of 'six', *è*) means 'the long *ē* vowel is retained'.

The results of the inquiry are set out in the accompanying map which shows what percentage of the eight words has breaking in which regions. It should be stressed that the words chosen are all of them ones where breaking *is* found in some places; consequently the percentages of it seem very high, with a large region having 100 per cent. This, it is important to understand, does *not* mean that 'all words with literary Sc. G. *eu* have breaking to *ia* in this dialect', and so proportionately with the other percentages. If all words with Sc. G. *eu* were studied the percentages would of course be very much lower, as the work of Robertson and other writers on Gaelic dialects proves that they really are. The value of the present figures is purely a relative one; they simply indicate that some parts of the Highlands have breaking more often than others, and show which parts these are.

When the collections of the Survey are analysed and published it will be seen that some isoglosses contrast very strikingly with others. Some for instance divide the Highlands roughly east and west, others roughly north and south. There are, however, a number in which the map of Gaelic Scotland appears—to simplify considerably—as a segment of two or more concentric circles. The innermost area comprises what I have called[4] the 'central' dialect, which is on the whole an innovating one and relatively homogeneous; the outermost, the 'peripheral' region, consists of several more or less fragmented dialects which differ more greatly one from another but have certain features in common, particularly the tendency to preserve older forms where the central dialect innovates. The exact outlines vary, of course, rather greatly, from isogloss to isogloss, but it is possible to say, in very broad terms, that the central dialect covers the Hebrides as far south as Mull and sometimes further, Ross exclusive of the north-east corner,[5] Assynt,[6] Inverness-shire, western Perthshire, and mainland Argyll roughly north of Loch Awe; while the peripheral dialects comprise Caithness and Sutherland exclusive of Assynt, the north-east corner of Ross, Braemar, eastern Perthshire, the rest of mainland Argyll with Kintyre, and Arran. Moray and the adjacent lower region of the Spey, the wide valley of Strathspey from Rothiemurchus to the Moray border, may go with the peripheral dialects, linking up with Braemar and east Perth. It will be seen from this that the innovating central

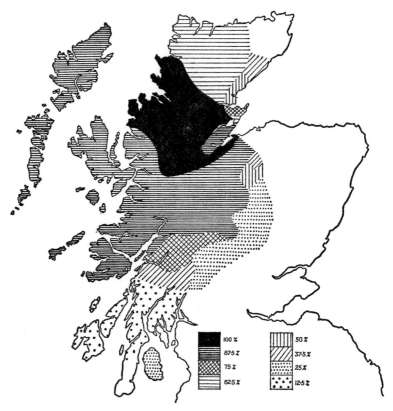

100 %	50 %
87·5 %	37·5 %
75 %	25 %
62·5 %	12·5 %

dialect seems to have spread outwards, reducing the older dialects to a more or less narrow rim, which it has broken through to the sea in the neighbourhood of Inverness. Certain features suggest that the main path of this break-through was the Great Glen.

The map on this page is a fairly typical example of this situation. The percentage figures represent the proportion of the eight words or phrases listed above in which breaking has taken place. It shows

that the parts of the Highlands with a very high proportion of diphthongization are the Hebrides as far south as Mull and Lismore, mainland Ross-shire except a small corner in the north-east, Nairnshire and
all mainland Inverness-shire except Strathspey, a small part of north
Perthshire in the Tummel region, and part of the Appin district of
north-west Argyll on the east shore of Loch Linnhe; the southern
boundary running thence eastwards along the ridge of the Grampians
(but penetrating south across the ridge to Tummel), and then north-
wards in a sinuous line to the mouth of the Beauly Firth. It takes up
again in the Cromarty Firth and follows the Ross-Sutherland boundary north-west, includes Assynt in west coast Sutherland, and reaches
the Atlantic at Edrachillis Bay. Most of the northern part of this,
marked black on the map, has breaking in all eight words, 100 per
cent, even *Seumas*, whence *Siamas*, and it is remarkable how this
neologism has penetrated eastwards down the Great Glen to Fisherton
on the Beauly Firth, past Inverness. In the rest all the words other than
Seumas have breaking, hence *sia*, *fiar*, etc., giving 87.5 per cent of
the total. The map is of course slightly simplified because of its size
which makes it impossible to show minor deviations; in the area marked
as having 100 per cent the informant from Loch Broom in Wester
Ross had in fact only 87.5 per cent, since he used *Seumas*; and in
that marked as having 87.5 per cent some dozen informants did not
use the word *sgreuch* (notably in the northern half of Harris), which
slightly lowered the percentage, but the *sgriach* which surrounded
them everywhere showed that if they did it would have been *sgriach*.
The fair-sized area with 75 per cent breaking in northern mainland
Argyll, penetrating into north-west Perthshire in Rannoch, is probably to be regarded as belonging to this high-percentage central
country which it borders. It will be observed that in fact the parts
with 75–100 per cent do correspond quite closely to what has been
defined above as the 'central dialect', and this part of north Argyll
does generally go, or tend to go, with that dialect. Round the periphery,
broken through only in the rather narrow district between the Cromarty Firth and Nairnshire, the percentages are strikingly lower, in
some places very much lower. Firstly, all Sutherland but Assynt and
the east coast has 62.5 per cent, that is to say, *feur*, *gun deunadh* and
Seumas remain without breaking. In the case of *beul* > *bial* it is characteristic of almost the whole of this part of Sutherland that the diphthongized /biaL/ has developed further to /bja:L/.[7] East of this, the

coastal strip to the north, from Helmsdale in Sutherland to Braemore in Caithness, shows a very great drop, to 37.5 per cent, the only words of the eight with breaking being *sia*, *a' chiad*, and *diag*; while the coast of Sutherland south of that has 50 per cent, with breaking in these three and also *bial* (= /bjɔːL/). In the Nigg peninsula and past Tain along the south side of the Dornoch Firth, in northern Easter Ross, the influence of the great Central dialect has made itself felt, giving 75 per cent, but the southern part of that peninsula preserves *feur*, *gun deunadh* and *Seumas* un-diphthongized, like the greater part of Sutherland. Coming to the more southerly section of the periphery, from Moray round to Kintyre, there is only 37.5 per cent of breaking in Moray (*sia*, *a' chiad*, *diag*, as in Caithness and Helmsdale); and 50 per cent to the south-west of that in Strathspey (*sia*, *a' chiad*, *diag*, *sgriach*; but close to Moray *sgreuch* is not recorded and it is therefore impossible to say whether it is really 50 or 37.5 per cent). Beyond this to the south the drop in the percentage is striking; Braemar in Aberdeenshire, and almost all Gaelic-speaking Perthshire apart from Tummel[8] and Rannoch, shows only 25 per cent of breaking—the two words being everywhere *a' chiad* and *diag*. To the west of this, most of northern Lorne, and Tyndrum over the border in Perthshire, has 37.5 per cent (*sia*, *a' chiad*, *diag*, as in Moray and the south-east border between Sutherland and Caithness);[9] but the 25 per cent is taken up again in Arran, with *sia* and *a' chiad*, but not *diag* or the rest. In the case of *sia* in Arran a development comparable to that affecting *bial* in much of Sutherland has produced /ʃaː/,[10]; a well-known Arran feature. Finally, all the rest of Gaelic-speaking mainland Argyll (southern Lorne, Mid-Argyll, Knapdale, Cowal and northern Kintyre), and the islands of Easdale, Colonsay, Jura, Islay and Gigha, has diphthongization in one word alone, *a' chiad*, giving 12.5 per cent.[11] In conclusion, one may note that except for the region marked black on the map, with 100 per cent (including *Siamas*), every part of the Highlands and Islands has breaking in one or more of the eight words and non-breaking in one or more; and that in the latter case the only example which has diphthongization everywhere[12] is *a' chiad* 'the first'.

NOTES

1 The present article is limited solely to the evidence collected by the Survey; hence the work of Robertson and others on this subject is not discussed here. In general it agrees closely with the Survey's collections.

2 p. 194. O'Rahilly says that Old Irish *ē* in this situation gave everywhere *ia* except in the case of *ē* arising by compensatory lengthening. This is not quite clearly phrased; it would be more intelligible if one said that Archaic Irish *ē* before non-palatalized consonants had become *ia* by the Old Irish period except in the case of *ē* which arose by compensatory lengthening; but that words with this latter *ē*, and others such as new loanwords which also had *ē*, have undergone diphthongization in some of the modern dialects (as described in this article).

3 *Trans. Gaelic Soc. Inverness*, xxv, 89.

4 E.g. in a lecture to the First International Congress of Celtic Scholars, Dublin, 1959.

5 The Nigg peninsula and the hinterland between Tain and the Sutherland border.

6 The south-westernmost part of Sutherland, south of Kylesku and Eddrachillis Bay.

7 This has not happened in Assynt, nor in the south-east corner of the 62.5 per cent country where it borders on the 100 per cent.

8 The informant from Tomintanda in the eastern part of Tummel, bordering between the 87.5 and 25 per cent countries, had 62.5 per cent, with *beul*, *sgreuch* and *Seumas* unbroken.

9 The informant from Kilchrennan on Loch Awe, next to the north Argyll district with 75 per cent, had 50 per cent, showing in addition *fiar*.

10 One Arran informant, from Tormore on the west coast, had *a' cheud*, and therefore breaking in only one word, *sia*.

11 The informant from Inverlussa in Jura, with 50 per cent (*sia*, *diag*, *fiar* *sgriach*) was wholly aberrant.

12 Except with the Arran and Jura informants just mentioned.

TERENCE M'CAUGHEY

Ní bhfuil

Professor T. F. O'Rahilly has offered an explanation of the apparent eclipsis after *ní* in the form *ní bhfuil* (*Irish Dialects*, 44ff.). This eclipsis he takes to be more apparent than real: 'in origin', he says, 'the *bhf-*(=*bh*) here is not eclipsis in the ordinary sense, but a glide developed between the *i* of *ní* and the following *u-*. The existence of these "eclipsed" forms can be traced back to the latter half of the fifteenth century, and they may possibly be older still'.[1]

Professor O'Rahilly sees the 'eclipsis' in the *fu-* forms of the verb *do-gheibhim* as having the same explanation. Indeed the tendency towards the semi-vocalizing of initial *u-* can be seen elsewhere in Gaelic; for example Cois Fhairrge *uaim* [wem′],[2] Gort a' Choirce [wʌəm], and central Outer Hebrides [v(uə)m].[3]

Given this tendency, it is hard to disagree with O'Rahilly's explanation of the *fu-* forms of the verb *do-gheibhim*. But is what came to be written *ní bhfuil* to be explained in the same way? O'Rahilly says of the form *ní bhfuil* that it may go back even further than the fifteenth century. It is the contention of the present article that a form which was in *actual fact* originally eclipsed existed long before the fifteenth century, and further, that the existence of this form (together, no doubt, with the tendency to semi-vocalize *u-* already discussed) exerted some force on the emergence of the forms *ní bhfuair*, *ní bhfuighidh*, etc.[4]

(1) *The Old Irish situation.* A variety of vocalization appears in the three biggest collections of Old Irish glosses. Strachan (*Trans. Phil. Soc.*, 1899) observed that the distribution differs in different kinds of sentences. Thus, in the Relative, *fil* occurs 89 times, *feil* or *fel* 4 times (Wb. 4c 1, 13c 26, 33b 18, in a gloss in the second hand, Ml. 47c 17). *File* occurs 61 times (decreasingly frequently relative to *fil* as time goes on), *fele* occurs once only. As dependent of the Substantive Verb the distribution is as follows:

Wb.: -*fel* occurs in forms of three or more syllables (with exceptions).
Ml.: -*fel*, -*fil* occur.
   -*fail* occurs once only, and for the first time.
Sg.: -*fil*, -*fail* only.

Strachan (*loc. cit.*, p. 56) did not accept the etymology of *fil* proposed by Sarauw (RC. 17, 276ff.), i.e. that it was an imperative form in origin from a verb cognate with the Welsh *gweled*, from a root **wel*, and he seems to have thought of the initial of *fil* as neutral in quality.[5] There seems, however, to be no reason for doubting that the *f-* was originally palatalized and became depalatalized (at least in some dialects)[6] during the Old Irish period. It seems probable that this depalatalization began in forms where -*f(a)il* was preceded by a pronominal infix.[7] From there it spread in the O. Ir. period to forms without the infix, and in the late O. Ir. and Mid. Ir. period to the Relative. The earliest and indeed the only example of the form *fail* as Relative in the *Thesaurus* is in the Carlsruhe Bede glosses (Bcr. 18c 4), dated *circa* 850 by Zimmer (cited Thes. II, x–xi). Mid. Ir. MSS. give examples of a further spelling, -*fuil*, *fuil* (rel.).[8]

(2) *The change in mutation after ní-.* As is well known, the adverb of negation *ní-* in O. Ir. sometimes geminates the initial consonant of the immediately following conjunct of the verb. In Mid. Ir. however, *ní-* aspirates the initial consonant of the immediately following active verbal form, in the MSS. generally expressed in the case of the voiceless stops. The fact that this aspiration occurs (with few exceptions) in the case of *active* verbal forms would seem to argue in favour of the suggestion that aspiration after *ní-* comes from a petrifying of the lenition which normally follows the neuter infixed pronoun in Old Irish.[9] If the aspiration now following *ní-* is to be explained in this way, it should not be expected that the process would immediately or automatically spread to *ní* plus *fil*, for *fil* in O. Ir. is in a different category from other verbs. *Fil* governs the accusative, and its grammatical object is its notional subject. In sentences with a pronominal subject, -*f(a)il* would be preceded much more often by a masculine than by a neuter infixed pronoun. In the case of -*fil*, therefore, the *masculine* infixed pronoun would be the one to become petrified. It is not surprising that the scribal tradition after the O. Ir. period, observing that all other finite forms were aspirated after *ní-*, and notoriously confused as it is on how to use infixed pronouns in any case, should

have shown then, and for so long after, the aspiration which *ní-* was seen to cause in all other verbs. *Ní fhuil* (a common spelling) would, as O'Rahilly points out, represent a pronunciation not far removed from what was later to be represented orthographically *ní bhfuil*, i.e. (N'i: wil'), and had the advantage of orthographic consistency, even if it represented something which in point of historical fact was inconsistent with what normally happened after *ní-*. It is not till the latter half of the fifteenth century[10] that we have evidence of scribes beginning actually to show a pronunciation of the type [N'i: wil'], representing it by *bhf-* and in so doing reproducing an 'eclipsis' heard in pronunciation, of whose historical ground they were, however, unaware.

If the contention of this article is conceded, then the form *ne vell* / *ne vel* of the Fernaig MS. is in origin *ní bhfeil*, but was understood as *ní bheil*, as the back-formation *am beil* [m̜ bel'] in Wester Ross dialects today clearly shows. *Ne el* of the Dean's Bk. is a mixed written form where *ne* = *chan* of speech.

NOTES

1 Eg. 1781 (transcribed 1487) has *ní bfuil*, cited O'Rahilly, *op. cit.*, p. 44.

2 de Bhaldraithe, *The Irish of Cois Fhairrge*, p. 87.

3 Carl Hj. Borgström, *The Dialects of the Outer Hebrides*, pp. 190, 238. On this tendency, see further *Duan. Finn*, III, 302.

4 And these in turn on the development of the form *ní bhfaca*. It is interesting to note that in Irish the past tense of *do-gheibhim* resists 'regularization' and retains its *f-* without mutation (unlike *tug*, *tánaig*), and in Scottish the *f-* is reduced not to zero but to |h-|, thus [huər'—xa duər'] like [huk–xa d̪uk].

5 Not so, however, Thurneysen, *Grammar*, pp. 105, 479 or Pedersen, *Vgl. Gr.*, I, 542. Thurneysen notes without comment in his paragraph on the abandonment of palatalization in proclitics that *fel* and *fail* occur beside *fíl feil* 'who is'.

6 It could be dangerous to place too much weight on the evidence of Mod. Sc. Gaelic, but the forms [m̜ vel', xa N'il'] in the majority of dialects suggests that not everywhere did the change pal. to neutral occur. In Sutherland, of course, the forms are [val', xa nal'].

7 Of the three exx. of *-fail* in Ml., one (44b 12) has a pronominal infix *ní-s-fail*, and two (69c 7, 92a 9) are followed by nominal objects.

8 It is worthy of note that *fail* as Relative does *not* occur in Ml. whereas *-fail* (dep.) *does*. AU has *conidfail* 958, *ni fail, ni fil* 894 (Ó Máille, 155); SR *fail*.
-fuil makes an appearance in PH and LU (e.g. 6302).

9 The only other plausible explanation would be the spread of the lenition usual after *nícon-*.

10 See note 1.

KENNETH MACDONALD

Unpublished verse by Sìlis Ni Mhic Raghnaill Na Ceapaich

Four of the following pieces ascribed to Sìlis Ni Mhic Raghnaill na Ceapaich (c. 1660–c. 1730), daughter of Archibald, chief of Keppoch, and wife of Alexander Gordon of Camdell and later of Beldorney, in Banffshire, are preserved in the MS. collection of the Rev. Alexander Irvine[1] (1772–1824), minister of Rannoch from 1799 to 1805, of Fortingall from 1805 to 1806, and of Little Dunkeld from 1806 until his death. Irvine was a prominent figure in that wave of antiquarian interest and literary activity which in part gave rise to, and was in turn greatly stimulated by, the activities of James MacPherson and the ensuing Ossianic controversy. He made his own collection of Ossianic and other Gaelic verse with a view to producing a work entitled, in the characteristic prolixity of the time: 'The Lives of the Caledonian Bards, ancient and modern, with historical, critical and philological observations upon their principal compositions, accompanied with several dissertations on Celtic literature and history in general.' The work itself never appeared, presumably through lack of subscribers, but a prospectus bearing the title and a note on the author's aims survives among his papers. J. F. Campbell made use of Irvine's collection of Ossianic verse in his Leabhar na Féinne,[2] but a further collection of papers, in the main consisting of Gaelic verse by seventeenth- and eighteenth-century authors, came into the possession of the National Library of Scotland in 1961, and is at present designated MS. Accession 3184. This box of papers contains one quarto-sized black-covered notebook divided into two sections separately paginated, the first section containing seventeen poems ascribed to Iain Lom and one ascribed to Mac Iain Luim, while the second section, headed 'Orain Ghaidhleach agus Laoidhean Le Silis ni' Mhic Raonail', contains sixteen pieces, including the following

76

four not found elsewhere. In 1914, these Irvine papers were lent by a member of the Irvine family to the Rev. Angus Macdonald of Killearnan, who copied a number of songs, including three by Sìlis, into a notebook which is now MS. 3781 in the National Library.

A copy of some Ossianic poems collected by Irvine, and now designated MS. Accession 2345 in the National Library, is accompanied by part of a letter written, shortly before his death, by Irvine's son, the Rev. Alexander Robertson Irvine, minister of Blair Atholl, to his own son, Alexander Irvine Robertson, later for many years minister of Clackmannan. This fragment is of interest as it identifies one of Irvine's principal sources:

The Manse, Blair Athol.   January 23d 1867

My Dear Alister,

Say to Mr. McNeill that the poems he refers to were for by much the greater part taken down by my father from the recitation of Mr. McDonald of Dalchosnie[3] grandfather of the late Sir John McDonald in the period between 1800 and 1804. It may have been a year or two earlier but certainly not later. The old gentleman had an extraordinary store of similar poetry, which my father had not time to take down. He had acquired it from his father and grandfather, who had gotten and preserved it in the same way, in their memory. They were of the family of Keppoch in Lochaber and it was there the poems were learnt by the McDonalds of three generations above mentioned. I cannot say of course through what channel the poetry first came into the family, but that it was in existence early in the last century is manifest, for the McDonalds of that time were a longlived race, and if you only go back for two generations from the old gentleman whom my father heard repeat the poems, you will reach the '45, or an earlier date, but it is quite safe to go back much farther, tho' I cannot legally prove it to be so.

There are a fragment or two among the poems taken down by my father from other old people in Rannoch at the same time as the others, but I can't say which they are. I am supposing Mr. McNeill has got a correct copy of them. Ask him, when you give him the information in this note, where he got them and let me know.

You may tell him as a proof of the singular gift of memory of many of these old reciters, that old Dalchosnie had a vast store of songs, some of which were taken down by his son Robert[4] who was at home when my father was in Rannoch, and these, or at least many of them, are still in the possession of his son Dr. McDonald of Strathardle. I have heard old Rob sing some of the songs for a whole night. And both sets of poems, the heroic taken down by my father and the lyrics jotted by Robert, were but a small part of what the old man could repeat.

That Dalchosnie, with his strong Keppoch connections, was one of the principal reciters on whose repertoire Irvine drew, doubtless accounts for the relative prominence of the two Keppoch bards, Iain Lom and Sìlis, in the Irvine Collection.

In the text of Sìlis's poems here given, the orthography has been normalized.

§ I

The son Gilleasbuig, to whom this song is addressed, was apparently Sìlis's firstborn, and was doubtless named after his grandfather, Archibald of Keppoch. The somewhat obscure allusion in the first two lines of the first stanza may possibly mean that he was an illegitimate child of doubtful paternity. There is evidence in some of Sìlis's extant verse to support the tradition, recorded by John MacKenzie, 'that in her young days she was very frolicsome'. Gilleasbuig's disappearance overseas is referred to in another of Sìlis's compositions— Oran Cumha air Bàs a Fir agus a Nighinn:[5]

> Tha Alasdair 'san Fhraing
> Is tha Iain fada thall,
> Tha Gilleasbuig air chall 's chan fhaighear e.

Oran a rinn i do Ghilleasbuig a Mac.

> Mo laochan mo laochan
> Mo laochan Gilleasbachan,
> Mo laochan mo laochan
> Mo laochan Gilleasbachan,
> Mo laochan mo laochan
> Mo laochan Gilleasbachan,
> Cas dhìreadh ris an fhuaran,
> Nì 'n cuartachadh feasgair dhuinn.

Mas tù Gilleasbuig Gòrdan
'S fearr còir air a' chinneach thu,
'N àm cur o dhaoine 'n òrdugh
Bi seòlta deas innealta;
Le d' phaidhir dhag is gòsaid,
Each cròitheach is pillean air,
Bi sgiobalt ann ad dhiallaid
Le d' shrianaibh 's le d' stiorapaibh.

'S dar a thig an Diùc sin
Bidh sùrd air mo ghillean-sa
'N àm dhìreadh ris na stùcaibh
Gu dlùth ris na firichibh;
Dar a nì thu crùban
'S e t' fhùdar gun innis e
Le gunna caol nach diùltadh
Air ùdlaich an daimh chinn-deirg.

'S gur iomadh sgeul a fhuair mi
Chuir truas agus mulad orm,
Thug rudhadh as mo ghruaidhibh,
Dh'fhàg droch snuadh 's droch cular orm;
A' chiad gineal so dh'àraich mi
Gun fhàillinn gun uireasbhuidh,
E dh'fhalbh uainn air sàile
Gun aon fhios càit an d' fhuirich e.

§ 2

Sìlis's daughter, Màiri, the subject of this light-hearted song, is also addressed in the song entitled in Patrick Turner's collection: 'Oran a' tabhairt comhairl' air na h-igh'nean òga'[6] and in 'Oran do Rìgh Seumas nuair bha e anns an Fhraing'.[7]

Oran do Mhàiri a Nighean.

Mo Mhàiri mo Mhàiri,
Mo Mhàiri bi spéiseil.
'S math a thig a' mhuslin dhuit
Cuide ris a' phéarluinn,

'S ribeanan air uachdar ort
Cho uallach 's tha 'n Dunéideann.

Bidh gùn do 'n t-sìde Shasannach
Is aparan ga réir ort;

Bidh fàinneachan a Hamilton
'Gan ceannach air gach féill dhuit.

Na cluasan 'sam bi lubagan
Bidh ruban anns gach té dhiubh:

Cha mhise bhios 'ga cheannach dhuit
Ach daoin' òg' a bhios an déidh ort.

Cha leig mi thar an abhainn thu—
Bidh Somhairle an déidh ort;

Cha toir mi d'Fhear Thom-Mhuilinn thu
O's cuilean d' an mhuic bhreun e;

Cha toir mi thu do 'n Bhàillidh
'S e air a chràdh mu d' dheighinn.

Cha toir mi Chloinn-a-Ghriogair thu
Na luchd nam biodag geura;

Cha toir mi luchd na sìthne thu
Mus toir iad 'fhrìth an fhéidh thu.

Bidh Iain òg do choimhearsnach
Cur a ghnothaichean an céill duit;

Tha oighre air a' Cheapaich ud,
'S ann a b'ait leis aige fhéin thu.

Gur dalt' a Chirstan Stiùbhart thu
'S gun d' òl thu sùgh a féithean;

A Rìgh! gur ait an gnothach leam
Gur comhalt thu Rìgh Seumas.

'S gun tig Rìgh Seumas fhathast oirnn
Nam biodh an rathad réidh dha;

Ge fada leibh gun tigheachd e,
Cha deach an t-slighe réiteach.

§ 3

In addition to the following, three other songs by Sìlis on the battle
of Sheriffmuir are extant.[8]

Oran air Latha Sliabh an t-Siorraim.

'S i sgeul a thainig an dràsd oirnn
A dh'fhàilnich air mo chiall,
Mu dheighinn Clann Choinnich 's Clann Domhnaill
A thuiteam còmhla air an t-sliabh.
Thug Morair Hunndainn as a chasan
'S beagan each nach b' fhiach,
'S bha gach caiptean air an casgairt
'S mo mhac-sa air dol diom.

Gur olc a' chlisg' a fhuair an dùthaich
Le fùidse nach b' fhiach,
A theich 'na theann-ruith bharr na machrach
Mam facas an gnìomh;
Dh'fhàg e mnathan anns a' bhasraich
Toirt am fuilt a nìos,
'S cha robh neach a chual' a' chaonnag
Nach do chaochail nial.

Ge bu lag mise, ghlac mi misneach
'S thubhairt mi ri càch:
'Beir uam an sgeul meallta breugach,
Na tugaibh éisdeachd dhà.
Gar am bi ann ach Gòrdanaich 's Clann Domhnaill
A thachairt còmhla anns a' bhlàr,
Cha toir an saoghal orm a shaoilsinn
Nach tug iad aodann dhàibh '

Glé mhoch an là-'rna-mhàireach
Man d' àrdaich air a' ghrian,
Bha buaidh-làrach air mo chàirdibh
Mar a b' àbhaist riamh;
Thug sibh deannal leis na lannaibh
Gu cruaidh daingean dian,
'S bha fuil is faobh is claignean sgaoilt
Aig luchd a chur ar n-aobhar sìos.

'S e 'n Rìgh a bha 'gur còmhnadh
'Nur n-ònaran leibh fhéin,
Nuair a theich iad uaibh, ur càirdean,
'S ur nàimhdean 'nan gleus;
Cruas ur làmh an ceann ur lann
A' gearradh cheann gu feur,
Sgathadh chluas 's a' sgoltadh chnuaic,
'S a' cur na ruaig 'nan déidh.

Ach mallachd aig a' phàirtidh
A dh'fhàg sibh 'nur teinn,
Mar bha cùirt an Rìgh 's Mhorair Hunndainn
Ri plundrainn 'nur déidh.
O! gur iad mo rùn na saoidhean
A chuir an aodainn ri gleus
Measg nan cùrsanaibh dùbh-ghorm
Bu dùbailte sréin.

Mo chreach lot àrmainn Mhùideartach
Bu chliùthar a bheus,
B' e sud an seobhag sùil-ghorm
Fhuair cliù measg nan ceud;
Dol cho dàn' an uchd do nàmhaid—
Sud a chaill thu fhéin,
Ach 's goirt an cridh' a fhuair do chàirdean
Dar a dh'fhàg iad thu 'nan déidh.

Thuit Morair uasal òg Shrathmór
'S mo chreach! bu mhór am beud,
Am planntais deas dàicheil
Nach d' fhàs ach mar gheug.

Gar am facas riamh do mhàthair,
Chualas cainnt a thuirt a beul:
'An taobh a chaidh am fear a b' àirde,
Rachadh càch 'na dhéidh.'

Mo dhiùbhail dà Iain Grannda
A bh' air an àraich gu fuar,
B' iad sud na spailp[9] dhaoin' uaisle tapaidh
A chùm an t-sabaid uainn,
'Gam biodh na teaghlaichean[10] fial, farsaing
Nach do chleachd a' ghruaim;
Mo chreach! ar clann 's ar mnathan uaisle
Toirt a nuas an gruag.

Chaill sibh òigridh shèimhidh, sheòlta
D' an tugas móran gràidh,
'Gan robh m' eòlas o thùs m' òige—
Leam gur bròn an call
Le miad an dùrachd anns a' chùis ud
'Chur air lùths an lann,
Tuiteam le luaidh ghlas 's le fùdar,
'S gum b' e mo dhiùbhail iàd.

§ 4

The two following stanzas appear in the MS. without heading, immediately after a version of the well-known lament for Lachlan MacKinnon, the blind harper. They suggest that Sìlis herself played the harp, but that its music was no longer tolerated in the household—there may have been a reaction to the traditional culture of which the harp was a part when Sìlis's son, James, succeeded to his father's estates.

Do bheatha, a chlàrsaich, a rìs
An d' éis domh do thilgeadh uam,
Nam faodainn do chumail asteach
Cha rachadh tu mach ri luaths;
Bu bhinn leam iuchair do theud
Bhith 'ga gleusadh goirid uam,
B' ait leam do chom buidhe binn
Bhith 'ga seinn làmh ri m' chluas.

Nam bu bhean mi 'gam biodh oighreachd
Bhiodh tu daonnan 'na mo chaidreabh,
Bu bhinn le m' chluais bhith 'gad chluinntinn
Nuair a dhùisginn anns a' mhadainn;
B' annsa na fidheal, is beus
Orgain cha teid mi g'a luaidh,
'S b' e mo roghainn thar gach ceòl
Fuaim do theud roimh d' bhòrdaibh cruaidh.

§ 5

The following hymn appears in MacLagan MS. 165 in Glasgow
University Library, headed: 'Le Sìli Ni Mhic Raghnaill air faighinn a
cainnt an d'éis a bhith trì bliadhna gun bhiadh, gun deoch, gun
chainnt.' While in some of its details this statement is manifestly
incredible, it is clear from Sìlis's lament for her husband and daughter
that, sometime before her husband's death, she did suffer from a
serious and evidently protracted illness:

'S tric a shileadh tu na deòir
'S tu 'gam fhaicinn am sgleò,
'S O! cha chaomhnadh tu do stòras a chaitheamh rium.[11]

This illness probably played an important part in the development of
the strong religious consciousness to which Sìlis gave expression in
the hymns of her later life. It was probably the reference to 'waking',
in the first stanza of this hymn, which led to its association with Sìlis's
illness, but the reference to 'rest' and 'sleep' and the imagery based on
morning household duties suggest that it is simply a morning hymn.
It is notable for the sustained metaphor in which sin is envisaged as a
seven-headed monster.

Taing dhuit, a Dhia, chionn do ghibhtean,
On a tha mi nis air dùsgadh;
Thug do ghràs dhomh tàmh is cadal,
'S inntrig 'sa mhadainn as ùr orm.

Fadaidh teine do ghràidh am chridhe,
Sguabamaid a rìs an fhàrdach:
'S math bu chòir an tigh a réiteach
Am bi Mac Dhé a' gabhail tàmha.

Sguabamaid amach luath a' pheacaidh
'S na stadadh i air ar n-ùrlar,
Eagal gun las i ar n-òtrach
Bàthamaid le deòir ar sùl i.

Fuadaicheamaid uainn amach
A' bhéist air am bheil na seachd cinn,
A shluigeas sinn uile 'na craos
Mas urra i dh'fhaotainn oirnn gill.

Uabhar, sannt, tnù is craos,
Leisg, farmad agus fearg—
Sin na cinn a th'air a' bhéist
Bhios gach aon là 'sa bheinn a' sealg.

Tàirnidh i faghaid mun cuairt duinn;
Mur robh ar buachaillean glic
'S gun dean sinn d' an comhairlean feum,
Marbhaidh i sinn féin 's ar sliochd.[12]

Ach saighead a chur 'na ceann-aghaidh:
Bhith leanailteach air na h-àithntean,
Bhith dol gu tric air ar n-ùrnuigh,
'S a' chreid a shloinneadh d' ar pàisdean.

Saighead a chur ann a cridhe:
Do chainnt a bhith dlighe dearbhtach;
Dh'aon nì gum faic no gun cluinn sinn
Cuireamaid cùl ri bhith feargach.

Saighead a chur ann a beul:
Ar cainnt a bhith céillidh glic,
Ar deòir a bhith air ar sùilean,
'S dol air ar n-ùrnuigh gu tric.

Saighead a chur ann a casan:
A bhith leanailt nan ceart cheuman
Gu imeachd an deidh ar Slànuigheir
Air a bhàir a rinn e féin duin.

Saighead a chur ann a gàirdean:
Gun do làmh gu meirl' a shìneadh,
Ma bhios uireasbhuidh no càs ort,
A shireadh air càch gu slobhalt.

Ma gheibh sinn air a' bhéist ud tadhal,
'S ar saighdean a chaitheadh air chòir,
Caillidh i a saothair 's a sealg,
Bidh ise marbh 's bidh sinne beò.

There are the following printed sources for Sìlis's songs, and for such scanty information about her life as we possess:

1. 1776. Raonuill MacDomhnuill, *Comh-chruinneachidh Orannaigh Gaidhealach*, p. 286.
2. 1786. Eoin Gillies, *Sean Dain agus Orain Ghaidhealach*, p. 141.
3. 1804. A. and D. Stewart, *Cochruinneacha Taoghta de Shaothair nam Bard Gaeleach*, pp. 357, 366.
4. 1806. *Co-chruinneachadh Nuadh do Dh'Orannibh Gaidhealach*, pp. 50, 186.
5. 1813. Patrick Turner, *Comhchruinneacha do Dh'Orain Taghta Ghaidhealach*, pp. 106, 135, 157, 302.
6. 1841. John MacKenzie, *Sàr-obair nam Bàrd Gaelach*, pp. 58–60.
7. *c.* 1848. *Orain na h-Albain*, a collection of Gaelic Songs with English and Gaelic Words and an Appendix containing traditionary notes to many of the songs. The piano-forte accompaniment arranged by Finlay Dun. pp. 28, 36 and Appendix, p. 2.
8. 1870. Archibald Menzies, *Comhchruinneacha do Dh'Orain Thaghta Ghaidhealach*, pp. 29, 178.
9. 1878. William MacKenzie, 'Leaves from My Celtic Portfolio II' in *Transactions of the Gaelic Society of Inverness*, vol. VII, pp. 114–16.
10. 1879. Unpublished poems with accompanying notes contributed by 'D. C. M.' to the Inverness weekly newspaper, *The Highlander*, 27 June and 25 July 1879.
11. 1886. Colin Chisholm: 'Unpublished Old Gaelic Songs' in *Transactions of the Gaelic Society of Inverness*, vol. XII, pp. 162–6.
12. 1890. A Maclean Sinclair, *The Gaelic Bards from 1411 to 1715*, p. 168.

13. 1893. *Comh-Chruinneachadh de Laoidhean Spioradail*. The hymns by Sìlis in this collection are identified by John Lorne Campbell in 'The Sources of the Gaelic Hymnal, 1893', *The Innes Review*, vol. 7, 1956.

14. 1896. A. Maclean Sinclair, 'Old Gaelic Songs' in *Transactions of the Gaelic Society of Inverness*, vol. XX, pp. 15–19.

15. 1900. Keith Norman Macdonald, *Macdonald Bards from Mediaeval Times*, pp. 18, 92–3.

16. 1904. A. and A. Macdonald, *Clan Donald*, vol. III, pp. 421, 576–7.

17. 1904. Douglas Wimberley, *A Short Family History of the later Gordons of Beldornie, Kildrummie, and Wardhouse*.

18. 1909. J. M. Bulloch, 'The Gordons of Wardhouse and Beldorney' in *Transactions of the Banffshire Field Club, 1908–09*, pp. 11–61.

19. 1911. A. and A. Macdonald, *The Macdonald Collection of Gaelic Poetry*, pp. xix, 82.

20. 1918. W. J. Watson, *Bàrdachd Ghàidhlig*, 3rd edition, 1959, pp. 125–33.

21. 1963. Annie M. MacKenzie, 'Lochaber Bards' in *Scottish Gaelic Studies*, vol. X, pp. 38–42.

NOTES

1 v. Scott, *Fasti Ecclesiae Scoticanae*, vol. 4, p. 159.

2 *Leabhar na Féinne*, pp. vii, xxv–xxvi.

3 John MacDonald of Dalchosnie, Captain in Keppoch's regiment at the time of the '45 rising, A. and A. Macdonald, *Clan Donald*, vol. III, p. 434.

4 The Rev. Robert MacDonald, Irvine's successor as minister of Fortingall. *Clan Donald*, vol. III, p. 437; *Fasti*, vol. 4, p. 179.

5 *Orain na h-Albain*, p. 36.

6 Turner, p. 296.

7 Turner, p. 106.

8 Turner, pp. 135, 302; *Transactions of the Gaelic Society of Inverness*, vol. XX, p. 15.

9 MS. sgailp.

10 MS. Teolachain.

11 *The Highlander*, 27 June 1879.

12 Alternative reading: Marbhaidh sinn i féin 's a sliochd.

Notes on some scribal terms

Valuable
use in rev.

(*a*) SELLAD, *examining, testing*

In his monograph 'On the Colophons and Marginalia of Irish Scribes,[1] Plummer writes '. . . the excuse most frequently alleged [for a scribe's shortcomings] is the badness of the writing materials and implements. . . . And so the Irish scribes are continually making trial of their pen, their ink, and other implements on the margins of their MSS.' Plummer cites[2] examples of *probationes pennae* giving the more usual *fromad* (al. *promad*) *pind* and its variant *fechain glesa pind*. For this expression of trial there is, however, another word, *sellad*, which appears to have been favoured by scribes of medical manuscripts.[3]

Sometimes the word stands alone, in a contracted form, *sell⁻*, immediately following the last word of a section or text;[4] at other times it is written in full, *sella*[5] and *sella sin*.[6] But when it occurs in the following context its meaning is clear: *Seallad pinn ann so sis agus dar lium ni bene in gleas na in litir,*[7] *Seallad droich duibh ar leang Ema*[inn].[8]

Sellad is glossed *fégad* in the Lecan Glossary 344[9] and since *fégad* 'often implies close observation or examination'[10] a similar interpretation could perhaps be applied to *sellad* in this case.

(*b*) GAIBID, (i) *takes down from dictation*, (ii) *chooses, excerpts, edits*

Many Irish translations of medical, religious and other non-Irish texts contain colophons giving the names of the author/compiler, the translator, the amanuensis and the scribe of that particular copy. The following is an example: . . . *curob amlaid sin do críchnaigid do thoil Dé tróccairigh in leabar so .i. Almusor*[11] *ó Tadhg húa Chuinn,*[12] . . . *Isead dobo slán don Tigearna in tan do crichnaigeadh in leabar so ó Laidin a nGaeidilg .i. míli bliadan 𐤆 cccc. bliadan. Et Nicol hua hIceadha*[13] *do gabh*[14] *a nGaeidilg 𐤆 is é lá do críchnaigid é ó Laidin a nGaeidilg .i. Céadain in Braith. Donnchad Ó Bolgaidhi*[15] *do graiffin*[16] *in leabar so . . . Anno Domini isin bliadain atám .m. .cccc. lx. viii.*[17]

(i) The phrase *do gab* in a colophon signifying the work of the amanuensis is translated by Plummer[18] 'took down from dictation', by Flower[19] 'made the first copy'. But when the finished work of the Irish amanuensis is more closely examined it would appear that he was not merely the scribe who just 'took down from dictation', his function might also include that of (ii) 'editor', who *chooses* or *excerpts* suitable parts of the text to be copied into the manuscript, sometimes perhaps inserting extraneous but appropriate material which he thinks (and maybe with the approval of the translator) would suit the compilation.

In his introduction to Smaointe Beatha Críost[20] Cainneach Ó Maonaigh o.f.m. has shown[21] that Domhnall Ó Conaill, the amanuensis of Tomás gruamdha Ó Brucháin, the translator,[22] incorporated in the translation a passage, not in the text of the Meditationes Vitae Christi, which shows a close relationship to a passage in the Irish version of De contemptu mundi, a text for which Ó Conaill was also amanuensis but to another translator, Uilliam Mac Duibhne. Ó Maonaigh also notes [23] the similarity in grammatical structure and language in these two texts—no doubt due to the influence of Ó Conaill.

If the work of Nicol Ó hÍceadha as amanuensis to Tadhg Ó Cuinn were examined it might yield a similar result. Otherwise it is difficult to accept for Ó hÍceadha, a man well-versed in different branches of Irish medical learning, the role of merely the scribe who took down from Ó Cuinn's dictation.

Whether the amanuensis made the first copy from his notes is hard to say. In the colophon to the Life of St. Féchín,[24] attributing the translation to Nicol Óg Mac Aba Cunga and stating that it was *Ua Dubthaig do gab 7 do scríb*, there may be a suggestion that it was not always the case for one person to take on what was normally the function of two.[25]

NOTES

1 Brit. Academy Proc. xii 12–14.

2 *Op. cit.*, 14 n. 6–8.

3 For its occurrence in a non-medical manuscript see NLI G1 f. 53v.

4 TCD h. 3.15 p. 53 inf. marg.; NLI G1 f. 53v.

5 RIA 2306 p. 13a20, NLI G11 p. 381b34.

6 2306 p. 13a14.

7 NLI G8 p. 35 sup. marg. 'Here below is a testing of pen and methinks neither the instrument nor the letter is good.'

8 G8 p. 34 sup. marg. 'Testing bad ink on . . .(?) of Éamonn.' The scribes of this manuscript also use the more usual 'fromad' and 'féchain' in a similar context, *ibid.*, p. 33 sup. marg.

9 ACL i 57.

10 Dict. Ir. Lang. F col. 58.

11 = Commentary of Geraldus de Solo on the ninth book of Rhazes' Almanzor. The author is more often referred to as *ugdar an leabair so* or *in tí do thracht in leabar so*, 3C19.

12 For other translations attributed to Ó Cuinn see NLI G11 p. 67a, in which he is cited as *baisiler a fisigeacht*, and RIA 23 M 36 p. 18. The more usual expression signifying the translator is *do chuir (an leabar so) a nGaedhilg*; other expressions include *do tinntoidh sin cetus a Laidin.* Sloane 3567 f. 12b, *do tarraing ó Laidin a nGaedhilge*, 24 P 3 p. 195, *do rinne trannslasion as Laidin uirthe*, 24 P 3 p. 241, *do ronadh an leabar so*, 23 F 19 f. 24v, *do cuireadh so a nGaoidhilg le*, Eg. 89 (BMi 222), *fer a curt[h]a a nGaidilg*, 24 P 14 p. 170.

13 A translation of the Aphorisms of Hippocrates is attributed to Ó hÍceadha in collaboration with Aonghus Ó Callannan in Eg. 89 (BM i 222); see also ed. Regimen Sanitatis I xxviii where J. Carney gives reasons for believing that the translation of the Regimen may also be the work of these two men.

14 *do fuair* in the text on Materia Medica in h. 3. 4.

15 For information on this scribe see Cat. Ir. MSS. NLI, Fasc. i, G11.

16 More often *do scríbh*.

17 NLI G11 p. 248. '. . . in like manner this book i.e. Almanzor was, by the will of merciful God, finished by Tadhg Ó Cuinn. . . . The Lord had completed one thousand and four hundred years when this book was finished from Latin into Irish. And Nicol Ó hÍceadha took it down from dictation in Irish and the day it was finished from Latin into Irish was Spy Wednesday. Donnchad Ó Bolgaidhi wrote this book . . . Anno Domini in the year we are 1468.'

18 *Op. cit.*, p. 16, n. 4. Plummer's statement in this note about Uilliam Mac Duibhne and Domhnall Ó Conaill being 'the same translator and scribe as in note 1 above' can be somewhat misleading, giving the notion that these two colophons are from different texts, whereas in fact it is the colophon to the same text but in different manuscript copies of that text.

19 BM ii 547.

20 Dublin Institute for Advanced Studies, 1944.

21 *Op. cit.*, xvii.

22 For the colophon see *op. cit.*, xvi, 221.

23 *Op. cit.*, xvii.

24 NLI G5 f. 5v, Plummer, *op. cit.*, p. 16, n. 4.

25 On the other hand Gordon Quin states in his edition of Stair Ercuil ocus a bás (ITS xxxviii, p. xxxix): 'It therefore seems to one very likely that we have in H. 2. 7 the autograph copy of these two tales' [SE and Irish Lives of Guy and Bevis] 'and that they were both translated and written down by Uilliam Mac an Leagha'.

BRIAN Ó CUÍV

A poem attributed to
Muireadhach Ó Dálaigh

Among the few poems attributed to Muireadhach Albanach Ó Dálaigh which have so far remained unpublished is one addressed apparently to a Scottish patron whose first name was Amhlaoibh. The only copy I have seen of this poem is in a seventeenth-century manuscript in the Royal Irish Academy, A iv 3, pp. 863–5. I publish it in the following pages as it is a cultural link between our two countries of a kind which Angus Matheson held very dear.

One other poem by Muireadhach Ó Dálaigh to a Scottish patron has come down to us, that beginning *Saor do leannán, a Leamhain,* and published by Skene *(Celtic Scotland,* iii, 454–5) and also by McKenna *(Aithdhioghluim Dána,* i, 173–4). This latter poem was for Alún 'mac Muireadhaigh', 'Mórmhaor Leamhna', whom McKenna (following Skene) identified as Alwyn, first earl of Lennox, whose floruit is said to have been about 1200.[1] There is a certain amount of confusion about the early earls of Lennox and their pedigrees, and conflicting statements have been made about them by various scholars. Thus McKenna *(op. cit.,* p. 172) says of the first earl 'Born probably about 1130, he would have been an old man at the time of the poet's sojourn in Scotland'. On the other hand Miss Ethel Stokes, who wrote the relevant portion of the article on Lennox in *The Complete Peerage,* vii (ed. Doubleday and Howard de Walden), 585ff., describes the poem beginning *Saor do leannán, a Leamhain,* which she considers was made for Alwyn, the first earl, whose floruit she puts '*circa* 1150', as 'a Gaelic poem composed, as was customary, on his coming of age'. But it is out of the question that Ó Dálaigh composed the poem in the middle of the twelfth century. According to Anderson *(Early Sources of Scottish History,* ii, 300) 'King William gave the earldom of Lennox (during the minority of Alwin II) to his brother David.' This appears from charters of the period 1178–82. Anderson also states 'Alwin II appears as earl of Lennox 1208 × 1214. . . . He was succeeded, within the same period, by Maldovenus'.

Now, apart from the earls of Lennox, there is a problem about the date of Muireadhach Ó Dálaigh's supposed flight to Scotland.[2] If it took place after 1214 the 'Mórmhaor Leamhna' would, according to Anderson, have been neither Alwyn I nor Alwyn II but Maeldoven, who is not mentioned by the poet. On the other hand in the genealogy of Donnchadh, a fifteenth-century Mórmhaor Leamhna, found in T.C.D. H. 1. 7, Mac Firbhisigh's Book of Genealogies, etc., the line is traced back through Baltar, Amhlaoibh, Donnchadh, Amhlaoibh Óg, Amhlaoibh Mór, Ailín, Ailín Mór, Muireadhach, Maoldomhnach, Maine Leamhna, Corc to Lughaidh.[3] There are clearly omissions in the earlier generations here, but what is of interest in view of the poem presented now is the occurrence of three Amhlaoibhs in the genealogy, the earliest of them being, it would appear, a son of the second earl. It would seem reasonable to suggest, on the basis of references in the poem and of the other evidence already referred to, that the Amhlaoibh whom Ó Dálaigh addressed in his poem was either a son or a grandson of the second earl.

The poem contains various complaints by Ó Dálaigh about his treatment by Amhlaoibh, who, he feels, has been inclined to ignore him or abandon him. He considers himself entitled to twenty milch-cows, swift Scottish foals, and choice land (§ 2), but he has become displeased with his lot (§ 3). Provided that he gets twenty milch-cows he is prepared to leave Amhlaoibh's territory, for he has always been given to travelling (§ 6). Indeed, he had planned to depart altogether from Amhlaoibh and go to Ireland to the descendants of Muireadhach (§ 7), but he had been stayed in this course (or perhaps 'maintained') by the 'mórmhaor' (§ 8). He has received rewards from Arbhlatha's son (§ 10) and his association with the 'mórmhaor Leamhna' has caused Amhlaoibh jealousy (§ 12). He reminds Amhlaoibh of his distant ancestors, including Oilill, Lughaidh and Corc (§§ 12–15), of his kinship with the people of Munster and the Mainigh (§ 16), and tells him that he knows the family of both his parents (§ 18). He has brought Amhlaoibh a fine poem (*duan*) from Ireland and he is now adding to it, as is fitting, a lay (*laoidh*) (§§ 19–20). He concludes by expressing once more his regret that he should be abandoned by Amhlaoibh (§ 21).

In preparing this poem for publication I have adhered closely to the manuscript version while expanding contractions silently and adding lenition marks where I thought them necessary. I have used round brackets to indicate places where the manuscript is difficult to read, and angular brackets where letters in the margin have been lost. I have used square brackets in § 10 where I have added a syllable required by the *deibhidhe*-rime.

NOTES

1 McKenna says his 'name and title occur in charters of the year 1205 and 1214'. According to Miss Stokes the charters granted between 1208 and 1214 were given by 'Alwyn, Earl of Lennox, son and heir of Alwyn, Earl of Lennox, with the consent of Maldoven his son and heir'.

2 See *Studia Hibernica* i, 56–69.

3 See Skene, *op. cit.*, p. 476.

1   Mairg thréigios inn, a Amhlaoíbh
      an ghuirt úaine ubhallmhaoíl,
          giodh mór do ghnaoí 'gus do ghráin
          ní lór mur taoí 'gum thógbháil.

2   Fiche loilghioch budh dleacht damh,
      searraigh urlomha Alban,
          rogha gach fóid challúir chaoímh
          ód mhallshúil óig, a Amhlaoíbh.

3   A Amhlaoibh, a fhabhra donn,
      ní buidhioch inn dot fhearann,
          bheith aguibh ar Aird na nEach,
          mairg do chagair mo chuibhreach.

4   Ní currach ní críathrach bog
      do dhleisinn d'fhagháil agad,
          cuid don chill do dhligh duine,
          a ghil fhinn, dá almhuire.

94

5   Munab áil leat ar mo laoídh
crodh is fhearann, a Amhlaoíbh,
bean th'fhearann is íoc an crodh,
ní dhleagham dhíot do dhomhan.

6   Cuir fiche loilghioch ar láimh
go ndearnoinn t'fhearann d'fhágbháil,
sirfiod ionadh, a chíabh cham,
ór siobhal ríamh do-rónsum.

7   Do thogras imtheacht uile
úaibh, a chneasbháin chúlbhuidhe,
do bhoing ré hÉirinn n-ealaigh
go cloinn méirsheing Muireadhaigh.

8   Ní nech úaibh, a fholt na raón,
do fhosd mé acht an mórmhaor,
tearc don tslúagh nár fheall orm-sa
acht an sdúagh sheang shúlmhall-sa.

9   (Fiche) bó ionnlaogh áloinn
dhamh ód ghnúis mur gheallámhoinn,
(baile) saór a Srath Leamhna,
rath taóbh ris an tighearna.

10   Buar is mean is mál bracha
fúair meisi ó mhac Arbhlat[ha]
maith an fear agá bhfoghar
mean is braith is bóthoradh.

11   Maith an treas a-táthar sonn,
dá airghi d'airghibh agum,
a Dhé do mheisnigh mheathaigh,
dá sheisrigh do sheisreachaibh.

12   Ó'd-chualuis, a chúl na sgath,
mur fúair mé mórmhaór Leamhnach
fásaidh, a chúl barrlag bog,
tnúdh agas farmad ionnad.

13   Cuimhnigh clann chúlchas Chonghail,
       maith th'aigneadh rét ollamhnaibh,
         clann Ghofraidh cuimhnigh 'mad chuing,
         a Mhuimhnigh shochraidh shéghainn.

14   Cuimhnigh ós cionn do leanna
       Lughaidh mór mac Oillealla,
         cuimhnigh Oillill, a athair,
         ós an mBoirinn mbraónsgathaigh.

15   Cuimhnigh Corc mór mac Leamhna,
       cathuidhe na claoinTeamhra,
         einioch Cuirc Chaisil cuimhnigh
         an fhuilt mhaisigh mhíondruimnigh.

16   Do iadhsad 'mád t'aighidh ngil
       na Muimhnigh is na Mainigh,
         na Mainigh is na Muimhnigh
         airigh agas athchuinnghidh.

17   Dá ttugthá uile dod aoídh,
       a dhuine óig, a Amhlaoíbh,
         atád sáirfhir, a bharr bog,
         a-nall ré a n-áirimh iomad.

18   <M>uinntior h'athar aithnidh damh
       is muinntior mhaith do mháthar,
         <re> sloinneadh liom-sa um laoídh,
         a choinniol fhionn-sa, a Amhlaoíbh.

19   Má thugas dúan 'na dúain bhinn
       dhuid, a Amhlaoímh, a hÉirinn,
         do laoídh, a rí, a-nos do-ním,
         ní bhí fros gan a froisín.

20   Ní bhí bó álainn gan oigh,
       ní bhí gamhnach gan ghamhain,
         dúan mholta linn gona laoídh,
         a chorcra fhinn, a Amhlaoibh.

21   A Amhlaoímh, a chais chorcra,
a chara 's a chomhalta,
th'éigios baird as binn a laoídh,
mairg thréigios inn, a Amhlaoíbh.

Notes on the poem

1 c '*gus*: *is* MS.; but this leaves the line a syllable short.

3 d *chagair* (:*aguibh*); but MS. has *chogair*.

4 c–d 'one has become entitled to a portion of the church-land (?) by virtue of what he has brought from over-seas (?).

5 c–d 'take your land and pay (out) the stock; I do not require your property from you'.

6 a *ar: ar mo* MS.

7 d I do not know what Muireadhach is referred to here. Could it be the Muireadhach, son of the Mórmhaor Leamhna who, according to AU, slew the chief of Ceinél Fearghusa in 1215, or perhaps the Muireadhach who, according to O'Flaherty (*Ogygia*, p. 384), took part in the Battle of Clontarf on Brian's side?

9 b *gheallámhoinn*: apparently a compound of *geal* and *lámhann* ('glove').

  c *Srath Leamhna: Srath* (here : *rath*) is common in Scottish place-names.

10 c–d This couplet is cited in *IGT* ii, ex. 2046: *maith an fear aga bhfaghar · mean is braich is bótharadh.*

11 c This line is satisfactory metrically, but I am not sure what it means; perhaps 'o God, to give courage to a coward'.

12 d *farmad*: MS. has *formad*, but this will not rime with *barrlag*. However, the form *farmad* is not cited as an alternative in *IGT* ii § 11 where *formad* occurs.

13 I do not know to whom Ó Dálaigh was referring with the phrases *clann Chonghail* and *clann Ghofraidh*. The phrase *a Mhuimhnigh* would be in accord with the supposed descent of the people of Leven from Corc of Caiseal, alluded to in § 15.

14 d The Boireann is far from the traditional territory of Oilill Flann Beag.

15 For Corc see *Aithdh. Dána*, i, pp. 172–4. We may doubtless infer that Corc was an ancestor of Amhlaoíbh. So the references in § 16 to *Muimhnigh* and *Mainigh* may be interpreted as being to Amhlaoibh's descent from Corc of Munster through Maine Leamhna.

19, 20, 21 The references to *duan* and *laoidh* suggest that a *laoidh* was a composition of less importance than a *duan*. I do not know exactly what the poet intended in § 19 *d* with the words *fros* (lit. 'shower') and *froisín*. His use of the term *bard* in the phrase *th'éigios baird*, apparently in reference to himself, is interesting in view of the supposed inferior status held by the *bard*.

MÁIRÍN O DALY

Úar in Lathe do Lum Laine

INTRODUCTION

This poem, which survives in one MS. (LL 145[b]) only, is a dialogue between a woman and a man, who address each other as 'Lom Laine' and 'Tethna'. It has been understood as spoken by Ailbe[1] daughter of Cormac mac Airt but it appears from the poem that the *ingen úi Chuind* mentioned is not Ailbe, who was known for her wisdom and judgment[2] rather than for any romantic episode in her life, but another daughter of Cormac. Elsewhere in LL we find a list of Cormac's daughters: *deich n-ingena do Chormac . . . Ailbe Gruadbrec Treithne Lethleór ꝛ Gráne . Lemuin Letherthe la Scéithi Admor Ainge Fásse Talinne . . . Innerb*, 4917f.; and *Ailbe Treithne Grane gle . . .*, 7020. The list is the same in each case but with orthographical variations. Another daughter not mentioned in this enumeration is Sodelb, see ZCP xviii 422. Our poem must belong to some lost tale about 'Tethna'. It might seem that 'Tethna' is the 'Treithne' of the LL list but the circumstances indicated are so reminiscent of the story of Gráinne, not the Tóraigecht but the earlier[3] and less romantic version in ZCP i 458, that I am inclined to regard 'Tethna' and 'Lom Laine' (lit. 'the bare one of L.') as pseudonyms for Gráinne and Díarmait and the form Treithne as perhaps deriving from this poem or the tale to which it belonged.[4] In the short passage in ZCP i 458f. Gráinne is married to Finn and lives with him though she hates him. To this tradition must also belong the quatrain occurring in the commentary to ACC:

ut dixit *Gránni ingen Cormaic fri Find:*

> *Fil dune*
> *rismad bude lem diuderc*
> *ara tribrind in bith ule*
> *a meicc Maire cid diúbert,* LU 514ff.

99

In *Early Irish Lyrics*, p. 236, Gerard Murphy writes 'this quatrain . . . seems to be the earliest reference extant to Gráinne's love for Díarmait' and he ascribes it to the ninth or tenth century. Gráinne, indeed, would seem to be in Irish literature the prototype of the eloping wife (or daughter). Cf. *'Grainde luid lat, a Lughaidh'*, Laws iii 532.11. Before this sentence we find *'Cuirm lium; lemnacht la cat'* said to have been spoken by Cormac úa Cuinn to Lughaidh, son of the king of Connacht or, according to another and more likely version, by Cairbre Lifechair son of Cormac, when defending his foster-brother (Lugaid, presumably) against Cormac's demand for the payment of damages for Lugaid's having eloped with Gráinne (see O'Curry Transcripts 1694) and cf. Leb. Gab. 30 § 29.

From our poem we may infer that 'Tethna' and 'Lom Laine' are in love but that there is some obstacle to their union, probably that 'Tethna' is married already, and that any relationship between them is likely to lead to the death of both. It also appears that Lom Laine is associated with Almu.

The third quatrain breaks the sequence of phrasing in §§ 2, 4, 5 and although identical in metre may perhaps not originally have belonged to the poem. This is also suggested by the way this quatrain and § 2 appear in Scél Baili Binnbérlaig, RC xiii 220 (Harl. 5280, f. 38ª):

ut dicitur:

> *Aboll Aildinde ardai*
> *ibor Baili, becc forboi,*
> *cia dobertar au laidhib*
> *ni tuicid daine borba.*

Et *amail adbert ingen Cormaic ui Quinn* [*.i. Aillbi*] (this is omitted from RC but is in MS.):

> *Es fris samlaim Aluime*
> *fri hibor Traga Baili*
> *fris combaroim aroili*
> *frisan abaild a hAilli.*

The 23 N 10 text differs from that in Harl. 5280 only in orthography. So that in Scél Baili § 2 is ascribed to Ailbe but § 3 is not. § 3 also appears in the Dindshenchas of Aillend, Rennes § 17, where it is introduced merely by 'ut dicitur'.

The only other quatrain that I have found cited elsewhere is § 7 which occurs with glosses in H. 3.18 (referred to as H below), p. 4, from which it has been published by Meyer in ZCP viii 107:

> Flaind line nacham luaidh
> nad rot bréccat meschoin[a] mūaid[b]
> mainbad leca[c] Lugdach Liss
> eoin bicc Baile[d] not beitiss.

It occurs also in Egerton 1782, f. 52 col. 1:

> A flaind line nadam luáid
> nadatragbat messchoin muáid
> ɔnenptis (leg. menptis) lecca luidgech liss
> eoin bicc bale notbetis .i. poc 7 pudar.

The language of the poem is Old Irish. Note deponent fritot-samlur §§ 2, 4 and final vowels. I see no reason for placing it later than the ninth century.

The metre is Rannaigecht (a mixture of r. mór and r. bec) except for § 7 which is a type of deibide (see Deibide docheil a chubaid, Murphy Metrics, p. 66).

The poem has been printed with translation and notes in MS. Mat. p. 476ff. but O'Curry did not realize that it was a dialogue and the translation is very faulty.

I reproduce the glosses from the diplomatic edition of LL as I find it quite impossible to read as much of them as the editors of that edition have read.

1   [T.]   Úar in[e] lathe do Lum Laine[f]
                  i lleith leinne oc[g] aige áin;
     [L.L.] is úar cid d'ingin ú[i] Chuind
                  foilces[h] a moing a lloing láin.

2   [T.]   Is fris samlaim Lom Laine
                  fri ibar Rātha Baili[i];
     [L.L.] fritot-samlur[j], a Thethna,
                  frisin [n-]abaill a hA[i]li.[kl]

[a] .i. di bhrai.   [b] .i. fir étaidh.   [c] .i. ruici 7 athis.   [d] .i. poic 7 meirtrech.
Cf. Eoin baili .i. bet 7 mebul, nó póc 7 pudhair, Harl. 5280, p. 64 marg. inf.
  [e] Read a? Line hypermetric. Read láa?   [f] Luine, MS.   [g] ic, MS.   [h] f-, MS.
[i] Baile, MS.   [j] -samlor, MS.   [k] hAle, MS.   [l] .i. a hAlind.

3   Aball* Ailinne[m] arda[e]
             ibar Baili, bec ṅ-orbba[i]
             ce dobertar i llaïdi[n]
             nis-tucat daíni[o] borbba[i].

4   [T.]   Is fris samlaim Lom Laine
             fri dam† [n]dūbartach [n]Drigrend;
    [L.L.] fritot-ṡamlurp[p], a Thethna,
             fri eilit[q] [n]Dromma Drigrend.‡

5   [T.]   Is fris samlaim Lom Laine
             fri slatta(ib) findchuill Aille[r];
    [L.L.] is fris samlaim-se Tethna[i]
             [f]ri scatha(ib) uachtair bainne[s].

6   [T.]   A Luim Laine, in ránac[t]
             co lLicc da Berg ac Srúb Brain?
    [L.L.] [u]ránac co[u] Ferta Magen
             fri[v] Suide Lagen anair.

7   [T.]   A Luim Laine, nacham lūaid,
             [w]nacham thaidlet[w] meschoin mūaid;
    [L.L.] mainbad[x] leca Luigdech lis
             eoin bic Baili[y] rot betisz[z].

8   [T.]   Cridṡerc mo menman míne
             ingenrad[aa] Temra tūade;
    [L.L.] 7 cridṡerc [bb]mo anman[bb]
             gillanrad Alman úare.

9   [T.]   A Luim Laine, nacham lūaid,
             a grāin gaile, a greit ṡlūaig,
             ma rop samlaid-seo ar sét,
             fo-d-irfe ar n-éc (i n)nach úair. U.

[m] Alinni, *MS.*   [n] llaide, *MS.*   [o] dáine, *MS.*   [p] -samlar, *MS.*   [q] eilte, *MS.*
[r] Áille, *MS.*   [s] báinne, *MS.*   [t] ranacais, *MS.*   [u–u] ranacus, *MS.*
[v] ra, *MS.*   [w–w] nad rot bréccat, H (*see Introd.*).

Translation

1 Cold the day for Lom Laine competing in splendid horse-racing(?), clad only in(?) a mantle; cold too for the daughter of Conn's grandson who is washing her hair in a full vessel.

2 To this I liken Lom Laine—to the yew-tree of Ráth Baili; I liken you, Tethna, to the apple-tree of Aile.

3 The apple-tree of noble Alenn, Baile's yew, small the heritage; if they be put into songs, ignorant people do not understand them.

4 To this I liken Lom Laine—to the combative ox of Drigriu; I liken you, Tethna, to the hind of Druimm Drigrend.

5 To this I liken Lom Laine—to the branches of the whitebeam of Aille; to this I liken Tethna—to the sheen(?) on the top of milk.

6 O Lom Laine did you reach as far as (*or* have you come from(?)) Lecc Da Berg at Srúb Brain? I reached as far as (*or* I have come from(?)) Ferta Maigen to the east of Suide Laigen.

7 O Lom Laine, do not (seek to) sway me; let not the eyes of a jealous husband light on me; were it not for *leca Luigdech lis* you would have the little birds of Baile (*or* the little birds of Baile would beguile you(?)).

8 Dear to my gentle mind are the maidens of the people of Temair; and dear to my soul are the youths of cold Almu.

9 O Lom Laine, do not (seek to) sway me, o valiant terror-inspiring one, o champion of the host; if this is to be our path, it will some day bring about our death.

ˣ reading of H. manibetis, *MS.*   ʸ Baile, *MS.*

ᶻ not beitiss, H. ?*Leg.* not bréct[a]is. *The difference between* betis *and* brectis *in a MS. would be very slight.*

ᵃᵃ ingen rig, *MS.*   ᵇᵇ⁻ᵇᵇ manman, *MS.*

* U( )find ath- oll- ul-·   † oendam eti( ) h( ) in( ) tib( ) imda ard( ).

‡ oenelit mael eter ardaib imda isind ailen 7 muinter Oengusa dia lenmainside i ruis in daim.

Notes on the poem

§1 *i lleith leinne.* (O'Curry, MS. Mat. p. 477 translates 'in half a cloak').
i lleith means 'under the protection of, depending upon, trusting in':
lecam ar ráma úan isa muir 7 fo-n-cerddam i lleth ar Tigernai, Ériu,
xi, 137. *nít erpi i lled nach áili* 'thou dost not trust thyself with any one
else', Wb. 1ᵈ10. *caingne in tsenaidh . . . do lecon i lleith na ndea* 'to trust
the disputes of the Senate to the gods', CCath. 4549. Perhaps the
lenn was a lighter garment than the *bratt* which sometimes, at any
rate, was fleecy: *brat ríabach rolómar,* BDD² 539. 790.

Lom Laine. If, as I have suggested, this is a sobriquet for Díarmait
úa Duibne, the second part might be a place- or people-name.
There is no rhyme to indicate the quantity. A tribal name *moccu*
(sic leg.?) *Láne* (:*máre* gsf. of *már*) occurs in Fél. Dec. 6, glossed:
.i. sentuath sen ro boi i ndesciurt Herenn aliquando, 7 díb sein do Gobbán,
p. 256. On the same page we find '*Gobbain .i. o Chill Lamraige i
n-iarthur Osraige.*' In Duan. Finn i xxxiii 9 Gráinne addresses Díarmait
as '*a laoich Locha fionn-Charmain*', and *Cochrann máthair Diarmata
meic Duib m. Duibne* was descended from Cathaīr Mār according to
Corp. Gen. p. 45. This would place her among the Laigin. O'Curry,
MS. Mat. p. 477, refers to the occurrence of this or a similar name in
a surname in the annals: *Corbmac Ua Lumluini, fer leighind Cluana
Ferta Brénainn, iarsma shuadh Ereann ina aimsir décc,* FM an. 1170.
*Corbmac Ua Luimluinn espoc Chluana Ferta Brenuinn . . . d'ég ina
naoimhshenoir cianaosda,* an. 1259 (*Luimlin,* ALC). Another member
of this family is mentioned at an earlier date in Ann.Inisf. an. 1076:
*Flathbertach mc. Luim Laene, in fer legind 7 anchara Dé, quieuit in
Christo i lLis Mor.* It is difficult, however, to see any connection
between this family name and the name in our poem.

ic aige áin. aige is vn. of *aigid* and is used of horse-racing: *mag . . . mó
a aighe .i. a graifne ech,* Corm.Y 898. *imma áig iar níth aigi ech i n-íath,*
LU 8669 (FB 50). *for aighe eoch,* St. Ercuil 203. *án* 'splendid, noble,
glorious' is frequently applied to horses and paired with *athlam* and
lúath. Here I think *aige* is not used quite as a vn., in which case it
could hardly be qualified by an adj., but rather as a substantive.
Cf. *oc geran 7 ac acaine moir,* LL. 407ᵇ19 (TTr. 2165), and for *oc* in
the sense of 'engaged in' cf. *bale i rrabe oc na clessaib,* LU 8568 (FB 43).
The phrase *aigid áin* is not uncommon but I have rejected this as our
text would imply the existence of an *o*-stem, nom. *án* g. *áin,* and of
this I find no evidence.

§§2, 3 *ibar Rātha Baili . . . in [n-]abaill a hA[i]li. aball A[i]linne . . . ibar Baili.* Here, I suggest, we have two different traditions, the second deriving from the first. The first reference I can find to Baile and Aile together is their occurrence in the Táin as place-names on Medb's route *sairdes a Crúachnaib Aii . . . for Cend Ferna for Baile for Aile,* LU 4606. *for Medhe in Eoin, for Baili, for Aile . . . for Cend Ferna,* TBC Stowe 300. Méide in Eoin was 'east of Áth Leathan in Crích Conailli Muirthemne', Hog.Onom. That there was a famous tree at Baile appears from: *dar Breg Ross dar Braine/ . . . /sech bun Baile in bile,* TBC 3323–5 = *re taeb baili in bili,* TBC² 2527. § 2 may indicate that besides the *bile (ibar)* in the place called Baile there was also an *aball* in Aile (but does the *findcholl Aille (:bainne)* represent yet another variant?) and that from these two trees derive two different legends, that of Baile Binnbérlach and Aillenn daughter of Fergus Fairrge *(senathair rīgraide Lagen,* Corp.Gen. p. 99) whose unhappy love-story is told in Scél Baili Binnbérlaig, RC xiii 221ff., and that of Crem Marda who abducted Aillenn daughter of Lugaid rí Laigen. In this tale (Rennes Dindsh. 17) Aillenn died of shame and an apple-tree grew from her grave (i.e. *aball Aillinne*) while a yew-tree grew from the grave of her lap-dog whose name was Ailbe. The yew-tree was called *Ibur Baile .i. Ailbe tre delidin* (i.e. through metathesis).

§4 *Drigrend . . . Dromma Drigrend.* For the second O'Curry reads *Drignend,* wrongly, I think (cf. LL 18186). One or other, probably the first, which presumably is the gen. of a place-name, is very likely an error. A proper name *Dricriu,* the gen. of which would be *Dricrenn* (cf. *Bricriu, Bricrenn*) occurs in the Tripartite Life: *Driccriu (Dricriu,* Trip. 186.5, Lism.L. 406) *is hé pá rí Hua nGarrchon ar chind Patraic in tan sin,* Trip.² 2178. Dricriu was married to a daughter of Loígaire mac Néill. He behaved badly to Patrick and consequently, we may assume, was deprived of issue since it is Cillíne (his brother?) who welcomed Patrick who appears in the genealogy of the Úi Garrchon (Corp.Gen. p. 39). I find no other reference to *Druimm Drigrend* and none to the *dam* or the *eilit* referred to here.

§5 *findchuill.* See Bertoldi, ZCP xvii 177ff.

scatha. The usual meaning is 'shadow, shade', but with our ex. cf. perhaps *co scathaib scoth for cach maig* (of Paradise), SR 971.

§6 *in ránac / co lLicc. . . /ránac co Ferta (ranacais . . . ranacus,* MS.). I suggest that this originally read *in ránacc / ó Licc . . . / ránacc ó Ferta.*

Examples of the spelling -*cc* in pret. sg. are few for the compd. *ro-icc*
but there are several from Wb. for *do-icc*. The -*cc* seems to be very
rare in ater O. Ir. and in Mid. Ir. and only reappears, perhaps due
to an archaizing tendency, in Mod. Ir. texts (see RIA Contribb. s.v.
do-icc). The final -*c* of *ránacc* may consequently have become detached
from the verb and attached to the follg. preposition. *Lecc da Berg*
and *Ferta Maigen* are unidentified. There was a place *Srúb Brain* in
the N.E. extremity of Inishowen, and another in Kerry which was
one of the three *airderca Hérenn*, Triads 60.

Suide Laigen still so called. Anglicized Mount Leinster. In the story
of Baile mac Buain, the bearer of false tidings says to Baile: *Di Tuaig
Inbir tiagoim ⁊ tar ais budthuaid anussai o Slioab Suidiu Laigeon*; and
to Aillenn: *a fochlai Erend o Tuaig Inbir ⁊ secha so co Sliab Suidi
Laigen*, RC xiii 222. 19ff.

§7 The translation of line *b* is based on the glosses from H. 3.18 cited
in Introd. Perhaps we should see here an echo of the slaying of
Delgnat's *meschu* by her jealous husband, Leb. Gab. 34 § 32.

leca Luigdech lis. This phrase occurs elsewhere but in no instance
is the context very enlightening:

> *Comul scartha fri Riab ñDerg*
> *is delg i cridi cró cnis*
> *Cu Chulaind do bith i n-iñgnais*
> *dirsan menbad leca lis.*

> *Menbad leca lis Lugdach*
> *lasa rumnad cach ñderba*
> *ba romoch ar n-étarba*
> *fri mac na Tri Find Emna*, LL 14476ff.;

and

leacht Conrúi hi Sleib Mis | lecht Lugdach fo leccaib leis (.i. e féin ro
(= *ra) marb hi cumaid a mna*), RC xxiii 319 § 10 = *lecht Luighdech
fo leccuib liss (.iii. lecca liss Luigdech .i. gress ⁊ ruicci ⁊ mebul*), 324
§ 10.

In spite of this gloss and the dat. pl. endings in the RC text, I
think *leca* is singular (*menbad leca* in LL citation, *mainbad leca*, H.).
The meaning 'shame' would suit the Aided Derb Forgaill text, Derb
Forgaill implying that to part from Lugaid and Cú Chulaind would

be unbearable sorrow were it not that the shame of living in her mutilated state would be yet more painful. *leca* also occurs in the Finn and Gráinne story (ZCP i 458) mentioned above* perhaps in the same sense: *is mithig son dunn scarad fri leca tromdruisi cotber fri* (*fi*, MS.) *bru breitheamon ar ni theit nach n-om a coiri.*

ēoin bic Baili. These are mentioned in the Dindshenchas of Hirarus (Rennes Dindsh. 117 and LL 22111ff.). '*Eóin Baile batar oc tathaigid Cairpri Lifechair do Raith Cairpri.* "*Tortha, tortha,*" *a do dib;* "*Tiagu, tiagu*", *in deda aile. Secht coecait oidhchi badar oc fochetal do, 7 ciped teach ind Ere a mbeith Cairpre taircitis chuccai. Cetheora poca insin in Meic Oicc. Ros-delb i rricht cethri* [*n-én*] *co mbidis oc togerad* (*togairad, LL*) *caem nErenn*', Rennes Dindsh. 117. *togerad* is translated 'girding at' 'mocking' by Stokes. Perhaps it is a vn. formation from *do-gair*, meaning 'summoning, calling to'. In the Dindshenchas the object of the birds seems to be to call away the beautiful ones of Ireland at the instigation of Óengus in Macc Óc, presumably to lure them away to the other world. Cf. the gloss on 4d where the Óengus mentioned is probably also the Macc Óc. Cf. also:

> *Eoin Bale batar thall tair*
> *i tír Cairpri Liphechair*
> *co mbitís na tretaib trell*
> *ic brécad naeden Herend*, LL 22128ff.

§8 Here I think the speakers imply that they would regret leaving their companions, a necessary consequence of an elopement.

§9 *ma ro* is unusual but cf. *ma ro loídib lammis*, Fél. Feb. 27 (*mad ar, mad i, mor a*, v.ll.).

NOTES

1 MS. Mat. p. 476.

2 See Tochmarc Ailbe, ZCP xiii 254ff. Cf. *aigillidh ingin i Cuinn |...| is i bainbretiomh gan feall | is fearr a n-inis Eireann*, Duan. Finn ii 130 § 22. *Aillbe cháidh | in bhean dob fearr ciall do mnáibh*, § 23; *gaois Ailbhe i n-inghin Domhnaill*, DDána 99.1 (Gofraidh Fionn).

3 Meyer, *Fianaig.* Introd. xxiii says of it 'the piece perhaps belongs to the ninth century' but Murphy, Duan. Finn iii Introd. p. lix writes '10th or 11th cent.?' and on p. 19, n. 1: 'the frequent use of *ro*-forms in narrative

* Introd. [p. 99].

suggests that a 9th cent. date is too early'. This is true of the general language of the tale but I believe it to derive from an earlier original. The rhetorics spoken by Cormac and Coirpre suggest a date at least as early as the ninth century.

4 When writing the Introduction I had overlooked O'Curry's reference to the poem *ibid.* p. 467, where he says it was 'written by Ailbhé' but 'written on the occasion of the elopement of . . . Grainné . . . with Dermot'.

Worker on Gaelic Atlas see p. 65

MAGNE OFTEDAL

Some sources of error in linguistic field work

To the experienced linguistic field worker there will be little or nothing new in the reflections set down here. It is my hope, however, that they will, to some extent, help other linguists to assess the reliability of data collected in the field. I also hope that my remarks may open the eyes of young students of linguistics not only to the many pitfalls to be avoided in field work but also to the inspiring challenges offered by this, perhaps the most fascinating part of linguistic study.

There are almost as many kinds of linguistic field work as there are different categories of linguistic material. One investigator may want to make an intensive study of the structure, or part of the structure, of one 'idiolect' (the speech of one particular person); another may want to record the terminology of, say, navigation in a particular linguistic area; a third may be studying place-names; a fourth may want data to throw light upon the history of a given dialect; a fifth may wish to investigate the interplay between the two languages of one or more bilingual communities, and so on. The most extensive form of field work is the collection of data for a linguistic survey of a larger area, usually to be published in the form of a linguistic atlas. The present writer has attempted field work in several of the branches of study mentioned above, and his reflections are based partly upon his own experiences in Norway, in Norwegian settlements in America and in the Scottish Gaidhealtachd (where he has done both intensive and extensive research), partly on his second-hand knowledge of the experiences of other workers in these and other areas.

Some sources of error may be found in the field worker's implements. Paper and writing tools of inferior quality have made many good field notes difficult to read and easy to misinterpret. A special warning must be given against the use of ball-point pens in linguistic field work: most if not all such pens are apt at times to leave a series of dots or dashes on the paper where a connected line is intended, so that the symbol ŭ may come to look like ü, or o like c or ɔ. The most recent piece of the field worker's standard equipment, the tape recorder, which has rapidly become an indispensable companion to traditional writing materials, may also cause many errors if not selected and used with all possible precautions. There is, for instance, the question of tape speed. A low-speed recording may be so indistinct, because the higher frequencies are lacking, that it is almost useless for any other purpose than the study of quantity, stress and pitch. $1\frac{7}{8}$ inches per second is definitely too slow; $3\frac{3}{4}$ inches is better and may be sufficient in many cases, but for really satisfactory results a speed of $7\frac{1}{2}$ inches should be used whenever possible. On the other hand, little or nothing is gained by a high tape speed unless a very good microphone is used. It is also of the utmost importance that the distance from the informant's mouth to the microphone be the correct one, and that the recording level be watched at frequent intervals and adjusted whenever necessary.

A tape speed higher than $7\frac{1}{2}$ inches per second is probably not to be recommended for field work. A speed of 15 inches, as used in studio recordings, requires studio conditions in order to give appreciably better results than $7\frac{1}{2}$ inches, and such conditions cannot be provided where field recordings are made—in the informant's home or even in the open air. What can be done, however, is to avoid extraneous sounds as far as possible (other people talking, babies crying, noises from animals, machinery, etc.). The quiet evening hours are usually best for the tape-recording sessions. One noise which the beginner often forgets is the ticking of a clock, unnoticed by both informant and field worker but clearly registered by the microphone and perpetuated on the tape. There must, therefore, be no clock going in the room where the recording is being made. If the clock cannot be removed or stopped, the recording session must be held in another room. Even a wrist-watch may occasionally cause disturbing noises. On one or two occasions I have had to ask my informant to put his wrist-watch in his pocket because he could not talk naturally unless he placed his hands in front of him on the table, only an inch or two from the only place where it was possible to put the microphone.

Even the best tape recordings made in the field have their limitations. In rapid speech, for instance, it is often very difficult to distinguish between **s** and **f** or between **d** and **r**. Moreover, the tape registers not only words and sounds that belong to the informant's normal speech, but also every tiny slip of the tongue, of which there may be many in a few minutes' conversation. Most of them are small enough to pass unnoticed (and accordingly uncorrected) by the speaker, but are mercilessly picked up by the microphone. If the field worker fails to hear properly a word he is writing down in phonetic script, he may ask for one or more repetitions, and as it is a physical impossibility for any speaker to produce an utterance twice in exactly the same manner, the field worker is able to circle in the true or 'intended' pronunciation by eliminating slips of the tongue.[1] Not so with a tape-recorded word. Every time it is played back it will come out exactly alike, and the person who transcribes the tape runs the risk of perpetuating an error—and the more so the more exact and conscientious he is. In consequence, the ideal use of tape recordings includes a thorough check-up with the informant after transcription, but this is unfortunately rarely feasible because of the extra costs and labour involved.

Most errors in linguistic field work originate, however, not in the technical equipment but in various human factors. Failure to obtain completely reliable material may be due to shortcomings on the part of the field worker or of the informant, or it may originate in an unsatisfactory *rapport* between the two.

Let us first consider some of the qualities required in a good field worker. Needless to say, he must have a first-class training in phonetics and general linguistics, theoretical and practical. He must have a good ear for shades of sound and be able to perceive, identify and describe them quickly. He should preferably also be a good imitator and able to reproduce the sounds he hears, after a minimum of practice. This is desirable because his descriptions of the sounds are usually given in terms of articulatory phonetics, and except in the case of interdentals and sounds where labial action is involved—that is, cases where articulation is partly visible—the field worker has no other means of observing the articulations than reproducing them himself and feeling what he must do with his tongue, velum, glottis, etc., in order to produce a good imitation of the sounds.

The field worker's *knowledge of the language* or dialect he investigates is an important but rather complex factor. It is theoretically (and indeed, sometimes also practically) possible for a good field worker to obtain excellent results with a language of which he is completely ignorant when he starts his work. In one respect this might be considered the ideal situation, as the investigator goes to his task without any preconceived ideas. In practice, however, an ideal situation does not exist. During his field work the trained linguist cannot help beginning to analyse the language as his work progresses, and this conscious or subconscious analysis will gradually influence his perception of the sounds and sound sequences, so that his final field notes may be very different from his initial ones. He will hear sounds and shades of sound which he did not notice at first, and may have to go over the whole material again with his informant. If he has no opportunity of doing this, the reliability of each item of information will depend on the stage of work at which it was taken down.

If, on the other hand, the field worker is acquainted with the dialect to be investigated, through the medium of a closely related dialect or standard language, he must be on his guard against several pitfalls: (a) he may imagine that he hears distinctions of sound which exist in the more familiar idiom but not in the dialect under investigation; (b) he may, inversely, fail to hear distinctions which occur in the dialect under investigation but not in the more familiar one; (c) a phonemic distinction may occur in both dialects but be overlooked in the one under investigation because the actual contrast in sound is less than or phonetically different from that found in the more familiar idiom; and (d) some words and inflections may have different meanings in the two dialects, and this may pass unnoticed because the field worker considers it unnecessary to record meanings.

The situation which comes nearest to being ideal is that in which the investigator is recording his own dialect, drawing the material either from his own speech or from that of another person belonging to the same speech community in the narrowest sense of the word. Among the most dangerous sources of error in this situation is the fact that the investigator, being a trained linguist, has a more or less complete mental picture of the structure of the dialect from the very beginning. If this mental picture is the result not of a previous systematic analysis but only of a general impression, it may be wrong, and the material he takes down may be distorted by subconscious attempts to make it conform with the preconceived pattern. The conscientious investigator will, however, probably discover his mistakes sooner or later, and as he usually has the opportunity of working leisurely in this situation and of re-examining every item of his material, his output will, as a rule, be more reliable than any other kind of field material.

We have now examined some of the qualities required in a good field worker, and have arrived at the question: What qualities are required in a good informant? The answer depends very much upon the purpose of the investigation. But, except in the rare cases where the whole object is the investigation of one idiolect without regard to comparative linguistics, historical or geographical, the most essential requirement is that the informant be *representative* or typical of his dialect community or a certain subdivision of it, such as an age group, an occupation, a group characterized by its comparative wealth or education, etc., according to the nature of the investigation and the sort of material looked for. In this context the word 'representative' has at least three different meanings, also dependent on the purpose of the investigation: (*a*) an informant may be typical of *the majority of speakers* within his community or the subdivision of it to which he belongs; (*b*) he may be typical of *strictly local speakers* as opposed to inhabitants of extraneous or mixed parentage; or (*c*) he may be typical of *those speakers who have preserved the largest amount of archaic features* in their speech (these are usually, but not always or necessarily, old people).[2] Finding a representative informant is one of the field worker's most difficult tasks, and one that may take a long time if he has to do it on his own. Very often he has to ask for advice and assistance from well-informed local residents such as public servants, clergymen, or school-teachers, but as these are often incomers they may not know the population or the dialect well enough to give perfectly reliable information.

Once a number of presumably representative speakers have been singled out (in whatever sense we use the term 'representative'), it remains to decide which of them is the most suitable in other respects. In order to reach a decision the field worker often has to interview several subjects tentatively. This is time-consuming but relatively easy work, and it may often yield interesting incidental information. Here the beginner must be given a double warning: he should be on his guard against all types of shortcomings in his prospective informants, but at the same time he must not give up any of them until he has made sure that he has found the best of them all. He should not, for instance, abandon a prospective informant merely for having no upper front teeth, because precisely this person may very well turn out to be the best informant in all other respects. Sometimes, of course, a physical deficiency may be so pronounced as to render linguistic interviews impossible or very wearisome both to informant and field worker. Deafness or general physical debility may be very hard to overcome, and prolonged interviews with persons suffering from such ailments may irritate them unduly or even be harmful to them. Even so, some such persons may make excellent informants if the field worker has enough time and patience to interview them in very short sessions, giving them ample time to rest.

Obviously, good health—including a perfect set of teeth—and a clear voice are invaluable assets in an informant, but they may at times be outweighed by another informant's *mental* equipment, which is after all more important. Most field workers start by assessing the intelligence of prospective informants, on the assumption that intelligent people can be relied upon to possess a large vocabulary, to be well informed about the society they live in, and to understand what the field worker wants from them. While this assumption is doubtlessly correct, it cannot be reversed to the effect that people with an intelligence around or below the average always have a smaller vocabulary, know less about their environment, and are more difficult to work with. This would be very far from the truth. Some of my best informants would probably not have rated very high in an IQ test, but nevertheless they possessed a surprisingly rich vocabulary, seemed to know practically everything about community life and activities and were very easy to train to the routine of answering questions (although some of them did not quite understand the purpose of the questioning nor seem to care much about understanding it). Indeed, these unsophisticated but well-informed and easily trained informants are often more reliable than the very intelligent, who not infrequently are inclined to show off their knowledge of some literary or standard language and sometimes even to suppress the genuine dialect forms if they consider these inferior. As Professor Hans Kurath puts it, 'The ideal informant is one who cannot help talking the way he does.'[3] Very often, however, the field worker is put off the track by his local advisers, the people he asks for information about informants, as they are only too liable, out of sheer helpfulness, to direct him to persons reputed for their learning. In my work in the Scottish Gaidhealtachd I have attempted to avoid such informants by telling my advisers that I preferred persons who could not read and write Gaelic. But I have not always succeeded, and among the errors I have to confess to personally is that of having sometimes selected informants who were too sophisticated.

The reader may now begin to wonder why I have not yet mentioned such qualities as willingness to co-operate, a friendly attitude and a talkative disposition among the characteristics desirable in the informant. The reason is that I regard these qualities not as features of the informant's personality but as part of the good *rapport* that must be established between informant and field worker. And this *rapport* is, in nine out of ten cases, the field worker's responsibility, and his only. The informant is not begging for the favour of being interviewed; it is the field worker who begs a favour of him, and he must not let himself forget this for a moment.

If 'reluctant' or 'unco-operative' informants exist at all, they must be very few. Persons with a true reluctance to be interviewed would hardly consent to act as informants in the first place. The experienced field worker knows that once a person has consented to co-operate and the first interview has begun, he will feel important and proud of being able to furnish the investigator with the information wanted, and will balk or back out only if the field worker makes a wrong move.

But wrong moves are easy to make. A good field worker must be tactful almost in the extreme. He must acquaint himself with local customs, superstitions and religion, and take great care not to do or say anything that may offend the local population. He must also find out all he can about his informant's personal views in moral, religious and political issues and not contradict him in these questions unless the informant himself asks for his views. Even then he must be extremely cautious, unless he discovers that the informant is of the argumentative type who will welcome an occasional discussion as a break in the monotony of questioning. A natural shyness or diffidence on the part of the field worker may make it difficult for him to make contacts at first, but this can be learned by experience (as in the case of the present writer), and once the contact has been established, modesty—whether congenital or acquired—is a great asset to the field worker, as it makes the informant feel more at his ease. It should be added, however, that this modesty must be genuine. The investigator must feel—not only pretend—that the informant has something to teach him. It is a capital mistake for a field worker to arrive in a community and announce that he wants to make an investigation—a word that will immediately create distrust. He has come to *learn*, and this is what he must emphasize.

The field worker who neglects to learn this attitude will sooner or later begin to irritate his informants, who may then—and with good reason—take a dislike to him and either refuse to co-operate at all, or else answer his questions perfunctorily and haphazardly in order to get it over with, or, in extreme cases, deliberately try to mislead him as a sort of revenge for having wasted their time.

Failure on the part of the field worker to observe these rules of modesty or common decency is thus a very dangerous source of error (although, I hope, not a very frequent one). The field worker's ability to deal with people determines to a large extent the value of his output, and—if I may indulge in wishful thinking for a moment—it would be a useful control if we could have, in addition to the field worker's customary description of the informant, the informant's candid opinion of the field worker!

In many field situations there are difficulties arising from the language or languages used in communication between informant and field worker. If the investigator does not understand and cannot make himself understood in the informant's language, he must either find an informant with whom he can communicate in some other language known by both, or use an interpreter. The latter alternative may lead to innumerable mistakes and should be avoided whenever possible. In such areas as the Scottish Gaidhealtachd, where nearly everybody is more or less bilingual, the difficulties are small, but even there misunderstandings may arise if the informant's English is poor or the field worker's knowledge of Gaelic is deficient (not to speak of such cases as my own, where the field worker is a foreigner to whom English is a second language whose intricacies he cannot be expected to master completely). Errors arising from such misunderstandings are usually in the area of meaning, not in that of sounds and forms.

In a not too distant future we may envisage more technical devices which will eliminate many errors frequently made today. I feel fairly confident that before very long we shall have portable recorders for video-tape to be played back through a TV set, so that we can watch and study the informant's mouth movements while we listen to his speech. Perhaps, if the danger of harmful radiation can be eliminated, we shall also have some sort of portable X-ray-film camera to record the movements of tongue, velum, and larynx. But even with such equipment we cannot eliminate errors altogether. Indeed, we must be prepared to discover new sources of error in the new vistas that will then be opened up to us. It is human to err, and not only that: because we are human we are bound to err.

My homage to the man whose memory this volume celebrates, I wish to extend to his people, the Gaelic speakers of Scotland, of whom he was a worthy representative. I have worked among them frequently during the last sixteen years, and hardly anywhere else have I found such hospitality, generosity, and genuine interest in the welfare of a total stranger who arrived uninvited and unexpectedly in their midst. Not only did they tolerate my work among them and my exploitation of their time and patience, but also they helped and encouraged me in every possible way. The numerous errors I have made in recording and in analysing their dialects are entirely due to failures of my own and not to any shortcomings on the part of the intelligent, well-informed, and friendly Highlanders and Islanders of Gaelic Scotland.

NOTES

1 But here is another pitfall. Some of the apparent slips may be forms that really belong to the dialect but are used only in connected speech. The informant should, therefore, first be asked to repeat the whole of the utterance in which the suspicious form was heard, and only then, if considered necessary, to repeat the word in isolation.

2 On this subject, see Professor Angus McIntosh, *Introduction to a Survey of Scottish Dialects* (Linguistic Survey of Scotland Monographs, no. 1, Edinburgh, 1961), pp. 86ff. This little book, especially Chapter 6, contains many more interesting and useful observations on the subject of informants, and I recommend the book strongly to everybody interested in dialect work.

3 *Handbook of the Linguistic Geography of New England*, Providence, Rhode Island, 1939, p. 49.

ANNE O'SULLIVAN

Verses on Honorific Portions

The following verses are taken from a vellum MS. in the National
Library of Ireland, MS. Gaelic 3, f. 22ᵛᵃ. This, together with Gaelic
MS. 2, originally formed one MS. They were separated at a re-binding
at the beginning of the last century probably when already in the library
of Edward O'Reilly. The present binding is of green vellum with
O'Reilly's book plate inside the front cover. At his sale in 1830 it was
no. 10 and Gaelic 2 was no. 11. A priced copy of the sale catalogue
(T.C.D. Gall. II 32. 48, no. 2) notes that they were not sold at the
auction, but another copy which belonged to Myles John O'Reilly
of the Heath House, Queen's co. (T.C.D. MS. N, 5. 22) shows that
they were afterwards acquired by John O'Donovan. He may have sold
them directly to Sir Thomas Phillipps from whose library at Chelten-
ham, where they were numbered 7021-2, they came to the National
Library in 1931. Sir Thomas in Gaelic 2 has written Cooper MS. in
pencil but this is just an example of the sort of confusion that inevitably prevailed in his vast collection because neither of these MSS.
occurred in the Austin Cooper sale in 1831 at which Phillipps acquired
Gaelic MSS. 17-20.

A number of subscriptions would indicate Adam Ó Cianáin as the
scribe of the greater part of these manuscripts and he has been identified by O'Reilly as the canon and learned historian of Lisgoole, co.
Fermanagh, who died in 1373. However, the following verses would
not seem to bear out his learned character and see also Miss Knott's
comments in her edition of the Irish Grammatical Tracts, Metrical
Faults, *Ériu*, xvii, Supplement, p. 293, where she is inclined to think
that the subscription on f. 78ᵃ may have been taken over from the
scribe's exemplar. There is also the possibility that another Adam of
this well-known learned family is intended. O'Reilly in his *Irish
Writers* while attributing this MS. to the canon mentions another
Adam as the scribe in 1450 of the poem *Ériu ard inis na ríg* in a vellum

MS. in his possession. The poem occurs in MS. Gaelic, 2 f. 36ra suggesting perhaps an uncertainty in O'Reilly's mind about Adam. He also lists him as the scribe of a poem written on vellum in 1430 beginning *Eol dam aiged erca gnimh*. This poem occurs in our MS. (Gaelic 3, f. 24vb) and must be the one meant by O'Reilly as the only other vellum copy known to me (Brit. Mus. Eg. 1783 f. 43^{v})* was apparently written in 1517. This was used by O'Reilly and afterwards appeared as no. 553 in William Monk Mason's sale in 1858 (*B.M. Cat. Irish MSS.* ii 263).

The chief contents of Gaelic MS. 3 are genealogical, pseudo-historical, legal and grammatical but ff. 22ra–25rb contain an interesting collection of poems which may be in the Ó Cianáin hand though it is smaller in size than the main body of the writing and the superficial appearance is different. The folio on which the verses occur is headed *a Lebar Glind Da Lacha in begsa sís.*† The Book of Glendalough, otherwise known as the Book of the O'Duigenans, is one of the lost Irish MSS. It is possible that it may still survive fragmentarily and unrecognized among the nameless medieval volumes, but no other copy of these verses is known to me.

The verses deal with the distribution of a pig‡ at a feast, presumably at Emain Macha, where the several cuts are graded according to the rank or occupation of the receiver. There are several texts§ dealing with this social custom but ours differs from the others in that it begins with the lowly and works up to a climax in King Conchobhar, legendary king of a golden age. This may follow a seating arrangement where apparently the lower orders sat on the floor in the inner rows near the fire and the higher on the outer on some kind of raised platform,¶ but it seems more likely that we have here a

---

* Printed by Kuno Meyer, ZCP, ix, p. 175.

† Under this heading and immediately preceding the present verses is the poem *M'aenaran dam isa sliab* (10 qq). ed. J. Carney, *Éigse*, ii, pp. 107–13. The *begsa* may, however, cover all the material to f. 25^{r} as a genealogy on 23^{r} also quotes Lebar G. Da L. as its source. On f. 25^{v} a poem by Giolla Brighde Mac Con Midhe has been written in in a later hand.

‡ Some of the names of the pieces mentioned are used especially of a pig.

§ Met. Dinds. i 24; Laws i 48, ii 232, iv 344; IT iii 188. These are all in general agreement. Book of Leinster (LL) lines 3638–789 (pp. 29^{a}–29^{b} facs.) are very schematic and probably fanciful.

¶ Críth Gablach par. 46. Lãnellach Tigi Rích 7 Ruirech, ed. M. O'Daly, xix, p. 81ff. and the LL texts cited above.

parody meant to be recited for entertainment somewhat like the verses in the Leabhar Breac *Aislinge Meic Conglinne*. Our text also mentions occupations not found elsewhere and one suspects that they may be *ad hoc* inventions of the author.

The language is Mid. Irish but there is nothing to help precise dating. The neut. art. in st. 3 is probably meant for the poss. pron. 3 *f.* as a feature of the composition is the change from the definite article before the name of each piece of meat in stt. 1, 2 to the fem. poss. pron. in 3 *et rel.* A similar variation is found after the prep. *do, dona/dia.* What the *a* in *dia* refers to is not clear. It seems to be *fem.* in st. 3 *d,* 6 *c* but *pl.* in 4 *a,* 5 *d.* Perhaps the *fem.* is meant to refer to *Emain* and the *pl.* to the nobles or the mutation may be a scribal error. The spelling *-bathlaigh* indicates relative lateness (see notes). There are some inaccuracies in the text and metre which is an imperfect type of *casbairdne.*

1   Comrainter in airigid
           bad oirdirc in midhemnus
       is eadh in fáth faramn*us*
           bidh cach fora dligedus.

2   An tairr dona trenferaibh
           in druim dona *dr*anairibh,
       in cend dona sgelaigibh
           in cos dona duanairibh.

3   A cruachait do crosanaibh
           ma cennaib coirigt*ir*
       a nndelg dia fiadhaigibh
           a hairni dia hoinmidib.

4   A cnama dia namsairib
           is amlaidh sin certaigtear
       a cruib dona slichtairib,
           a scaim dona rechtairib.

5   A ruip dona rathmogaib
           —is airigid *in*bathlaigh—
       a gaili dia primlegaib
           a muine dia ningairtib.

6   A cascairin comadas
      dona degmnaib dilmainib,
      a blonac dia hollamnaibh,
      a haighe dia righflaithibh.

7   A cara gan cuntabairt
      don fir oirdirc ollbladach
      a cumang ni turbadach
      do Conchobhar comramach.

2*b* *dranairibh*: first two letters badly stained in MS. It could be *duanairibh* and the latter in *d* a mistake for something else.
3*b* one syll. short. Read imma ? *c dia* dissyllabic here though monosyllabic elsewhere.
*in*5*d gairtib* makes a faulty rhyme.

Translation

1 Let the special piece be distributed: let the selection (of portions) be obvious: the compelling reason is that everyone is intent upon his proper share.

2 The stomach to the strongmen, the back to the snarlers(?), the head to the story-tellers, the leg to the rhymers.

3 Its rump to jesters—they are got up with head-dress(?)— the[1] spine to its hunters, its kidneys to the[1] buffoons.

4 Its bones to the[2] attendants—thus is it fixed—its trotters to the slaughterers (?), its lungs to the stewards.

5 The intestines to the household slaves(?)—it is the special portion fit for boors—its belly to the[2] principal physicians, its entrail fat to the[2] nurses (?)

6 Fitting its curving lean part for the noble free ladies; its lard to the[1] ollavs, its limbs to the[1] chief princes.

7 Without doubt its loins—not mean the portion—to the very glorious pre-eminent triumphant Conchobhar.

[1] *lit*. its.   [2] *lit*. their.

GLOSSARIAL NOTES

1 *dligedus = dliged.*

2 When used of animals *tairr* usually refers to pigs. The other texts do not mention the tairr but cf. *Feis Tighe Conáin* 553 where it goes to the man of the house. The *trénfer* is likewise unknown in the other texts but cf. TBC 5530: *Trioscatal trenfer tigi Concobair is é cuires an líg a n-airdi.* The only ex. of *dranaire* (if this is the word) known to me is the name of a Fenian hound where it is rendered 'The Snarler' (Oss. Soc. iv. 204). In Met. Dinds. and LL the *druim* goes to the *drúth.* Perhaps our character might be translated *the one who grimaces or grins.* Single -n-, however, presents a difficulty. In the other texts the *cenn* goes to the *ara* and the *sgélaige* does not figure. The *duanaire* and his *cos* are likewise absent.

3 *crochet* 'upper thigh, rump', Contribb. Cf. *de croch[t]aib saildi*, Mon. Tall. p. 128. In Met. Dinds. the *ollam filed* is classed with *rí, súi, brugaid* and they get *láraig* and *lóncrochit.* In Laws i 48 *rí, espoc, súi* get the *lárac* and the *crochet* goes to *fresabbratt rig.* In IT iii 188 the *crochet* goes to the *sai litri.*

crossán, some type of ribald rhymer who, we know, wore some kind of bizarre get-up. Here it is probably intended in the sense of the follg.: Moyle Issa called crossan ffyn a' (= o') King, archpoet of Ireland in that kind of metre called crossanaght, Ann. Clonmacnoise anno 1137. Patrick Crossan or Crosbie . . . whose ancestors had been chief rhymers to the O'Moores and the O'Connors, O'Donovan, Top. Poems p. 28. *crossan* gl. *scurra*, Ir. Glosses 14. In the Lives of the Irish Saints it generally answers to Lat. *praeco*, Plummer MS. Notes.

delg translated spine on the basis of: *hó lorcc dromma delg* gl. *spina*, Ml. 51ᵃ8. Neither the *delg* nor the *óinmit* figure in the other texts. The *óinmit* here may be equated with the type of person mentioned in Laws iv 344. 9.

4 *amsaire = amus*, some kind of servant. Neither he nor the *slichtaire* and their pieces are mentioned in the other texts. The *slichtaire* I take to be connected with *slechtaid* slaughters, cuts, hews. But it may be derived from *slicht* and mean tracker, as suggested to me by E. G. Quin. I would also like to thank Prof. MacCana for other useful suggestions. In Met. Dinds. and LL the *rechtaire* gets the *mael.*

5 Cf. *rathbuige* rath-builder. The *rathmog* and his *rop* is absent in the other texts.

bathlach is a later spelling for *bachlach*, see IGT Decl. par. 11. In Met. Dinds. and LL the *liaig* gets the *mael.*

muine is used of the lard that lines the intestines of pigs.

dpl. of *ingairid*(?) but *ingartaibh* would be the form required for rhyme.

6 *cascairin* (*cas* + *cairin*). *cairin* I take to be dim, of *cara*, leg, ham, thigh. Cf. *muccaid iar maidi a charann*, IT iii 85. 27 (Bruchst. i 37 § 88). *cairin.i. feoil gan tsaill*, O'Cl. In Laws i 48 the *rígain* gets the *les*.

The *ríflaith* and the *áige* are not mentioned in the other texts. That the *áige* was well regarded is shown in TBFr. 126: *no rannad cach n-ágae cona a chlaidiub 7 ni aidleth toinn na feóil* (of a carver).

7 *cumang*, the narrow part, I take to be the centre loin, still the choicest cut of an animal.

That Conchobhar was regarded as the king *par excellence* is also shown by the *Ériu* xix text: *ar-sesar Conchobhar cētath*, Conchobhar shall be placed in the chief seat.

E. I. ROWLANDS

Iolo Goch[1]

§ 1

A *cywydd* by Iolo Goch in praise of Sir Roger Mortimer was discussed by John Lloyd-Jones in the *Bulletin of the Board of Celtic Studies*, vol. xi, pp. 114–18. He showed that the bard had detailed knowledge of certain Irish affairs at the end of the fourteenth century, and was fully aware of the problem facing Mortimer in his campaigns in Ireland.

The poem, consisting of 134 lines, is considerably longer than the average praise poem, but for most of its length it deals with the status and standing of Mortimer who has but recently come of age, is heir-apparent to Richard II, is descended from the princely house of Aberffraw, and is rightful leader of four nations, Welsh, French, English and Irish. It can hardly be a coincidence that Iolo Goch lists the nations in this order: numerous references by late medieval Welsh bards seem to indicate that, if they were to be listed in order of precedence in honour, this would be the order inevitably presenting itself to the mind of a Welshman of that age. In the last twenty-two lines of the poem Iolo Goch deals specifically, and of course optimistically, with the task facing Mortimer as the leading figure in Ireland, this being also the task with which the earl was immediately concerned. These last lines of the poem as printed in IGE (2), p. 48, are quoted below with a translation.[2]

O hyder o uchder ach	'Through confidence from the height of breeding
Hy goresgynny Gonnach	Boldly wilt thou conquer Connaught.
15 *Dos drwy'r môr, a distryw'r Mydd*	Go over the sea, and destroy Meath
I flaenau'r wlad aflonydd;	To the furthest parts of the unruly country;

Tref tad i tithau yw'r Trum,[3]	The town of Trim is from thine own father:
Tau gestyll teg eu hystum.	Thine are castles fair of shape.
Tegwch gwlad Fatholwch fu	This was the fairness of the land of Matholwch,
20 *Calon Iwerddon orddu.*	Heart of black Ireland.
Dyrchaf dy stondardd, hardd hwyl,	Raise thy standard, a beautiful sail,
Diarchar yw dy orchwyl.	Thy progress is irresistible.
Gwna fwysmant, bid trychant trwch	Make an ambush—may 300 be struck down—
25 *Macwy mawr â Mac Morwch*	Mighty lad, upon Mac Murchadha.
Tor rwyg a brath tu rhag bron[4]	Cut, rend and strike, straight ahead,
Draw i Galys drwy'i galon.	Yonder to Kellistown through its heart.
Brysia a chleimia achlân	Make haste, and claim completely
Gwlad Wlster, glod Elystan.	The land of Ulster, thou of Elystan's fame.
Llyna gyfoeth llawn gefalc,[5]	That is a dominion (?) filling a false boundary,
30 *Myn di yn dau min Dwndálc.*	Demand it as thine on the edge of Dundalk.
Yn ôl daly Grednel, fy nêr,	After capturing Great Niall, my lord,—
Ci ffalstwf cyff o Wlster,	Ulster dog from a stock of false growth—
Ti a leddy, clochdy clod,	Thou, belfry of fame, wilt kill
Bobl Wlster bob ail ystod.	The people of Ulster with every further blow.'

As the historical background of this extract has been admirably discussed by Lloyd-Jones, it will suffice here to make further comments on two matters arising from consideration of the last three couplets (lines 29–34).

In IGE (2), p. 413, the word *gefalc*, occurring in line 29, is simply listed in the vocabulary with no attempt made to elucidate its meaning. Lloyd-Jones suggested that it was probably a borrowing from the English *gavelock*. More consideration should be given, however, to a variant reading given in IGE (1), p. 55, *viz. geufalc*. Though but one MS. gives this reading, the others giving *gefalk* or *gofalk*, it is likely that *geufalc*[6] is correct in the sense of 'false balk'. The only reasonable explanation of the form *geufalc* is that it is a compound of *gau* 'false' and *balc* < English 'balk'. Such a word is suitable in the context, for Ulster, thus, would be described either as a dominion 'full of wrongful impediments' hindering its reduction by Mortimer, or as a dominion 'within a false boundary'.[7]

That Iolo Goch had already used the word *balc*, towards the beginning of the poem (p. 45, line 22), gives support to this suggested interpretation. The relevant line is

Balc arnad, bual corniog   'There is a balk on thee, horned
                                buffalo.'

According to IGE (2), p. 405, *balc* here means 'bwlch, bai', i.e. 'gap, fault'. This can scarcely be credited, for the line occurs in a section of the poem where the bard refers to the coming of age of Mortimer and exhorts him to act in the manner ordained for him. In Welsh idiom, *bai arnat* 'there is a fault on thee' signifies 'thou art at fault'. The tenor of the whole poem proves that *balc* here can not be equated with *bai* 'fault'. The epithet *bual corniog*, 'horned buffalo', suggests strongly that Mortimer is exhorted to plough the land still unploughed, and this interpretation is of course borne out by a theme of the entire poem, which is that Mortimer's status is recognized everywhere but in Ireland, where he must use his power so as to substantiate his claim. It can be suggested that *balc* here has a secondary meaning of 'land still unploughed'. The concrete sense of the metaphor tallies well with the epithet *bual corniog*, with the following couplet,[8]

Nid oes ond eisiau arfer   'It is only necessary to wear
O arfau prydferth nerth nêr   Beautiful armour, the power of a
                                lord.'

and with the general theme.

This meaning must be secondary, however, for the syntax, with *balc* followed by a preposition, implies that the word is used figuratively. The meaning 'fault' being absurd in the context, it must be taken, therefore, that the primary meaning of *balc* here is 'hindrance, impediment', and that *balc arnad* means 'thou art impeded'. Clearly, this interpretation is very apt both in the immediate context and in the context of the general theme of the poem.

The poem can be regarded as a lengthy introduction to a brief discussion of Mortimer's Irish problem. A deeper analysis reveals an ordered, well-balanced and unified composition. It is sufficient, here, to note that having referred to the coming of age of Mortimer and the *balc*, the bard describes his personal soldierly qualities before proceeding to a listing of Mortimer's titles, claims and expectations. This is followed by a discussion of the relationship between him and each in turn of the four nations over which he should rule. There is on this evidence a definite connection between *balc* [IGE (2), p. 45, line 22] and *geufalc* [*ibid.*, p. 48, line 29]: after referring to an 'impediment' towards the beginning of the poem, there follows at the end of the poem a precise reference to the false 'impediment' (or to the 'false boundary') at Dundalk. The link between them is provided furthermore by the bald reference in the middle of the poem to Mortimer as earl of Ulster [IGE (2), p. 46, line 18].

A second point arising from Lloyd-Jones's discussion is that he takes *Grednel* to be a reference to Niall Mór Ó Neill. He regarded the form as a borrowing from an anglicized version of the name of the king of Ulster, i.e. either 'Great Niall' or 'Great Neill'. It does not seem that Lloyd-Jones had been able to find evidence of the occurrence of the presumed anglicized version of Niall Mór's name, but there cannot be any doubt about the rightness of his suggestion. I cannot venture to discuss the process whereby the Irish king's name came to Welsh through the medium of an English semi-translation, but it does seem more likely that the Welsh form would be based on 'Great Niall' rather than 'Great Neill', and one assumes that Lloyd-Jones included the alternative possibility mainly because of the peculiar form of the Welsh *Grednel*. It may be, however, that Lloyd-Jones has not only elucidated the meaning of the text here, but has also made possible a clarification of its form.

If, in line 31, *yn ôl* is emphasized it could be argued that the correct translation should be 'Hold back Great Niall. . . .' This is possible if Iolo Goch is taken to be referring simply to the defence of Dundalk. The poem, however, is an exhortation to Mortimer to assume control over his dominions, and it seems, therefore, that the main sentence in the last four lines of the poem should be taken as *Yn ôl daly Grednel, ti a leddy bobl Wlster*, 'After capturing Great Niall, thou wilt kill the people of Ulster'. If this is the correct interpretation, as seems more than probable, the emphasis must be on *daly*, not on *yn ôl*. An analysis of the *cynghanedd* in the line shows that *yn ôl* must be emphasized, whilst *daly* cannot be permitted to bear the slightest emphasis. As printed, the line forms a *cynghanedd draws fantach*, the only consonantal correspondence being between the *n* of 'yn ôl' and the *n* of 'nêr'. As Saunders Lewis has pointed out, one of the graces of 'strict' poetry is the occasional counterpoint between the emphasis required by meaning and the stressing demanded by *cynghanedd*. Nevertheless, as an absolute contrast between major emphasis required by meaning and utter lack of stress demanded by *cynghanedd* never occurs in medieval Welsh poetry, an acceptance of the text as printed in IGE would necessitate a rejection of the apparently correct meaning.

The form *Grednel* clearly is wrong, for if it represents a borrowing from a semi-translation of the name Niall Mór, it could not be a compound with the second syllable unaccented. *Grednel* must be an incorrect representation of either *Gred Nel* or of *Gred Nêl*. If 'Niall Môr' became 'Great Niall', a Welshman would presumably pronounce the name as *Gred Nïal*, for *Niall* in Welsh would have to become a disyllabic *Nïal* or an unlikely monosyllabic *Nil*. If indeed Iolo Goch did use the form *Gred Nïal*, the problem arising from the stressing of the line would be solved, for it could be emended to read[9]

'Nôl dal Gred Nïal, fy nêr.

The line would now contain *cynghanedd sain*, the stressed words being *dal* and *Nïal* rhyming, and *nêr* having a consonantal correspondence with *Nïal*. There would be absolute correspondence between the meaning emphasis and the *cynghanedd* stress.

There must be doubt about the form which the name of the Irish king of Ulster would have in Welsh. There is also some room for doubt about the correct interpretation of the meaning of *yn ôl* in line 31, but if the meaning strongly suggested by the context is to be taken, the line should be emended as proposed. Corroboratory evidence as to probability is afforded by an analysis of the *cynghanedd* in the poem. It is generally recognized that fourteenth-century bards used *cynghanedd sain* much more frequently than *cynghanedd draws*. In this particular poem of 134 lines, 20 per cent of the lines are in *cynghanedd draws* but 41 per cent are in *cynghanedd sain*. In the IGE text the line forms a *cynghanedd draws fantach*, a sub-type of *cynghanedd* of which there are only two other certain examples in the poem.[10] The line as emended has *cynghanedd sain lefn anghytbwys acennog*, a sub-type of *cynghanedd* of which there are no fewer than 22 examples in the poem. These lines can be further analysed into those where consonantal correspondence occurs only before the accent (16 examples) and those where consonantal correspondence is carried beyond the accent (6 examples).[11] In the emended line, the consonantal correspondence is only before the accent as in the great majority of lines of this subtype of *cynghanedd* in this poem. These statistics are, moreover, fairly typical of Iolo Goch's poetry generally. If the other arguments are regarded as valid, considerations arising from the analysis of *cynghanedd* usage strongly suggest the probability that the line as emended is correct.

§ 2

According to Professor Henry Lewis, the editor of the poems of Iolo Goch in IGE, it was natural enough that the bard, who held land in the lordship of Denbigh, should sing the praise of Sir Roger Mortimer, his landlord.[12] He also notes that most of Iolo's patrons had fought for the king of England.[13] In discussing the *cywydd* to Owain ap Tomas ap Rhodri (Owain Lawgoch), he notes[14] that Iolo Goch had composed poems in praise of Edward III, Sir Roger Mortimer, as well as numerous influential Welsh adherents to the royal party in Wales, and concludes that this poem, prophesying the success of the Welsh claimant to the principality, has been wrongly attributed to Iolo Goch.

It is true, of course, that Iolo Goch addressed poems to the king and his adherents in Wales. Yet conclusions concerning the bard's political beliefs do not justify a rejection of Iolo's authorship of the poem to Owain Lawgoch. There seems to be more force in the argument that Iolo Goch was renowned as the bard of Owain Glyndŵr, and that transcribers, having confused the Owain addressed in the poem with Owain Glyndŵr, wrongly attributed the poem to him.[15] There may be some slight justification for this view, but it is needless conjecture unless independent evidence is provided that Iolo Goch was not the author of the poem to Owain Lawgoch. An analysis of the political ideas of Iolo Goch, based on a list of the persons to whom he addressed poems, is no such evidence.

Some parts of Wales began to fall to the Normans soon after 1066, and within less than half a century about half of Wales was controlled directly by Norman barons. The other half of Wales remained under the control of native rulers until the campaigns of Edward I at the end of the thirteenth century. For well over a century before this, the rulers of Gwynedd, claiming the title of *princeps*, had gradually developed a policy of establishing their supremacy over the other Welsh lords, and this culminated in the final establishment of the principality of Wales by Llywelyn ap Gruffudd. Most historians recognize that the principality of Wales was the result of a long process aimed at safeguarding the relative independence of Wales by adapting and utilizing Norman constitutional and administrative theories and practice. This 'policy of Gwynedd' was revolutionary, and consequently often resented by the Welsh lords outside Gwynedd, but was understood and indeed advocated by the bards. After the Edwardian conquest, the bardic order remained more faithful to Welsh nationalistic ideals than any other section of the community, and this is, and always has been, one of the best known facts of Welsh history. What does not seem to be as well understood nowadays is that the bards were not simple dreamers and immature politicians. They were the most politically aware element in Welsh society, fanatical perhaps, but both intelligent and knowledgeable, by vocation closely connected with the centres of political power in Wales, by aptitude theorists and thinkers, by training the guardians of the traditions and culture of the Welsh as a Brythonic people. In the fourteenth century these bards were faced with the political complexities arising from the reduction of the principality to English rule. There were, therefore, many strands in the Welsh political thought of the period. Iolo Goch sang in his early days in praise of Edward III, and in his later days in praise of Sir Roger Mortimer. This is no reason why Iolo Goch should not also have been the bard who longed for the arrival of the fleet of Owain, grandson of a brother of Llywelyn ap Gruffudd, prince of Wales.

A sadly needed appraisal of the political content of the poetry of Iolo Goch cannot be attempted here. Nor can the history of that most abused century of Welsh history, the fourteenth, be reviewed.[16] Yet, a brief general statement must be made. The basic fact of Welsh politics in the period was the conflict of loyalties; on the one hand loyalty to the memory and to the ideal of a Welsh principality, on the other hand loyalty to the Crown. Some rejected the first loyalty outright; it is doubtful if any rejected absolutely the second. Yet, to most, the first loyalty was the more deeply felt, though it was almost always hidden: it could burst forth only at the expense of the second, and, therefore, did so only when circumstances made the inner conflict unbearable. Loyalty to the Crown, though occasionally withdrawn, could never be denied.

The greatest of Iolo Goch's patrons was Owain Glyndŵr. Owain was the offspring of a marriage between the direct descendant of the princely house of Powys and a descendant of the princely house of Deheubarth. This marriage had been arranged because there was a continuing loyalty to the Welsh principality.[17] There could be no direct claimants to the rights of the pre-eminent dynasty of Gwynedd, but intermarriage had infused the blood of the house of Gwynedd into the houses of both Powys and Deheubarth. Owain Glyndŵr was born to be prince of Wales, and Iolo Goch's realization of this is made abundantly clear in his poems to Owain. Yet Owain Glyndŵr did not, and could not, press his claim until the Crown had fallen to the usurper Henry IV. To almost all Welshmen, this usurpation meant the resolving of a rending conflict, so that abstract loyalty could now fuse with concrete action. It would be easy to argue that a Welsh labourer fighting for Owain Glyndŵr felt none of this and to make vague comparisons with peasant unrest in England, France and Bohemia, but this would simply be to confuse the basic with the incidental.

Iolo Goch was certainly fully conscious of the excruciating choices facing a Welshman in the second half of the fourteenth century. He knew his history and understood the theory of government. He must have been aware of how and why Edward I had forced Llywelyn ap Gruffudd to destruction,[18] and why he had then preserved the shell of the lost principality. Though believing in the sovereignty of Britain, Iolo also believed that the principality of Wales should be a reality and not an emptiness.

The poem in praise of Sir Roger Mortimer contains matter of Irish interest, but the real historical value of the poem is to the Welsh historian. The extant poems of the bard range from his measured eulogy of Edward III to his passionate review of the genealogy of Owain Glyndŵr, from the revilement of the self-righteous Grey Friar of Chester to a serene appreciation of the bravery of Sir Hywel of the Battleaxe, from the serious appraisal of the lot and station of the Labourer to an impudent rejoicing in Iolo's bardic office in his *Altercatio Animae et Corporis*. Against all this varied background is found crystallized, in one of the great poems of his old age, Iolo's political thought, his hopes, the strength of his convictions, the abusiveness of Iolo's hate and his approval of determination and bravery.

The effusiveness of Iolo Goch's praise of Sir Roger Mortimer was as natural and wholehearted as his yearning for the advent of Owain Lawgoch about twenty years earlier. Mortimer is addressed on his coming of age. The duties, tasks and honours now facing him are outlined. It is true that Sir Roger is lord of Denbighland in which lordship the land held by Iolo Goch was situated, but it is not to this that the bard refers. The poem is an exhortation on the coming into a power of tremendous potential of a descendant from Llywelyn ab Iorwerth, prince of Aberffraw. At the time, to Iolo Goch, it must have seemed a possibility that the conflicting loyalties inherent in fourteenth-century Welsh political thought could be brought into accord by the newly embarked-upon career of Sir Roger Mortimer. The bard calls upon him to assume the leadership that has come to him:

. . . *Wyr burffrwyth iôr Aberffraw.*	'Pure-fruited descendant of the lord of Aberffraw.
Draig ynysoedd yr eigiawn,	Dragon[19] of the islands of the ocean,
Dragon aer—darogan iawn	Dragon of battle—it is true prophecy
Ydd wyf—madws it ddyfod	That I make—it is time that thou shouldst come
Gymru lle rhyglyddy glod. . .	To Wales where praise is thy due.
Darogan yw mai'n draig ni	It is prophesied that it will be our dragon
A lunia gwaith eleni;	That will make action this year;
O ben y llew glew ei gledd	From the head of the lion with the valiant sword
Coronir câr i Wynedd. . .	One akin to Gwynedd will be crowned.
Teilwng oedd it gael talaith	Thou wert worthy to gain the crown
Aberffraw, f'ymandaw maith.	Of Aberffraw, my great lord.

Amserol, mi sy herod,	It is time—I am a herald—
It ddeffroi i gloi dy glod...	For thee to awaken so as to clinch thy glory.
Gwodrudd cerdd, gwaed y ddraig goch	Inspirer of song, the cinnabar
Yw'r sinobr y sy ynoch.	Within you is the blood of the red dragon.
Am hynny, bydd hy, baedd hoyw,	Because of that, be bold, vigorous boar,
A rho eto aur otoyw,	And wear again golden spurs.
Cael da yw coel dy awydd,	It is good—trust in thy ambition—
Cael gorfod, rhagod poed rhwydd!	To overcome. Mayest thou have success![20]
Gras Arthur a'i groes wrthyd	May the grace of Arthur and his cross be with thee.
A'i lys a'i gadlys i gyd.	And his court and his fortress wholly.
Gorau lle, ail Gaerllïon,	The best place, a second Caerllïon,
Y sy iwch o'r ynys hon.	In this island[? dominion] is yours.'

On two occasions it is stated that the time has come for Mortimer to assume his inherited leadership over the Welsh. This ties in firstly with the statement that Mortimer has come of age:

Mab fuost, daethost i dir,	'Thou hast been a lad, thou hast come to land,
Gŵr bellach a grybwyllir.	It is a man who will be mentioned from now on.'

Secondly, it links with the implications of the reference to Arthur and Caerllïon. The day had dawned for a new Arthur to take up arms, for the hero of the Welsh to prepare himself for the acceptance of the sovereignty of Britain.[21]

The ideal of Welsh separatism, so alive in the fourteenth century, died in the ruins of the cause of Owain Glyndŵr. There arose a new nationalism, a shifting unfocused turmoil of opportunism, often turbid with the bitterness of hate. The only fixed points, or positive factors in fifteenth-century post-Glyndŵr Welsh nationalism were a desire for equality in law with the English, and a belief that the Crown should be, in some way, Welsh. Clearly, there is some continuity with the sentiments expressed in 1395 by Iolo Goch, and, indeed, it was precisely the Mortimer, and therefore the Gwynedd, connection that made the Yorkists theoretically acceptable to the Welsh bards. It is also no accident that Iolo Goch identified Mortimer with Arthur at Caerllïon and that Henry VII named his eldest son Arthur. In spite of the element of continuity, the basic difference between the nationalism of such as Iolo Goch and that of the post-Glyndŵr bards must be recognized. There is sufficient evidence in his works, even excluding his poem to Owain Lawgoch, to show that Iolo Goch was a separatist, and this one would expect in the fourteenth century. He wanted a reintroduction of the Venedotian policy of establishing a Welsh principality separate from England though feudally subject to the Crown. He can be forgiven if he failed to realize the implication of the identification of the principate with the kingship in the person of Mortimer. Sir Roger was descended from Gwladus Du, daughter of Llywelyn the Great. He was also earl of March, representative of a long-established family of mighty Norman-Welsh landowners deeply involved in Welsh affairs. Not only were his claims to leadership rightful, he was also a man who should understand the relationship between Wales and England. If that was how Iolo Goch looked upon Mortimer, it was not how the Welsh bards looked, half a century later, upon Edward IV, for Welsh political ideals had by then been metamorphosed by the crushing of Owain. Edward IV was actually a king of England descended from the princes of Aberffraw. What the bards saw in him was a chance for Welsh equality and a rather nebulous hope for an avenging supremacy.

Iolo Goch saw Mortimer as the head of four nations. This recalls that the claim of Mortimer's ancestor, Llywelyn the Great, to have 'no less liberty than the king of Scotland' was later developed by Llywelyn ap Gruffudd into a more precise claim that the Welsh like the Gascons, the Scots, the Irish, the English formed provinces each with their own laws and rights under the ultimate feudal authority of the Crown.[22] Iolo Goch must have been the last of the Welsh bards who allowed this clear, mature and traditional Welsh political ideal to inform his political thinking.

§ 3

If Iolo Goch's interest in political affairs was as passionate and informed as a study of his poems leads one to conclude, an appreciation of this important strand in his poetry supplies the key to a true understanding of the part he played in the development of Welsh bardic poetry.

From the sixteenth century onwards students of Welsh literature have recognized that the fourteenth century was a critical period in the evolution of bardism. One result of the conquest of Wales by Edward I was the disruption of the bardic system previously centred upon the princely courts of Wales. The burden of patronage devolved upon the Welsh *uchelwyr* (i.e. the freemen, or, perhaps, the highest class of freemen) for the princely courts were gone. It is psychologically significant that Iolo Goch came to be regarded traditionally as Owain Glyndŵr's bard. In fact, though he was certainly patronized by Owain, Iolo was an itinerant bard who received the patronage of many lesser noblemen. Yet, according to popular tradition, Iolo Goch was the court-poet *par excellence*, though he lived a century after the Edwardian conquest.[23]

When recovery from the effects of the war of Glyndŵr began, around the 1430s, there began also the most flourishing century in the history of Welsh poetry. A continually increasing number of bards were given effective patronage by an expanding class of landowners, later to develop into the Welsh Tudor squirearchy. If sixteenth-century Welsh scholars were aware that the crisis engendered in the bardic order by the Edwardian conquest was one of patronage, it cannot be doubted that the fifteenth-century bards, more vitally concerned as they were, were endowed with a comparable capacity to analyse the obvious. This may partially explain the particular nature of the preoccupation of so many of these bards with the theory of patronage. It is significant that the ideal of patronage throughout this great century of bardism was symbolized by that granted to Dafydd ap Gwilym and to Iolo Goch, for the works of these two poets represent the decisive stages in the evolution from thirteenth-century court poetry to fifteenth-century praise poetry.

When the princely courts had gone, as a result of the Edwardian conquest, there was not an audience for the tremendous panegyrics of the court poets. No longer could the *laudes* to God and 'king' be sung by the *pencerdd* on the *teir gwyl arbennic*. Yet, for a century afterwards, *awdlau* were composed by bards in the traditional manner, for the practice was upheld both by bards and by conservative patrons. This could not last, however. Diction was too archaic, and the style of the *awdlau* was far too complex and difficult for the compositions to be comprehensible without much puzzling, if then. Although *uchelwyr* had had *awdlau* composed in their praise before the conquest, the central reason for the existence of the *genre* had been the ceremonies of the princely courts, so that the ceremonial solemnity and archaic pomp of the *awdlau* could not be maintained indefinitely when the bards had to rely exclusively for their patronage on the class of *uchelwyr*.[24]

In the mid-fourteenth century Dafydd ap Gwilym popularized a new type of poetry. It cannot be doubted that a light poetry of love existed contemporaneously with the ceremonial praise poetry of the princely courts. None of it is now extant. We cannot be certain what innovations were made by Dafydd ap Gwilym, either in content or form, when he composed his nature and love songs. It is very likely, however, that a major innovation was the introduction of *cynghanedd*, the intricate pattern of sound harmony used in court poetry, into a metre previously used for popular poetry only, a metre from amongst a type generically known as *cywydd*. Even if Dafydd was not the innovator,[25] there can be no doubt that a *cywydd* in *cynghanedd* must have been uncommon before his time, and it is unquestionably safe to regard him as a poet who raised nature and love poetry to a new level in content and form.

Dafydd ap Gwilym is rightly regarded as standing alone in the history of medieval Welsh poetry, for he was easily the greatest Welsh poet, and, as such, flourishing at a time of grave crisis in the bardic institution, it was inevitable that there were many distinctive traits in his poetry. But it is also true that he was a figure of prime importance in the development of bardic tradition, for the type of *cywydd* used by him, the *cywydd deuair hirion*, became the main vehicle of bardic poetry in the fifteenth and sixteenth centuries. It must also be remembered that during this period the poetry of love and nature remained an integral part of bardism, and that Dafydd ap Gwilym was the link between the songs of the earlier *bardd teulu* in the 'queen's' chamber and the light poetry, in *cynghanedd*, of the later middle ages.

Like other bards, Dafydd ap Gwilym composed praise poems in

the *awdl* metres. His *awdlau* were orthodox. There are a few poems, composed to patrons, that were not *awdlau*, however. These, like his popular poetry, were *cywyddau* and were in the relatively simple style of his love and nature poems. One must conclude that Dafydd, having exalted popular poetry by introducing the *cynghanedd* technique of court poetry into a *cywydd* metre, then took matters a step further by occasionally addressing a patron through the new poetic medium. In Dafydd's *cywyddau* addressed to Ifor Hael, the very metaphors used are comparable to those found in his love and nature poems.[26] This is significant as indicating that the relevance of addressing Ifor in *cywyddau* was that Ifor was a patron of Dafydd as a composer of love and nature poetry. Apart from tradition, such a theory is supported by a comparison with the poetry of Llywelyn Goch Amheurig Hen (a younger bard whose *floruit* must have been partly contemporaneous with Dafydd's). Llywelyn Goch too composed *awdlau* to patrons and was also a love poet using the *cywydd* metre. In a *cywydd* which begins as a nature poem describing winter snow, he goes on to describe his duties as a bard at the courts of his relatives and patrons, the powerful family of Nannau.[27] He states explicitly that, amongst other duties, he had sung his love poetry at the courts of his nephews.

Throughout the second half of the fourteenth century there were bards, from Dafydd ap Gwilym onwards, who distinguished sharply in practice between their twin offices of court poets and love poets, but who, on occasion, could compose subjective praise poetry to their patrons in the metre and manner of their love poetry. This was done at the courts of *uchelwyr* who had paid and maintained the bards for their services as singers of the light poetry of nature and love. An important step in the evolution of the bardic tradition is that the *cywydd* metre and style, in this way, became an acceptable medium for praise poetry.

The work of Dafydd ap Gwilym, followed by Llywelyn Goch and others, furnished the bards of the fifteenth and sixteenth centuries with the opportunity, which they took, of capturing the patronage of the numerous class of *uchelwyr*, cultured men, mostly of limited but sufficient wealth, who could not possibly have appreciated praise in the archaic manner of the traditional *awdl*, and for whom such eulogy would have been incongruous in any case. Yet, praise poetry required a closer connection with the traditional ceremonial poetry than was

afforded by the pattern set by Dafydd ap Gwilym. It was by Iolo
Goch that the link was provided.

Unlike any other fourteenth-century bard, Iolo Goch used the
cywydd deuair hirion as the normal medium of praise poetry, even when
he composed poems in honour of such as Edward III, Sir Roger
Mortimer and Owain Glyndŵr. Again, unlike his contemporaries,
he used in his *cywyddau* much of the diction, style and technique of the
awdl foliant. It would be quite wrong to give the impression that, but
for the metrical difference, a *cywydd* by Iolo Goch is exactly in the
manner of an *awdl.* A detailed analysis cannot be attempted here, but
it can be safely suggested that Iolo Goch introduced into the *cywydd*
the basic essentials of the *awdl* of praise. By accepting the metre as
well as some of the simplifications of diction and style in the *cywydd*,
but by returning also to the orthodox objectivity and employing the
traditional imagery, Iolo Goch set a new pattern, a pattern which was
necessary for the remaining centuries of bardism.

It might appear that the great bards of the mid-fifteenth century owe
more to the style of Gruffudd Llwyd than to Iolo Goch, for the poetry
of Gruffudd Llwyd, a younger contemporary of Iolo Goch, had, long
before them, some of the most distinctive characteristics of the poetry
of their time, in particular the easy conversational style and the care
for compositional unity. But Gruffudd Llwyd was almost certainly a
cleric and was essentially a religious poet, so that his few praise poems
are really in the personal and subjective pattern set by Dafydd ap
Gwilym, but with a religious or philosophical rather than a light-
hearted pleasure-loving slant. It is likely that Gruffudd Llwyd's contribution to the later development of bardism was philosophical rather
than stylistic, and that the similarities in style mentioned are to be
explained not so much as the result of the direct influence of Gruffudd
Llwyd but as coincidence arising partly from a gradual and increasing
mastery of the potential of the *cywydd* metre by fifteenth-century
bards, and partly from a rejection of the more extreme manifestations
of Iolo Goch's conservatism.

If the evidence for Iolo Goch's conservatism is clear and ample,
yet the truth is that the introduction of this reactionary element into
cywydd poetry was an innovation, and involved a total acceptance of
change in the whole system of bardism, a change seemingly not accepted,
or a necessity probably not perceived by other freer and less serious
spirits. It is a complementary fact that Iolo Goch was passionately

aware of traditional Welsh political ideals and had a wide and real knowledge of contemporary political affairs. This is indeed complementary, for it is not merely an analogical aid to an understanding of Iolo Goch's character, but is rather an explanation of his attitude towards his bardic craft and of his answer to the crisis in bardism. This answer, if congenial and instinctive, was also rational. A bard, trained in the bardic craft, could hardly have wrought a revolutionary change in bardic practice unless he did so deliberately. Conservative and self-confident by nature, yet forced by circumstances to adapt himself, Iolo Goch would not have found the key to the continued success of bardism simply by chance.

Of course, Dafydd ap Gwilym and Iolo Goch alone were not solely responsible for the development of Welsh bardism in the fourteenth century. They were the two great poets into whose works the evolutionary processes were clearly channelled. Others were involved, including the patrons.

Lewys Glyn Cothi[28] was in some ways very like Iolo Goch. Many of the fifteenth-century bards were obsessed by politics, but none was so utterly involved as he. Nor was anyone else so preoccupied with the nature of patronage. It is not surprising to find, therefore, that references to Dafydd ap Gwilym and Iolo Goch and their patrons are especially frequent in the works of Lewys Glyn Cothi. Ifor Hael was regarded as Dafydd's patron by Lewys Glyn Cothi like everybody else. There was no such unanimity by the bards in referring to Iolo Goch's patrons, but it is interesting to find that Lewys several times refers to Rhydderch in this respect.[29] In his *Altercatio Animae et Corporis*, Iolo Goch had listed Rhydderch ab Ieuan Llwyd of Glyn Aeron amongst his patrons.[30] This was the man whose name has been perpetuated in the famous *Llyfr Gwyn Rhydderch*, and a man, therefore, whose name will always have a place in the history of Welsh literature. Nevertheless, he cannot be counted amongst the most distinguished of Iolo's patrons, who included Sir Roger Mortimer and Owain Glyndŵr, and perhaps Edward III. To Lewys Glyn Cothi, however, Iolo Goch's patronage by Rhydderch, represented an ideal. Dafydd ap Gwilym too had patrons in Glyn Aeron, including possibly Rhydderch himself, and certainly his mother Angharad. Glyn Aeron is the only certain place where the respective spheres of the two bards overlapped. It is interesting to find that this overlapping occurs at a court and in a district where there was a live concern with literary affairs.[31]

Very near to Glyn Aeron was the commote of Caeo. The two districts are almost adjacent, and sufficiently close for their literary traditions to be well known each to the other, or possibly shared. There are references to Caeo which seem to indicate that there was another indirect but very significant link between Dafydd ap Gwilym and Iolo Goch, and again Lewys Glyn Cothi provides valuable evidence. He states apparently that Rhydderch held land in both Glyn Aeron and Caeo.[32] Lewys Glyn Cothi was a native of Caeo, and local pride may be part of the reason why the bard stresses the connection between Iolo Goch and Rhydderch. What is more important, however, is that Lewys Glyn Cothi testifies[33] to the strength and nature of the bardic tradition in Caeo in such a way as to throw further light on the implication of the contemptuous reference of the fourteenth-century Glamorgan bard, Casnodyn, to 'beird keith kaeaw' when eulogizing Ieuan Llwyd of Glyn Aeron, father of Rhydderch.[34] The more conservative bards, such as Casnodyn, were welcomed by the nobility of Glyn Aeron, but so were the bards of the *cywydd*. Was it to these that Casnodyn referred, or is his derogatory remark about 'the serf-bards of Caeo' to be interpreted literally? It is clear, at any rate, that there was a connection of some sort between Glyn Aeron and the bards of Caeo who were regarded as inferiors by Casnodyn. Ifor Hael of Glamorgan, chief patron of Dafydd ap Gwilym, was a half-brother of Morgan ap Dafydd of Rhydodyn in the commote of Caeo. Thus, and there are other corroboratory considerations, the literary life of the area may have had influence on Dafydd ap Gwilym.[35] As for Iolo Goch, he is known to have visited Caeo at least, and to have enjoyed the experience. According to his *Altercatio Animae et Corporis*, in a line which is sufficient proof of the jocular irreverence of its contents,[36] *Gwell Caeaw no naw o nef*, 'Caeo is better than nine heavens.'

Amongst the varying influences on Dafydd ap Gwilym and Iolo Goch, some were common and afford points of some contact. It is likely that the emerging *cywydd* styles of the period were found particularly congenial in Caeo and Glyn Aeron. The 'uchelwyr' of the two districts may well have played an important, though hardly a crucial part, in the development of Welsh bardism in the fourteenth century. Here, but elsewhere also, Iolo Goch sought and found patronage. More politically aware than his contemporaries, Iolo Goch understood better than his fellow-bards the need for a positive and constructive response to the crisis in bardism. His answer, it is possible, may have been more appreciated in Glyn Aeron than elsewhere. We know for certain that it was accepted by patrons all over Wales, including many of the most powerful figures in Welsh society. Thus did Iolo Goch make possible the great renascence of Welsh poetry in the fifteenth century.

NOTES

1 Henry Lewis, Thomas Roberts, Ifor Williams (ed.), *Cywyddau Iolo Goch ac Eraill*, Argraffiad Newydd (New Edition) (Caerdydd, 1937) contains the standard edition by Professor Henry Lewis of the poetical works of Iolo Goch. It is abbreviated in this article to IGE (2). There are occasional references below to IGE (1), the first edition published in 1925.

I take this opportunity to thank Mr. H. R. Loyn and Professor A. O. H. Jarman, both of whom read the typescript and made valuable suggestions.

2 Here, as in the other translations following, I have attempted to keep as closely as possible to the original, and without referring to possible alternative renderings.

3 This line is ambiguous. *Tref tad* normally means 'patrimony', and this meaning is undoubtedly present in the line. The caesura in the line comes after *tref*, however, indicating that *tad i tithau* is an adjectival phrase describing *tref* 'home, homestead, township, town'. As Lloyd-Jones pointed out, Mortimer inherited Trim from his father, whereas most of his Irish claims were through his mother. Although my translation does not convey the ambiguity of *tref tad i tithau*, or either meaning strictly, it does give a correct general impression of the ultimate meaning of the line.

4 I have quoted exactly as printed in IGE (2), except that the required accent has been placed on *Dwndálc* (line 30). My translation does imply, however, several minor un-noted divergencies from the printed text, particularly as regards punctuation. Attention must be drawn, however, to line 25 which I interpret as *Tor, rhwyg, a brath. . . .* The second half of the line is difficult: *tu rhag bron* seems to mean 'side against breast', a description of hand to hand fighting, but I have ventured, perhaps wrongly, to translate on the analogy of such phrases as *tu blaen*, etc.

5 I emend *gefalc* to *geufalc*, and discuss the matter further below. The context seems to imply that the bard describes Ulster as a dominion 'filling (i.e. within) a false boundary'. *Llawn* means 'full', however, suggesting that the translation should be 'full of false impediments'.

Llawn apparently occurs in some modern South Wales dialects in the sense of 'filling'. Because of the particular suitability in this context of interpreting the word thus, I have tentatively suggested that *llawn* here means 'filling'. If this is unacceptable *llawn geufalc* must be given the alternative rendering suggested below. Though, in deference to English idiom, I suggest as this alternative 'full of false impediments', in fact *geufalc* should be taken as an abstract noun. Lloyd-Jones's suggestion that *gefalc* means 'spear' suffers from the difficulty that the plural of a concrete noun would be expected after *llawn*.

6 In medieval orthography *geufalc* would appear as *geuualk*, *geuvalk*, *gevualk*, or *gevvalk*, forms which later transcribers could easily render as *gevalk*, *gefalk*. [Since this article went to press, I have had an opportunity to see several MS. copies of this poem. At least four other MSS. have *geufalc*, including Mostyn 143, which is older than all but one of the MSS. consulted by the editor of the IGE text. The reading *gofalk* is confined to MSS. copied by Wmffre Dafis or related MSS., and is clearly traceable to this copyist's misreading of an *e* as an *o*, two letters which can be easily confused in sixteenth-century script.]

7 See n. 5 above.

8 Though several different translations of this apparently simple couplet could be suggested, none would affect the argument.

9 The only emendation is the substitution of *Nïal* for *Nel* or *Nêl*. A disyllabic *Nïal* would require deletion of another syllable elsewhere in the line. *'Nôl* for *Yn ôl* is the obvious change as the contraction of *yn* to *'n* is fairly common after a consonant or at the beginning of a line in such phrases as *yn y, yn ôl, yn eithr*. Transcribers of medieval Welsh poetry were neither accurate nor consistent in such matters of detail as modern editors are well aware. *Dal* and *daly* are variant forms, cf. *hel, hely; bol, boly;* etc. The archaic forms do often appear after the fourteenth century, but the later forms, such as *dal*, had certainly appeared in poetry by the fourteenth century.
[I have since seen nine MS. copies of the poem. In only one of these is *daly* the form of the word, the eight others have *dal*. The Wmffre Dafis group of MSS. read *ynol dal gretnel gweler*, which clearly represents a crude attempt to 'correct' a line which the copyist thought was wrong in his original. Mostyn 143 has *vy ner yn ol dal ynel* rhyming with *Wlstel*, this being perhaps a more reasonable attempt at emendation. It is very probable that both copyists tampered with such a reading as that found in most MSS., i.e. *yn ol dal grednel fy ner*. As neither copyist was prepared to accept a caesura after *yn ol*, they emended the line drastically

in order to provide *cynghanedd* as well as to retain the required general meaning. As I have shown, this can be achieved quite simply by substituting *Gred Nial* for *Grednel.*]

10 Line 6, p. 48, is almost certainly wrongly edited, and should read *y sy ywch.* . . . The line would still be *cynghanedd draws*, but not *cynghanedd draws fantach* as in the printed text. [I have since ascertained that several MSS. read *y sy ywch.* . . .]

11 To give examples from the quotation already given, line 27 has correspondence in the *chl* of *chleimia* and of *achlân* but none between the *m* after the accent in *chleimia* and the *n* of *achlân*, whereas in line 13 there is correspondence in the absence of a consonant before the accent in *uchder* and *ach* and partial correspondence after the accent in both words in that *ch* occurs in both, though followed by *d* in *uchder*. There is complete correspondence in line 23 between the *tr* before the accent and the *ch* after the accent in *trychant trwch*.

12 IGE (1) p. xxxiii.

13 *Ibid.*, p. lxxiii.

14 *Ibid.*, pp. l–li.

15 *Ibid.*, p. li, and also pp. xxxv, xlvii.

16 No history of Wales in the fourteenth century has been published, and no historian has attempted to trace the history of the manifestations of the continuing loyalty to the native Welsh principality from the Edwardian conquest to the war of Owain Glyndŵr. With the exception of Professor Glanmor Williams in *The Welsh Church from Conquest to Reformation* (Cardiff, 1962) recent Welsh historians tend to play down the strong element of nationalism in fourteenth-century Welsh politics. The late Professor Glyn Roberts's paper 'Wales and England, Antipathy and Sympathy' in *The Welsh History Review*, vol. i, pp. 375 ff., is in many respects valuable and well-balanced, but makes no attempt to evaluate the strength and nature of Welsh separatist aspirations in the period, and fails to distinguish between the character of Welsh nationalism before and after Glyndŵr. For a full list of works relevant to fourteenth-century Welsh political history, see the *Bibliography of the History of Wales*, New Edition (Cardiff, 1962), Section FIb. A supplement has been published in the *Bulletin of the Board of Celtic Studies*, vol. xx, pp. 126–64.

17 This conclusion is, I think, inescapable because of (*a*) the previous history of Welsh loyalty to the native principality, (*b*) the subsequent

history of Owain Glyndŵr and (c) the content of Iolo Goch's poem eulogizing the ancestry of Owain. Yet, no Welsh historian has been prepared to draw this obvious conclusion.

18 It has been suggested that Llywelyn ap Gruffudd had precipitated the Edwardian Conquest because of his recklessness and foolhardiness, especially up to 1276. Recent opinion seems to be that these strictures are unjustified because, although events proved him to be wrong, his policy of defiance must have appeared reasonable at the time. I intend to discuss elsewhere an alternative thesis, that Llywelyn had no real choice as Edward I was bent on destroying him and his principality.

19 It could be argued with considerable justification that *draig* and *dragon* should be translated as 'hero', 'chieftain' or 'warrior'.

20 As is clear from my translation, I regard the IGE punctuation as being wrong in this couplet.

21 See Glanmor Williams, *The Welsh Church from Conquest to Reformation*, p. 213. See also Mary E. Giffin, 'Cadwalader, Arthur and Brutus in the Wigmore Manuscript', *Speculum*, vol. xvi, pp. 109–20. Dr. Giffin's article contains material that shows and explains Sir Roger Mortimer's interest in Welsh vaticination, and should be consulted.

22 For discussions of this constitutional and legal issue, see J. Conway Davies, *The Welsh Assize Roll* 1277–1284 (Cardiff, 1940), pp. 138–9; J. G. Edwards, *Littere Wallie* (Cardiff, 1940), pp. xlvii–li.
It is more than probable that Sir Roger Mortimer genuinely accepted that when crowned he should act as the head of a confederation of nations. There is clear evidence that he wished to be considered, and indeed to be, an Irishman in Ireland and a Welshman in Wales. Such a policy, inspired by Welsh political thought, could not be accepted at the time in either England or Ireland.
The policy of Edward IV towards Wales and the Welsh may be partially explained as a diluted continuation of Mortimer policy. Edward placed the whole of Wales under the control of William Herbert, earl of Pembroke, who was moreover the king's most trusted adviser. After Herbert's death, Edward established the Court and Council of Wales and the Marches. Whatever else may have been the purpose of this institution, it remains true that its establishment recognized the special position of Wales administratively, a Wales incidentally not markedly different in extent from that envisaged by Owain Glyndŵr.

23 Admittedly, Iolo Goch's traditional fame in this respect derives more from Owain Glyndŵr's position than from his own, but other bards

addressed Owain Glyndŵr and only Iolo Goch came to be regarded as his court poet.

24 In *Llên Cymru*, vol. vi, p. 236, I drew attention to the need to compare the ceremonies of the Welsh court poets with 'crown-wearing' ceremonial in England, for which see H. G. Richardson and G. O. Sayles, *The Governance of Mediaeval England* (Edinburgh, 1963), p. 397 *et seq.*, Appendix I, 'Coronations and Crown-wearings before the Conquest'. For the *teir gwyl arbennic*, 'the three special festivals', see the opening sections of any version of medieval Welsh law, the latest translation being by Melville Richards, *The Laws of Hywel Dda* (Liverpool, 1954). For a relevant discussion of the purpose and style of Welsh court poetry, see J. Lloyd-Jones, 'The Court Poets of the Welsh Princes', *Proc. Brit. Academy*, XXXIV (1948), pp. 169–70, 173–5. For a discussion of a change in Irish bardic practice as a result of political change, comparable though not similar to what happened to Welsh poetry after 1284, see J. E. Caerwyn Williams, *Traddodiad Llenyddol Iwerddon* (Caerdydd, 1958), p. 124.

25 Although Dr. Thomas Parry has maintained (see *Transactions of the Hon. Soc. of Cymmrodorion*, 1939, pp. 209–31) that subsequently lost *cywyddau* in *cynghanedd* had existed for about a generation before the time of Dafydd ap Gwilym, the arguments put forward are not convincing.

26 D. J. Bowen, in 'Dafydd ap Gwilym a Morgannwg', *Llên Cymru*, vol. v, pp. 164–73, pointed out the similarity between the imagery in the *cywyddau* to Ifor Hael and that in Dafydd ap Gwilym's nature poetry. Mr. Bowen was not concerned with the reason for this, but with proving Dafydd's authorship of the poems to Ifor Hael, a matter which should not have been in doubt but which had been questioned by Dr. Thomas Parry in his edition of the poetry of Dafydd ap Gwilym.

27 For the poem, see Ifor Williams, Thomas Roberts (eds.), *Cywyddau Dafydd ap Gwilym a'i Gyfoeswyr* (2nd edition, Cardiff, 1935), pp. 157–9.

28 Most of his extant works have been published, see John Jones and Walter Davies (eds.), *The Poetical Works of Lewis Glyn Cothi* (Oxford, 1837) [abbreviated PWLGC], and E. D. Jones (ed.) *Gwaith Lewis Glyn Cothi, Y Gyfrol Gyntaf* (Caerdydd, Aberystwyth 1953) [abbreviated GLGC].

29 See GLGC, p. 28, line 26; PWLGC, p. 98, line 43 (a probable reference); PWLGC, p. 315, lines 21–4 (a particularly full and interesting reference).

30 IGE (2) p. 78, lines 9–10.

31 Since this paper was prepared an interesting article by J. Beverley Smith on 'Einion Offeiriad' has been published in the *Bulletin of the Board of Celtic Studies*, vol. xx, pp. 339–47. Mr. Smith deals with the probable connection between Einion Offeiriad (to whom is attributed authorship of the earliest known Welsh bardic tract) and the family of Glyn Aeron, and he argues that this family played a vital part in the retention and in the development of Welsh bardic traditions in the fourteenth century. Also important is the connection between Einion Offeiriad and Sir Rhys ap Gruffudd, the most powerful Welsh nobleman of the first half of the century. Iolo Goch sang Sir Rhys's elegy *c.* 1355, see IGE (2), pp. 10–11, and Ifor Williams 'Rhys ap Gruffudd', *Transactions of the Hon. Soc. of Cymmrodorion*, 1913–14, pp. 193–203.

32 PWLGC, p. 204, lines 20–2.

33 PWLGC, p. 204, lines 19–30; p. 312, lines 23–8.

34 RP, col. 1246, line 7. See also Saunders Lewis, *Braslun o Hanes Llenyddiaeth Gymraeg* (Caerdydd, 1932), p. 53, where this reference is quoted more fully, and where it is suggested that Casnodyn was referring to poetry similar to that composed later by Dafydd ap Gwilym, and attention is drawn to the fact that the home of Dafydd's uncle and patron, Llywelyn, was not far from Caeo.

35 I have suggested elsewhere (*Llên Cymru*, vol. v, p. 143) that the literary tradition of Glamorgan may well have influenced Dafydd ap Gwilym. This I believe to be true, but here it is the influence of Caeo, also important, that is stressed.

36 IGE (2), p. 77, line 16.

DERICK S. THOMSON

The Harlaw Brosnachadh:
An early fifteenth-century literary curio

The most notable bardic dynasty in Scotland was that of the Mac-
Mhuirichs, reputedly descended from Muireadhach Albanach Ó
Dálaigh whose flight from Ireland is vividly recounted in *The Annals
of the Four Masters*, under the year 1213. There are numerous, if
sporadic, evidences of this family's activities in Scotland from the
thirteenth to the nineteenth century.[1] Here we shall be concerned
mainly with the *Incitement to Battle* said to have been composed by
a MacMhuirich before the battle of Harlaw in 1411.

Donald, Lord of the Isles, claimed the earldom of Ross by right of
his wife, the daughter of Euphemia, countess of Ross. Pursuing this
claim, and in particular seeking to assert his authority over those
lands of the earldom situated in the sheriffdoms of Banff, Aberdeen
and Kincardine, Donald invaded Aberdeenshire, and his forces were
engaged by an army led by Alexander Stewart, earl of Mar, at Harlaw.
It is thought that as a military engagement the battle was indecisive,
and there seem to have been heavy losses on both sides.[2]

There is extensive evidence that the MacMhuirich bards were for
many generations in the service of the MacDonalds of the Isles. The
ascription of the Harlaw Brosnachadh to a MacMhuirich can be
regarded as an item in that dossier of evidence, and there is no reason
to doubt that the family was in the MacDonald service long before
the fifteenth century. There is, however, some confusion as to the
name of the author of the Brosnachadh.

There are two previously unpublished texts of the poem in the
McLagan MSS.[3] The version in MS. 222 ascribes the poem to 'Lachlann mor Mac Mhuirich, aos-dana Mhic Dhomhnuill', whereas MS. 97
ascribes it to 'Ian Mac Mhuirich Bard Chlann Ranuill'. A note in
McLagan MS. 248 repeats the ascription of MS. 97 in identical terms.

In the McNicol MSS.,[4] on a single foolscap sheet, there is a copy of a document entitled 'Geneology of Neil McMhurich Bard to Clanranald's family', written by Neil McMhuirich in the presence of witnesses, and attested on 11 July 1775 one of the witnesses being Mr. William McLeod, Minister of the Gospel at Campbeltown. Part of this genealogy runs: 'Lachlan Mc Neil Mc Lachlan Mhoir do reinn prosnachadh Catha Chath-caireabhach 1411'. Although the genealogy is certainly inaccurate in some respects, we may note the evidence it gives of our poet's name, and the name of his grandson. Donald McNicol, in his *Remarks*, published in 1779 but mostly written soon after 1773, says that a gentleman in Argyllshire is 'possessed of Prosnachadh Catha *Chlann Domhnuill*, at the battle of Harlaw in 1411, composed by *Lachlan More Macvurich*, the Bard. . . . It contains four epithets upon every letter of the alphabet. . . .'[5] John MacCodrum, the North Uist bard, in 'Tàladh Iain Mhùideartaich', composed between 1763 and 1766, says:

> Bha Clann Raghnaill treun aig Arla
> Nuair bhrosnaich Lachlann am bàrd iad.[6]

MacCodrum was obviously passing on the MacMhuirich family tradition, as he had cultivated the acquaintance of the family.[7] Ranald MacDonald, editor of the first published version of the poem, in his Eigg Collection of 1776, ascribed the poem to Lachlann Mór. Hugh MacDonald of Kilpheder, in his statement of 1800,[8] ascribed the Brosnachadh to 'Nial mòr MacMhuirich'.

In this confusion of testimony it is worth noticing that the ascriptions which derive most directly from the MacMhuirich family favour Lachlann Mór's authorship. This is the case with Neil MacMhuirich's testimony of 1775, and with MacCodrum's casual reference noted above. This was the tradition accepted by the editor of the Eigg Collection, Ranald MacDonald, and it is known that both he and his father, Alasdair Mac Mhaighstir Alasdair, carried away MacMhuirich MSS. from Uist.[9] Yet a strong element of confusion persists, for McLagan MS. 97, which ascribes the poem to 'Ian Mac Mhuirich', calls the author Clanranald's Bard. This would seem to suggest that the version in MS. 97 is of island provenance. The version in MS. 222, on the other hand, ascribes the poem to Lachlann Mór, who is said to be MacDonald's *aos-dàna*. This seems to reflect the more accurate tradition, and we shall see that the version of MS. 222 is in many respects more archaic than that of MS. 97. It is also quite clear that Ranald MacDonald knew both versions, and produced a conflation of both.

An interesting light is thrown on the problem by a statement which occurs among the McNicol Papers. This is a statement written on 22 March 1871 and entitled 'Information regarding Rev^d. D. McNicol furnished by Dr Duncan McColl'. McColl makes this significant statement: 'MacNicol got much information from the Macdonalds of Ardshiel, rep^s. of the original M^c. D s of the Isles, and connected with M^c. D s of Dalness.' This suggests that McNicol may have had at one time a copy of the Brosnachadh corresponding to one or other of the McLagan versions (and it is thought that an important part of the McNicol Collection was in fact lost overboard in the West Indies by McNicol's son). There is evidence, also, that McNicol and McLagan worked over the same ground, and enjoyed to some extent the same circle of friends and contacts. But McColl's statement suggests a more interesting possibility. Ranald MacDonald's mother was Jane MacDonald of Dalness, and it seems likely that he, and his father, would have had independent access to the 'information' which McNicol is said to have got from the representatives of 'the original MacDonalds of the Isles'. In view of this, and in view of the evidence of the sources, we must consider the possibility that Ranald MacDonald had access to a more complete copy of the version in MS. 222.

The version of the poem in MS. 97 claims to be 'a true copy from an old MS. in galic character', and this is attested on 18 October 1775 by James MacIntyre of Glenoe[10] and James McLagan, Chaplain to the 42nd Regiment. Perhaps the date is significant, for we saw above that Neil MacMhuirich's genealogy, containing the ascription to Lachlann Mór, was copied on 11 July 1775 and witnessed by Mr. William MacLeod, minister at Campbeltown. It may be that this transaction gave rise to a search for a MS. of the Brosnachadh, and that two came to light. The evidence points to the MS. 222 version having come from a mainland source, where the connections of the MacMhuirichs with the 'MacDonalds South' were appreciated. The ascription in MS. 97 remains puzzling, for it envisages the MacMhuirich of 1411 as bard to Clanranald, which is not credible, yet does not follow what was apparently the Uist tradition that Lachlann Mór was the author.

On p. 8 of MS. 97 there is a postscript which runs as follows:

There was more noble blood shed in this battle (incomparably) than in any fought in Scotland for three centuries.—There were 30 Noblemen slain therein & about 16 Tribes of the Low country people quite extirpat. The retreat was followed 14 miles from the first stance of battle whereon they began, yet at ilka mile's rout they rallied, so that the victory was too dear to McDonald & his Highlanders. It was both fateague & darkness of the night that parted them. McDonald settled all Ross after this battle; and after the king came home from his imprisonment, he executed all those of his subjects that occasioned this cruel and unjust trouble in his absence, & was instrumental in destroying such a number of his valiant subjects in an unjust cause.—

The above was wrote as it stands on the back of the foresaid Galic MS.

Leaving aside the traditions and the historical interpretation implied by this passage, two points may be worth commenting on. The reference to 'three centuries' suggests that this note was written in the first half of the eighteenth century, and the use of 'ilka' suggests that it was not written by a Hebridean. As a conjecture, it may be suggested that the author of the note was the antiquary Walter MacFarlane. At any rate, if the point concerning 'ilka' stands, this Gaelic MS. in the old character was for a time at least in the keeping of a mainland person who used both Scots and Gaelic, and so it is not likely to have come to light in Uist after Neil MacMhuirich's statement in 1775.

Regarding the poem itself, much stronger evidence both of age and of authenticity can be derived from a study of the sources, and of related material of MacMhuirich provenance. Since the Eigg Collection is not widely available for consultation, and since the two McLagan versions are unpublished, it is justifiable to make a full edition, with variant readings. The basic text is that of McLagan MS. 222, pp. 25–6, supplemented by readings from McLagan MS. 97, pp. 6–7, and occasional readings from Eigg. All such readings from MS. 97 and from Eigg are printed within square brackets.

It is not the intention to restore rigorously a hypothetical fifteenth-century text, although in fact the edition goes some way towards that, because MS. 222 preserves a number of earlier forms. The intention is to bring the evidence of the sources into full play, in the hope that they will throw valuable light not only on the immediate question of the poet's identity, but also on linguistic points which are so meagrely attested in Scottish sources for the fifteenth century. Orthography is normalized, but forms which may provide evidence as to the dating of the poem are not modernized. The linguistic problems posed by the poem are discussed below.[11]

In its original form, it seems probable that the poem included two lines of epithets, that is four epithets, for each letter of the Gaelic alphabet. In our edition there is only one line of *u*-epithets, and in the MS. 222 text the entire *e*-section, the entire *o*-section, and one line of the *u*-section are missing. In the MS. 97 version the *h*-section is misplaced, coming after the *l*-section. *h*- was not properly regarded as a letter of the Irish alphabet, and there is a possibility that the *o*- and *u*-sections were pillaged at some stage in the poem's transmission, to provide an *h*-section, and that the *i*- and *a*- epithets in lines 17–18 were added at that time. It is clear that the section following the alphabetical series, i.e. lines 38–48, was intended to have alliteration in every line, and thus a line from the MS. 97 version has been rejected, since it does not fulfil this condition. The only other metrical requirement was that the line had seven syllables, and this criterion has been used in constructing the text. The author had used the conjunction *is* where his first epithet in a line was monosyllabic, in order to fill out the line. Conversely, he did not count the epenthetic vowel in lines 18 and 27 as a syllable; this is in line with bardic practice.

The numbers in the edition of the 'Brosnachadh' refer to the textual notes.

Brostughadh[1]-catha, Chlann-Domhnaill, Là Chatha Gharbhaich.
Le Lachlann Mór MacMhuirich, Aos-dàna Mhic Dhomhnaill.
    A[2] Chlanna Cuinn, cuimhnichibh[2]
    Cruas an[3] am na h-iorghaile[4]:
    Gu[5] h-àirneach[6], gu h-arranta[7],
    Gu h-athlamh[8], gu h-allanta[9],
5   Gu beòdha[10], gu barramhail[11],
    Gu brìoghmhor[12], gu buan-fheargach[13],
    Gu calma[14], gu curanta[15],
    Gu cròdha, gu cath-bhuadhach[16],
    Gu dùr[17] is[18] gu dàsannach[19],
10   Gu dian[20] is gu deagh-fhulang[21],
    [Gu h-èasgaidh[22], gu h-eaghnamhach[23],

Gu h-éidith'[24], gu h-eireachdail[25],]
Gu fortail[26], gu furachail[27],
Gu frithir, gu forniata[28],

15 Gu gruamach, gu gràineamhail[29],
Gu gleusta[30], gu gaisgeamhail[31],
Gu h-ullamh, gu h-iorghaileach[32],
Gu h-olla-bhorb, gu h-àibheiseach[33],
Gu h-innill[34], gu h-inntinneach,

20 Gu h-iomdha[35], gu h-iomghonach[36],
Gu [laomsgar][37], gu làn-[ath] lamh[38],
Gu làidir, gu luath-bhuilleach,
Gu mearghanta[39], gu mór-chneadhach[40],
Gu meanmnach[41], gu mìleanta,

25 Gu neimhneach[42], gu naimhdeamhail,
Gu niatach[43], gu neimh-eaglach[44],
[Gu h-obann[45], gu h-olla-ghnìomhach,
Gu h-oirdheirc[46], gu h-oirbheartach[47],]
Gu[48] [prap] is[48] gu prìomh-ullamh[49],

30 Gu prosta, gu [prionnsamhail],
Gu ruaimneach[50], gu ro-dhàna,
Gu ro-bhorb[51], gu rìoghamhail,
Gu sanntach[52], gu sèanamhail,
Gu socair, gu sàr-bhuailteach[53],

35 Gu teannta[54], gu [togarrach[55]],
Gu talcmhor[56], gu traigh-èasgaidh[57],
Gu h-urlamh[58], gu h-ùr-mhaiseach[59]
[60]Do chosnadh[60] [na][61] cath-làthrach[62]
Re[63] bronnaibh[64] bhar[65] biodhbhadha[66].

40 A Chlanna Cuinn Cèad-chathaich[67]
[A] nois[68] uair bhar[69] n-aitheanta[70],
[A chuileanan confadhach][71],
A bheithrichean[72] bunanta[73],
A leómhannan[74] làn-[ghasta][75],

45 [A onchonaibh iorghaileach][76],
Chaoiribh[77] chròdha, churanta
De Chlanna Cuinn Cèad-chathaich[78]—
A Chlanna[79] Cuinn, [cuimhnichibh
Cruas an am na h-iorghaile].[80]

Notes to Edition

1 MS. 222 has the older form *Brostughadh*; MS. 97 *Brosnacha*. The full title in MS. 97 is as follows: 'Brosnacha catha Chlann Domhnuill le Ian Mac Mhuirich Bard Chlann Ranuill, La Tharlà san bhliadhna 1411 edir Mac Dhomhnuill Innse Gall & an Eirthir ghallach, mu Iarlachd Rois.' The title in Eigg adds some further details, and runs as follows: 'Prosnuchadh-catha roinaidh le Lachun-Moir-Macmhuireach-Albinnich, do Dhomhnil a Iola, Riodh Inshagaill, agus Eairla Rois; la Machrich Cathgariach. Thugidh è June 11. 1411.'

2 Eigg *Chlannibh cuin, cuinhichibh.* The Voc. Pl. form *Chlanna* is what we should expect from a trained bard of the early fifteenth century.

3 Both MSS. *ann.*

4 MS. 222 *Iurghuille*, MS. 97 *Irghile*.

5 MS. 97 uses the form *ga* throughout, apart from three or four instances in which the form seems to be *go*. In this MS. *h-* is not prefixed to the epithets with initial *a-, e-, o-* and *u-*, except in the lines corresponding to 17–18 in our text—lines which seem to have been regarded as the *h*-section of the piece. Eigg adopted this usage; this is one of several strong clues that Ranald MacDonald used a version closely similar to, or identical with, that of MS. 97.

6 MS. 97 *àirnich*, Eigg *arnich*. The *-ich* ending is characteristic of MS. 97. Can this possibly be a derivative of *airne* (Mod. Ir. *áirne*) 'watch of the night, watching'? Otherwise, a tentative emendation is *àrnaidh*, cf. Meyer, Contt. *arnaid.*

7 MS. 97, Eigg *arronta*. Cf. Gaelic MS. 63 (Nat. Lib. of Scot.), p. 148. *na ha ghaielibh arronta* (SGS IV, 154). Glossed in the Stewarts' Collection 'bold, daring, confident'. I owe these references to Dr. J. L. Campbell.

8 MS. 222 *alamh*, MS. 97 *ailimh*, Eigg *athlif.* Eigg's spelling is perhaps influenced by MS. 97's *lanathlif* in line 21; or rather, to avoid begging the question, by a similar spelling in the source used by the editor of Eigg.

9 MS. 97, Eigg *allonta*. The original form may have been *allata*, becoming *allanta*, *allonta* by dittography, since the ending containing *n* occurs in the previous line.

10 MSS. 97 and 222 *beogha*.

11 MS. 222 *baramhuil*, MS. 97, Eigg, *baramhil*.

12 MS. 222 *brioghar*, MS. 97 *brioghoir*, Eigg *brioghor*.

13 MS. 97 *buanfhergich*, Eigg *buan-fhergach*.

14 Eigg *calama*.

15 MS. 222 *curranta*, MS. 97 *curonta*, Eigg *curonda*.

16 All sources *cath-b(h)uaghach*.

17 Eigg *duir*.

18 MS. 97, Eigg *'s*. The original intention was evidently to use *is* when the first epithet in the line was a monosyllable. MS. 222 comes nearest to reflecting this usage.

19 MS. 97 *dasunnich*, Eigg *daisunnach*. In MS. 222 the word is glossed 'bold'.

20 MS. 97, Eigg *dion*.

21 MS. 97 *deugh-fhulinich*, Eigg *deugh-fhuillin*. Both spellings, and especially that of Eigg, suggest the pronunciation with palatal *l*, as in the Mod. Sc. Gael. dialectal forms *fuiling*, *fuilig* (2 sg. imperative). MS. 97's form, standing for *deagh-fhuilingeach*, is a syllable too long.

22 MS. 97 *eisgi*.

23 MS. 222 has no *e*-section; Eigg has only one line of *e*- epithets, corresponding loosely to line 12 in MS. 97 and in our text. MS. 97 reads *eighnamhach*. The word seems to be related to Irish *eagnamh*, which the editors of the RIA Dict., E, Fasc. 11, suggested was a confusion of *ecna* and *engnam*, the sense being apparently 'prowess, valour'. It would be possible to conclude that the word in our text is in fact *eangnamhach*, with *n* + lenited *g* giving a nasalized *gh*, as in dialectal pronunciations of *seang* for example.

24 MS. 97 *eidi*, Eigg *éidi*. It is probably the past participle *éidithe* that is intended, but it seems likely that the final syllable was not pronounced. Both MS. 97 and Eigg have *'s* to link the two halves of this line; it has been omitted here.

25 MS. 97 *ericoil*, with *eireachdail* written in margin, in the same hand. *Eireachdail* 'handsome etc.' is well attested in Scottish Gaelic, and the sense fits here. The form *ericoil*, however, which purports to be that of an old MS., is scarcely credible. Eigg has *èicoil*, which might stand for *euchdail*; this is somewhat unlikely, as in every other instance the second epithet in the line is trisyllabic. The whole *e*-section may be regarded as suspect.

26 MS. 222 *Fortuil*, MS. 97 *fortoil*, Eigg *tortail*. The initial *t-* of Eigg no doubt arises from a printer's error. The capital F of MS. 222, in the eighteenth-century hand, looks like a capital T. MS. 97 has *'s* to link the two halves of this line; it has been omitted here.

27 MS. 222 *furachoil*, MS. 97 *furichil*, Eigg *furichair*. Eigg's spelling represents the form used in Classical Irish.

28 MS. 222 *foirn-fhiata*. Eigg links the two epithets with *'s*.

29 MS. 222 *graineamhuil*, MS. 97 *grainamhil*, Eigg *grainemhol*.

30 MS. 97 *glesda*, Eigg *gleusda*.

31 MS. 222 *gaisgeamhuil*, MS. 97 *gaisgemhil*, Eigg *gaisgemhol*.

32 MS. 222 *iorghuilleach*, MS. 97 *irghillich*, Eigg *erighilach*. Lines 17 and 18 in our edition are mis-placed in both MS. 97 and Eigg, where they occur after the *l*-section. The copyist of MS. 97 was, however, conscious of this misplacement, as the two lines, which come at the foot of p. 6, have a semi-boxing round them. It is clear from the arrangement in MS. 222 that these two lines were regarded as the *h*-section of the poem; thus the initial vowels of the four epithets are all different.

33 A doubtful reading. MS. 222 has *abhaiseach*, but MS. 97 has *athisich*, represented in Eigg by *athisach*. It is doubtful if these latter two are for *aithiseach*; although this form would make some sense, as 'reviling', the similar-sounding *athaiseach* means 'slow', and probably such an ambiguity would not be tolerated. *Aitheasach*

'successful' makes better sense. MS. 222's reading, however, can scarcely be evaded, cf. the Irish sense of *áibhéiseach* 'reckless, extravagant' given by Dinneen?

34 All sources *innil. Innill* is the gen. of *inneall*, used attributively, cf. RIA Dict. sub *indell.*

35 MS. 222 *iomadha*, showing svarabhakti pronunciation. MS. 97 has *ilich*, with *inmhich* written above it, and Eigg has *iolichdich*, presumably 'exultant'.

36 MS. 97 *iumaghonich*, Eigg *uima-ghonach* (leg. *iuma-ghonach*), presumably meaning 'inflicting many wounds'. It is likely, however, that it is the prefix *imm-* we have here, and that the adj. is formed from the verb *imm-goin* 'wages war, gives battle'.

37 MS. 222 *luasgar*, MS. 97 *laomsgar*, Eigg *laomsgir*. I have departed from the text of MS. 222 here, unless indeed *luasgar* represents a pronunciation of *laomsgar*; the form *lyṁskir* in the Book of the Dean (Watson, line 721) suggests that the *m* was lenited. Mac Mhaighstir Alasdair uses this word, in a passage which seems to echo the 'Brosnachadh' in other respects also:

> Thig do chinneadh féin ort,
> Na tréin-fhir laomsgair gharbh,
> Nam bearaichibh go reubadh;
> Nan leoghainnimh go creuchdadh;
> Nan nathraichibh graid-léimneach. . . .
> (1751 edition, p. 53)

38 MS. 222 *lan-ealamh*, MS. 97 *lanathlif*, Eigg *lain-athlif.*

39 MS. 222 *meardhannta*, MS. 97 *merradh*, Eigg *merragha*. The two latter forms represent *meardha*. This may be the original form, or alternatively we should perhaps read *mearghant*, to give a seven-syllable line.

40 MS. 222 *mor-chneathach*, MS. 97 *mór-chriodhich*, Eigg *moirchriadhach*. It is possible that, with the common variation of *cn-* and *cr-*, all these forms represent the same original, but it is more likely that the latter two represent a form *mór-chridheach*, which would give a somewhat less apt sense.

41 MS. 222 *mainmneach*, MS. 97 *menmnich*, Eigg *menimnach.*

42 MS. 222 *neimneach*, MS. 97, Eigg *nimhnich*. The latter form, besides showing the lenition of the *m*, is later than that of MS. 222.

43 MS. 97, Eigg *niata*. RIA Dict. regards *niadach* as a variant, possibly later, form of *niach*, an adj. formed from *nia*. See RIA Dict. sub *niata* for instances of the occurrence of this form along with *nemnecha* and *naimdemail*.

44 MS. 97 *nemheglich*, Eigg *naimheglach*.

45 MS. 222 has no *o*-section. Eigg has only one line of *o*- epithets, corresponding to line 27 in our text. The MS. 97 version does not prefix *h*- to the *o*- epithets.

46 MS. 97 *orradheirc*, representing a svarabhakti pronunciation.

47 MS. 97 *oirbhertich*. Note that svarabhakti pronunciation is not implied here.

48 MS. 222 *prata 's*. It may be conjectured that the final syllable of *prata* belongs to the following conjunction.

49 There is marked disagreement between the sources in the *p*-section. Eigg has conflated the two versions represented by MSS. 222 and 97, taking *priom-hurlambh* (leg. *priomh-urlambh*) and *proishoil* from the former, and *prap* and *pruinsamhol* (leg. *priun-samhol*) from the latter, and preserving the word-order of neither. The two lines in MS. 97 read

> ga prap 's ga priunsamhuil,
> ga proisoil ga puthirich,

and in Eigg,

> Ga prap, 's ga priom-hurlambh,
> Ga proishoil, ga pruinsamhol.

MS. 222's *prosta* is a word of fairly rare occurrence; it may be conjectured that this is the reason for its dropping out of the MS. 97 version, and its rejection by the editor of the Eigg version.

The reading of MS. 97, *priunsamhuil*, has been preferred to that of MS. 222, *proiseamhuil*, but the correct reading remains doubtful. MS. 97 is the only source for *puthirich*, which represents *pudharach*, an adj. formed from *pudhar* 'harm, injury'.

50 See comment on p. 162 below.

51 Eigg *ro-bhorib*.

52 Cf. *ba santaigi saigid* '. . . most eager in attack' (O'Donovan, *Magh Rath*, 216. 22).

53 MS. 97, Eigg *sar-bhuailta*. MS. 97 has *-ach* written in the margin opposite this line. The use of *sàr-* and *ro-* is frequent in alliterative passages.

54 MS. 97 *tenta*, Eigg *tenti*. *Teannta* may be the participial adj., meaning 'compact', referring to the close ranks of the MacDonalds.

55 MS. 97 *toggirrich*, Eigg *toggirrach*. MS. 222 has *toghannta*, a puzzling reading. Is this a variant of *toghdha*, 'choice, excellent; wilful, arrogant'? In MS. 222 the word is glossed 'forward'.

56 MS. 97 *talcar*, Eigg *talcarra*. MS. 222's *talcmhor* seems to be a formation based on *talc*, a variant form of *tailc* 'strong, vigorous'. But *talcar*, in the sense of 'determined, unyielding' would be an equally credible reading, and it is not surprising that confusion arose between the two words.

57 MS. 222 *traidh-easgidh*, MS. 97 *troigheachdich*, Eigg *froigheasgi*, with *f-* misprinted for *t-*.

58 In MS. 222 *urlamh* is substituted for *ullamh*. MS. 97 *urlabhich*, Eigg *urlabhach* may represent an original *urladhach*, cf. *urlaidhe* 'the act of smiting' (Glossary to *Duanaire Finn*). The RIA Dict. notes only the negative compound of this adj., see sub *-urladach*.

59 MS. 97 *urmhaisich*, Eigg *urmhaishaol*.

60 MS. 97, Eigg *ga cosnidh*.

61 MS. 97 *nan*.

62 MS. 222 *catha-larach*.

63 MS. 97, Eigg *ri*.

64 MS. 97 *bruinne*, Eigg *bruinnidh*. These variants provide interesting evidence of the age of the poem. *Ri* and *re* (<OI *fri*) normally take the accusative, but instances of dat. pl. following *re* are not uncommon. MS. 222 implies a nom. *brù*, and MS. 97 a nom. *bruinne*. It is doubtful, however, if the Eigg form stands for the nom. pl. *bruinni*.

65 Eigg *air*. The editor of Eigg apparently did not understand this line.

66 MS. 222 *beagh-bhui* (glossed 'enemies'), MS. 97 *biuidh* (substituted for earlier *biudhaidh*, which is stroked out), Eigg *buidhidhi*. The emendation *biodhbhadha*, instead of the normal gen. pl. *biodhbhadh*, is suggested *metri gratia*.

67 MS. 222 *Cuinn Cead-chathaigh*, MS. 97 *Chuinn Cheud-chathaich*, Eigg *chuin-ched chathach*.

68 MS. 222 *nois*, MS. 97 *Anois*, Eigg *A nios*. MS. 222's reading makes the line a syllable short.

69 Eigg *air*.

70 MS. 97 *aithneachaidh*, Eigg *aithinicha*. MS. 222's form is apparently a variant of *aithinte*, gen. of *aithne* 'recognition'.

71 Not in MS. 222. MS. 97 reads *A chuileanan confhach* (which is a syllable short), Eigg reads *A chiulenin conifidhach*. The form of the adj. in Eigg may suggest that the line was included in the second version the editor was using.

72 MS. 222 *bheithrichibh*.

73 MS. 222 *bunnanta*, Eigg *bunonta*.

74 MS. 222 *leoghannaibh*, Eigg *leoghinin*.

75 MS. 222 *lan-ghaisgidh*, Eigg *lainghasta*.

76 Not in MS. 222. MS. 97 reads *Ăr-chonabh iorghoileach*, which is a credible reading. Eigg reads *Aonchonibh irighilach*. Both these lines are a syllable short, and it is suggested here that the editor of Eigg, using a second version, very similar to that of MS. 222, but including this line, misread *A onchonibh* as *Aonchonibh*.

77 MS. 222 reads *a chraobh*, with 'no chaorabh' i.e. 'or *chaorabh*' written above. The *a* has been omitted, so as to give a seven-syllable line. This line is not in MS. 97, but Eigg reads *Do chaoiribh crodha, curonta*. MS. 97 has an additional line here, *A ghasraidh sgaiteach theum-bheura*; the lack of alliteration throws doubt on the authenticity of this line.

78 MS. 222 *a Chlannaibh Cuinn Cead-chathaich.*
MS. 97 *Do Chlanna Chuinn Cheud-chathaich.*
Eigg *Do clannimh chuinn, cheid-chathuch.*

79 MS. 222 *Chlannaibh*; MS. 97 originally read *Chlannaibh*, but a line
has been drawn through -*ibh*.

80 MSS. 222 and 97 both end at *Cuinn*, adding '&c'.

Translation

Clan Donald's incitement to battle, on the day of the battle of Harlaw.
By Lachlann Mór MacMhuirich, MacDonald's Aos-dàna.

<blockquote>

O Children of Conn, remember
Hardihood in time of battle:
Be[12] watchful (?), daring (?),
Be dextrous, winning renown,
5   Be vigorous, pre-eminent,
Be strong, nursing your wrath,
Be stout, brave,
Be valiant, triumphant,
Be resolute and fierce,
10   Be forceful and stand your ground,
Be nimble, valorous,
Be well-equipped, handsomely accoutred,
Be dominant, watchful,
Be fervid, pugnacious,
15   Be dour, inspiring fear,
Be ready for action, warrior-like,
Be prompt, warlike,
Be exceedingly fierce, recklessly daring,
Be prepared, willing,
20   Be numerous (?), giving battle,
Be fiery, fully-ready,
Be strong, dealing swift blows,
Be spirited, inflicting great wounds,
Be stout-hearted, martial,
25   Be venomous, implacable,

</blockquote>

Be warrior-like, fearless,
Be swift, performing great deeds,
Be glorious, nobly powerful,
Be rapid [in movement], very quick,
30 Be valiant, princely,
Be active, exceedingly bold,
Be exceedingly fierce, king-like,
Be eager, successful,
Be unflurried, striking excellent blows,
35 Be compact [in your ranks], elated,
Be vigorous, nimble-footed,
Be ready, fresh and comely,
In winning the battle
Against your enemies.
40 O Children of Conn of the Hundred Battles,
Now is the time for you to win recognition,
O raging whelps,
O sturdy heroes (lit. 'bears'),
O most sprightly lions,
45 O battle-loving warriors,
O brave, heroic firebrands,
The Children of Conn of the Hundred Battles—
O Children of Conn, remember
Hardihood in time of battle.

The Brosnachadh, if the tradition about it is reliable, may well have been composed in the vernacular, rather than in Classical Common Gaelic. If it was, in fact, intended to raise the spirits of Donald of Harlaw's host there was much to be said in favour of making it comprehensible to the soldiers, who cannot be assumed to have understood the language of the bardic schools. We cannot of course assume that the poem, as we have it in eighteenth-century sources, has not undergone modification. Yet it seems unlikely that it is a 'translation' from Classical Common Gaelic to the vernacular, for had this been attempted in the eighteenth century it is probable that fewer archaic features would have survived. What requires to be investigated is whether the Brosnachadh, in a form close to the extant versions, can be regarded as a credible production of the year 1411. The scheme of the poem both limits the range of this investigation and makes it more credible that such a production could be almost equally comprehensible in the eighteenth century and in the fifteenth, for by far the greater part of it consists of epithets whose form has changed little in the intervening period. Thus, epithets such as *beòdha, calma, cròdha, dùr, dian* and *làidir* have undergone no change in the period in question. Indeed the great majority of the epithets can be shown to have existed in the form in which we have them in the Brosnachadh, making allowances for faulty spelling in the existing versions. Nor can we too readily assume, in a century which saw the adjectival flights of Donnchadh Bàn and Mac Mhaighstir Alasdair, the former quite unlettered, that the vocabulary of this poem would present serious difficulty to monoglot Gaelic speakers of the eighteenth century, let alone the fifteenth.

There are several formations in the poem which deviate from the standard Classical language. Thus both MS. sources fluctuate in their usage regarding the Vocative Plural, each using the Dative Plural termination in the final lines of the poem, although not in the earlier instances. These can probably be regarded as copyist's errors. The termination of the 2nd Plural Imperative is here *-ibh* (line 1), which is a Sc. Gaelic innovation, but it is one already attested in the Dean of Lismore's Book in the early sixteenth century.[13] The plurals *chuileanan, bheithrichean, leómhannan* (lines 42–4) are of Scottish type also. The epenthetic vowel is written in four instances in the MS. 97 version, and in two in the MS. 222 version. Two of these show a Scottish-type epenthesis: *orradheirc* in MS. 97 and *iomadha* in MS. 222. The instance of epenthesis in compound words (e.g. *olla-bhorb*, line 18) is common in both Irish and Sc. Gaelic. O'Rahilly was not aware of its occurrence in south Argyll[14] but it was in fact recorded by Edward Lhuyd in Knapdale, e.g. *sheany van* (seana-bhean),[15] *kamy chosach* (cama-chosach),[16] *kályman* (calman).[17] The occurrence of these forms in MSS. 97 and 222 does not of course prove the occurrence of epenthesis in the original, although the presence of *olla-bhorb* in both sources points to that. In line 24 we have the form *mìleanta*, whereas *mìleata* (Mid. Ir. *mìleta*) is the standard form; the *-n-* presumably belongs to the adjectival suffix *-anta, -eanta*. The epithet *ruaimneach* (line 31) does not seem to be attested in Irish, although it may be connected with *rúam* 'fame, glory(?)'. This may be regarded as a Scotticism, as may *talcmhor* (line 36), *eireachdail* (line 12) and *dàsannach* (line 9) (Ir. *dásachtach*).

On the other hand, there are several archaic[18] forms in MSS. 97

and 222, which in themselves support a dating well before the eighteenth century. The occurrence of *athlamh* (line 4) in the *a*-section (rather than *ealamh* in the *e*-section) supports the fifteenth-century dating, as *ealamh* largely superseded *athlamh* in Scottish Gaelic. The form *bhar* (lines 39, 41), rather than *bhur* or *ur*, also supports the earlier dating, as do the forms *do* (line 38) (rather than *a*), *re* (line 39) (rather than *ri*), and the form *A nois* (line 41) (rather than *A nis*). In the phrase *gu deagh-fhulang*, *gu* (<*co*) perhaps retains its prepositional sense, while *fulang* derives from the verbal noun of *fo-loing*. The phrase would in that case mean literally 'with good enduring'; *deghfhuluing*, however, occurs as an adjective in a MacMhuirich passage to be quoted below. Eigg's form *naimheglach* (line 26) may point to an early MS. form, the more usual vernacular Scottish form of the prefix being *neamh-* or *neo-*. The forms *barramhail* (line 5), *gràineamhail* (line 15), *gaisgeamhail* (line 16), *naimhdeamhail* (line 25), *prionnsamhail* (line 30), *rìoghamhail* (line 32) and *sèanamhail* (line 33) also suggest an early dating (cf. *bliadhnamhail* in 1408 Islay Charter); *-amhail* was later reduced to *-ail*. The following words, considered as lexical items, would seem to have been obsolete by the eighteenth century: *àirneach, fortail, forniata, prap, prosta, sèanamhail, bronnaibh, biodhbhadha, aitheanta, confadhach*[19] and possibly *onchonaibh*. *Frithir* is a word of rare occurrence, although Mac Mhaighstir Alasdair used it,[20] and it also occurs in Turner's Collection of 1813;[21] these two instances, together with that in the Brosnachadh, might be added to those quoted in the RIA Dictionary.

The conclusions to be drawn from a study of the language of the Brosnachadh are as follows: (1) it is considerably older than the eighteenth century, (2) there is nothing in the language which is inconsistent with a fifteenth-century dating, and (3) it is possible that the poem was originally composed in vernacular Scottish Gaelic.

It is worth noting in passing that if the above conclusions were admitted, the text could be regarded as the earliest metrical text in vernacular Scottish Gaelic.[22]

The case for both a MacMhuirich and a fifteenth-century ascription is greatly strengthened by a comparison of the Brosnachadh with a Prose-poem on the Arming and Army of John of the Isles. This passage, from the so-called Red Book of Clanranald, can be consulted in Alexander Cameron's *Reliquiae Celticae* 11, pp. 258–64. The Prose-poem apparently refers to the fighting which took place between John and his illegitimate son Aonghus Og after 1476, and it gives details of the Highland lords (*armainn*) who supported John. The whole piece is constructed mainly on the alliterative principle. The following short extract, giving details of some of John's supporters, the Mac-Donalds, Clanranald, MacAllisters and MacDuffies, will serve to illustrate the principle:

> ...clanna díomsacha drechsholus dath-aluinn dásachta deghbhrethech dúasmhora Domhnuill 7 clanna réighe rathmhora ruaigmhera ro-dhána ribhrethacha raghnuill 7 clanna ionnsoigheach oirsgiathach alasdair 7 clanna díona dúra dannardha deghfhuluing duibh-shíthe. ...[23]

The Prose-poem is followed by a short metrical poem in praise of MacDonald; this also contains much alliteration.[24]

We have seen that in the Brosnachadh which purports to date from 1411 the MacDonalds are described by a series of epithets arranged in alliterative quartettes, and a brief comparison of the passage just quoted with the Brosnachadh will show a number of correspondences in the epithets used. A more extended comparison of the two works reveals an interesting pattern. The number of complete or partial correspondences between the two passages is high. Thus, if we compare the forms used in our sources for the Brosnachadh with those used in the Prose-poem, we find that the following epithets occur in both, in identical spellings: *beògha, bunanta, calma, cath-bhuaghach, dùr, dion, làidir, mìleanta, ro-dhána* and *socair*. In other instances there are only minor orthographical differences between the two passages, e.g. *alamh* (MS. 222)/*athlamh* (Prose-poem), *brioghar* (MS. 222)/*brioghmhora* (Prose-poem), *crodha* (MS. 222)/*cróghdha* (Prose-poem), *deagh-fhulang* (MS. 222)/*degh-fhuluing* (Prose-poem), *foirn-fhiata* (MS. 222), *forniata* (MS. 97)/*foirmata* (leg. *foirniata*) (Prose-poem), *graineamhuil* (MS. 222)/*graineamhal* (Prose-poem), *naideamhail* (MS. 222)/*naimhdemhla* (Prose-poem), *neimneach* (MS. 222)/*neimhneca* (Prose-poem), *sheanamhail* (MS. 222)/*sénamhal* (Prose-poem) and *urlamh* (MS. 222)/*urrlamh* (Prose-poem). In several other instances the correspondences are slightly less close, e.g. *confhach* (MS. 97), *conifidhach* (Eigg)/*confuigh* (Prose-poem), *dasannach* (MS. 222)/*dásachtacha* (Prose-poem), *èicoil* (= *euchdail?*) (Eigg)/*échtbhéogha* (Prose-poem), *lan-ghaisgidh* (MS. 222)/*lainmhileadh* (Prose-poem), *merradh* (MS. 97), *meardhannta* (MS. 222)/*mear, meara-menmn*[*a*]*c*[*h*] (Prose-poem), *onchonibh* (Eigg)/*onchu* (Prose-poem).

On analysing the correspondences between the texts of the Bros-nachadh and the Prose-poem, we find the following results. The total number of separate epithets in the MS. 222 version (including the nominal epithets *beithrichean, leómhannan*, etc.) is 70. The number of close or partial correspondences with the Prose-poem is 29. That is to say, over 41 per cent of the epithets in this version of the Bros-nachadh show some correspondence, usually a close one, with the epithets in the Prose-poem. In the case of MS. 97 the corresponding figures are 84 and 32, showing a percentage of 38. In the case of the Eigg version, which is a conflation of two versions, the figures are 76 and 34, showing a percentage of over 44. The fact that there are no *p-* epithets in the Prose-poem slightly increases the statistical significance of these figures. It is very doubtful if such a high proportion can be fortuitous; it seems to point inevitably to some direct relationship between the two passages.

A further, oblique, light is cast on the problem by a version of the Brosnachadh to which no reference has been made as yet in this discussion. This version was printed in A. and D. Stewart's *Collection of Gaelic Verse*, published in 1804. The Stewarts' version is considerably longer than those we have been considering, and the suspicion of forgery attaches to it much more readily than to earlier versions. As against four epithets per letter of the alphabet in these, the Stewart version usually has forty or more, although in a few instances the score is not so high. Although the Stewart version seldom agrees with the order of epithets in the earlier texts, it includes most of them, and generally in the first three lines of each alphabetical section. The Stewart text, especially in its orthography, is modernized. There are some unfortunate choices, as for example *imshniomhach* 'anxious', hardly an epithet to instil courage in the troops, and worse, *gang-aideach* 'deceitful'. Alliteration has conquered judgment here, as it never does in the earlier versions. Stewart uses both *athlamh* (in the *a-*section) and *ealamh* (in the *e-*section). In the *i-*section the word *idnearach* occurs, based perhaps on the word *idna* which William Shaw included in his Dictionary published in 1780, apparently not realizing that the *d* is lenited. It is significant that the Stewart version agrees closely with our text in the closing section, making, however, a sensible correction (S *Onnchonaibh*, E *Aonchonibh*).

On making a detailed comparison of the epithets in Stewart with those in the Prose-poem, the following statistics emerge. In the Stewart version there are 664 separate epithets. Close or partial correspondences with the Prose-poem amount to 64 instances, giving a percentage of 9.6. Of these correspondences, 30 are common to Stewart and Eigg. This makes the likelihood of a close original connection between Stewart and the Prose-poem even slighter.

After 1780, a Scottish Gael with lexicographical/rhetorical tendencies would have access to a considerable word-list, arranged alphabetically, namely William Shaw's Dictionary. A sample investigation of the *a*-section in the Stewarts' version shows that of the 42 epithets used, 30 have correspondences with words listed by Shaw. The number of correspondences with Robert MacFarlan's Dictionary of 1795 is only half as large, but MacFarlan had expressly stated (possibly a reflection, in passing, on Shaw) that he was not including obsolete words.

The conclusion to be drawn from this small investigation is that the Stewart version is an expansion of the Eigg version, probably undertaken by some industrious gentleman with a perverse interest in lexicography, and access to Shaw's Dictionary. It can with some confidence be dated between the years 1780 and 1804.

It is of course possible to conclude that the Harlaw Brosnachadh is posterior to the Red Book passage on the Arming of John of the Isles, but it seems more reasonable to conclude that Lachlann Mór of Harlaw is not a ghost figure, that his Brosnachadh was genuine, was known to his successors, and was used by one of them in the third quarter of the fifteenth century as a partial basis for the Prose-poem. It may be suspected, further, that the author of the latter was a grandson of the Lachlann of 1411, bearing the same name, and appearing momentarily in the year 1485 as a witness to a charter given by Angus of the Isles to the monastery of St. Columba in Iona. His name appears as *Lacclannus m^c muredhaich archipoeta*, which indicates that he was the chief poet of his family at that time.[25] It may be objected to this that in the Red Book passages the author is on the side of John, Angus's father. But Angus's star was in the ascendant by 1485, and it need not surprise us if the poet had changed his allegiance.

Although it is easy to see that the 'breath of poetry' is lacking in Lachlann Mór's Brosnachadh, it is equally clear that it finds a recognizable niche in the tradition of medieval verse. It may be regarded as a vernacular exercise in that rhetorical tradition which was cultivated by men of letters using Latin as their medium for verse. The Brosnachadh combines the alliterative technique with the rhetorical exercise of the alphabetical poem, of which one of the most remarkable examples is the poem on the Hawk and the Peacock (*De Accipitre et Pavone*), in which the verse paragraphs consist of lines beginning with each letter of the alphabet in turn.[26] Another famous example of alliterative technique is that of the ninth-century poet Hucbald of S. Amand, in his praise of baldness; here 'every word of the hundred and forty-six verses of which it is composed begins with the letter *c*'.[27] It is well known that Irishmen entered with zest into such rhetorical exercises, and these techniques have left their mark, tediously enough at times, on Irish and Scottish Gaelic literature, both in prose and in verse. Many examples of alliterative technique would be known to Lachlann Mór. One such was probably the poem sometimes known as 'Rosg Ghuill', a version of which is preserved in the Book of the Dean of Lismore.[28] Here the alliteration is not nearly as pervasive as in the Brosnachadh, but it is much in evidence, and it may also be significant that there are a good many correspondences in vocabulary between it and the Brosnachadh, as can be seen in the following quotation:

> Laoch armach mear
> feargach re *coir*;
> colg conbhfach air,
> onchu ar ghoil.[29]

The author of the Stewart version of the Brosnachadh, indulging his failing or his fancy, carried the alphabetical gimmick to absurd lengths, and in so doing sacrificed that impact which Lachlann Mór's verse still retains. The 1411 Brosnachadh shows us a medieval rhetorical technique applied with restraint to a subject of the Heroic Age.

NOTES

1 A summary history is contained in a paper which I contributed to the Gaelic Society of Inverness in January 1963. This appeared in Vol. XLIII of the Society's Transactions, pp. 276-304.

2 The Highland tradition was that Donald's army had been victorious. See, for example, Macphail, *Highland Papers*, I, 30-1, and Mac Mhaighstir Alasdair's reference *Nach sinn air beagan mhìltean linn/A thug linn fhìn Harlà.*

3 In Glasgow University Library.

4 In the National Library of Scotland. Unfortunately the McNicol MSS. are not numbered, nor is there a published catalogue; this makes precise reference difficult.

5 Rev. Donald McNicol, *Remarks on Dr. Samuel Johnson's Journey to the Hebrides*, etc. (London, 1779), 263–4.

6 W. Matheson, *The Songs of John MacCodrum* (Edinburgh, 1938), lines 1757–8.

7 We may note, in passing, other eighteenth-century evidence of know-ledge of the Brosnachadh: in the McNicol MSS. there is a poem, of the *aisling* type so well known in Ireland, ascribed to Hector MacLeod, the South Uist poet. This includes a section of *prosniche* of the MacDonalds, beginning 'Chlannibh milidh, mosglibh', using alliteration, and includ-ing several epithets which appear in the Harlaw Brosnachadh. (A version of this appeared in the A. and D. Stewart Collection, p. 287.)

8 Highland Society's Report, App. p. 40.

9 *Ibid.*, 276.

10 From a note in McLagan MS. 122 it seems certain that James MacIntyre was the 'gentleman in Argyllshire' possessed of a copy of the Bros-nachadh. McLagan says that MacIntyre possesses a MS. containing the adventures of 'Smerbie *mor*', and also 'Clann Uisneachan'. McLagan's statement is closely similar to McNicol's in *Remarks* 263, although McNicol does not mention MacIntyre in this context.

11 Pp. 161–3.

12 Instead of translating each of the epithets by an adverb I have, for the most part, used the formula 'Be (adjective, adjective)'.

13 See T. F. O'Rahilly, *Irish Dialects, Past and Present* (Dublin, 1932), 64.

14 *Ibid.*, 200.

15 J. L. Campbell and D. S. Thomson, *Edward Lhuyd in the Scottish Highlands, 1699–1700*, 214.

16 *Ibid.*, 149.

17 *Ibid.*, 131.

18 Using the word in a relative rather than a strictly linguistic sense.

19 But it may be noted that Mac Mhaighstir Alasdair used *confhach*. See the edition of the 'Birlinn' in *Sàr Orain*, ed. Angus MacLeod (Glasgow, 1933), line 461.

20 *Ibid.*, line 292.

21 P. 132.

22 It must ruefully be admitted that this would be an inauspicious starting point.

23 Alexander Cameron, *Reliquiae Celticae* (Inverness, 1892), vol. 11, 260.

24 *Ibid.*, 264.

25 Collections of Register House Charters, No. 517.

26 Quoted in F. J. E. Raby, *A History of Secular Latin Poetry in the Middle Ages* (Oxford, 1934), vol. 1, 216.

27 *Ibid.*, 249.

28 N. Ross, *Heroic Poetry from the Book of the Dean of Lismore* (Edinburgh, 1939), 60–8.

29 *Ibid.*, 64.

R. L. THOMSON

Edward Lhuyd in the Isle of Man?

The recent publication in *Edward Lhuyd in the Scottish Highlands 1699–1700* (Oxford, 1963; hereafter *ELSH*) of Lhuyd's original notes of two forms of the Scottish Gaelic equivalents of the classified vocabulary in Ray's *Dictionariolum* makes possible a closer examination of the material labelled as Scottish Gaelic in his *Archæologia Britannica* (hereafter *AB*), pp. 290–8 (and 41–179, cf. *ELSH*, pp. 229–31). The comparison of *AB* with the original notes is not without importance in assessing the value of the material printed in *AB*, and in showing how it might have been transformed in its passage from notebook to printed page. Lhuyd is not necessarily to be held responsible for the printed version, for this section (Tit. VIII) was compiled by his assistant D. Parry, but the work was very likely done at Lhuyd's suggestion, and perhaps even under his supervision. The editors of *ELSH*, Dr. J. L. Campbell and Professor D. S. Thomson, are undoubtedly correct in stating (p. 229) that 'nearly all these words [i.e. the Scottish words in *AB*] are clearly derived from the translation of Ray's Dictionariolum'; this is put beyond doubt by the erroneous gloss on *hircus* (s. Caprinum genus) being the same as that of the *Dictionariolum* VIII. 36, where it is misplaced from the following lemma. At the same time, the material printed in *ELSH* cannot be quite the only source, for two items in the Appendix to Tit. VIII (hereafter *Appx*), the glosses on *canis* and *mare*, do not occur there.

Of the 154 Latin lemmata in the *Appx* only 76 have Scottish equivalents (as against 95 Manx ones, and a complete rendering in Irish), but, as many items are separately recorded for two different dialects, and occasionally more than one word is given for each dialect, the total of Scottish words is 110. Of these no fewer than 85 suffer some change in passing into print. Many of these changes, often more than one in each word (there are in all about 130 of them), are systematic. Lhuyd had noted his Gaelic words in what is to all intents and purposes Welsh orthography, and, apart from difficulties with palatalized consonants and the frequent occurrence of [ə] in final syllables, where Welsh *y* is not an entirely suitable rendering, the method is reasonably effective. It is, of course, like the examples of early Modern English in the same orthography, capable of revealing features of pronunciation that are concealed by a traditional spelling.

Throughout *AB* Lhuyd modified the orthography of Irish and Welsh by substituting symbols from his General Alphabet (the germ of a true phonetic alphabet) in order to ensure an approximately correct pronunciation in cases where he thought the usual spelling might prove misleading, especially to English readers. He writes (*AB*, p. 1): 'The reason then, that I make use of this General Alphabet, is because it frequently removes those false Colours wherewith the different Orthography of these Languages have disguis'd their Words; in so much . . ., that such as are not acquainted with each Language, nor accustom'd to Etymological Observations, can hardly discern their Affinity.'

Thus he uses dotted y for [ə] (though his definitions, based no doubt on his own Welsh pronunciation of English, suggest [ʌ]) to avoid the misinterpretation [i] or [ai], Greek χ in case ch should be read as [tʃ], Hiberno-Saxon ȝ before e, i, and y to avoid the mis-reading [dȝ], dotted u for [u(:)] to avoid [ʌ] or [ju:], and so forth. He also supplies the circumflex accent as a length-mark.

It need cause no surprise, then, to find that in *Appx* Lhuyd's *y* becomes *ẏ* in some 28 cases, or that his *ch* becomes χ in 14, or that *u* on 23 occasions (8 of them dotted) is substituted for his *w*. These three classes alone account for half the total alterations made. It is rather less satisfactory to find that on 18 occasions a circumflex has been omitted, only once with a doubled vowel (frẏẏχ gl. erica) by way of alternative indication of length, or that on three occasions the dot over a vowel (of uncertain meaning) has been omitted, or that on four occasions (all quite plausible) the circumflex has been added. One acute is omitted (megan gl. arbor), and one added (gavín gl. vacca, s. Bos). On 13 occasions a grave accent is omitted; the function of this accent is not certain, but it seems likely that Lhuyd used it as in Welsh, to indicate the shortness of a vowel which, according to Welsh usage, would be or might be expected to be long. Its use in his notes was probably only for his own benefit; in *AB* it could be omitted, as his readers would not be likely to assume that any vowel was long unless so marked. There are three instances each of the substitution of *k* for his manuscript *c* and of 3 for his *g*, and in two cases double consonants, of uncertain significance, but perhaps affected by the traditional spellings *beann* and *coille*, have been simplified. There are also about a dozen unclassifiable changes, some implying a difference of pronunciation, some purely graphic. The information about the sources of the Gaelic words is notably less complete in *Appx* than in the *Dictionariolum*, and 27 items have lost their localizing prefix in the process of being transferred from manuscript to print.

Since practically all the head-words in *Appx*, with the exception of *mors*, *vita*, and the five verbs (*loquor*, *ludo*, *no*, *video*, *volo*) also occur in the *Dictionariolum* it is clearly not lack of material that caused so many of the Scottish words to be omitted from *Appx*, though there may have been some difficulty in finding them in a hurry. The most probable reason for the omission of nearly 60 items is that they were practically identical with one or other of the Irish words under the same heading; only two words having one form in the *Dictionariolum* and another in the Irish of the *Appx* are omitted (s. vv. *brachium*, *rastrum*). On the other hand, similarity of form is clearly no *regular* criterion for omission, for at least 50 of the 79 Scottish words actually entered are very similar to the corresponding Irish entries. There seems, therefore, to be some element of chance in whether Scottish examples were included in any particular case.

With these points about the Scottish material in the *Appx* in mind we may now turn to the Manx. The total number of items is larger than in the Scottish list, 95 in all, or nearly two-thirds of the Latin. The material is as follows. For comparison with *ELSH* the list is arranged in the same way, and to each item is added the normal modern (Biblical) Manx spelling and a representative spelling of the first Prayer Book of 1610, if it occurs there.

Acus	Snèd	snaid	snaidje (g.sg.)
Albus	Ben	bane	bayn
Amnis	Aon	awin	oanyn (pl.)
Annus	Blïen	blein	bleyn
Aqua	Wystèe	ushtey	uisky
Aratrum	'Tzeirach	shesheragh	
Arbor	Bille	billey	bille

Argentum	Arget	argid	argyd, argyt
Asinus	Assŷl	assyl	assyll
Avena	Koirkie	corkey	
Avis	Ien, nien	eean	æn
Auris	Klyss	cleaysh	kluash
Aurum	Eèr	airh	ayr
Bos	Dow	dow	dou
Taurus	Tarw	tarroo	teryuf, terriu (pl.)
Vacca	Bụa	booa	buo
Vitulus	Leigh	lheiy	lyei
Brachium	Ri	roih	rii
Cæruleus	Gorm	gorrym	gorym
Calceus	Breg	braag	brayg
Canis	Mawda	moddey	mody
Cannabis	Kadip	kennip	
Caprinum genus			
Hircus	Gaawr	goayr	goer, pl. goyr
Capra	Gaawr verin	goayr woirrin	
Caput	'Tchynn	kione	kian
Caro	Phil	feill	feyl
Catus	Chat	kayt	
Cervus	Fieigh	feeaih	fiiei (?)
Cibus	Bî	bee	bii
Cor	Krî	cree	kri
Cornu	Erk	eairk	eyrk, erick
Corpus	Korp	corp	korp
Dens	Phegil	feeackle	feakylyn, fiek- (pl.)
Digitus	Mer	mair	meyr
Dorsum	Drym	dreeym	drym
Equus	Kabyl	cabbyl	kapyl, kabyl
Equa	Lèr	laair	
Facies	Adyn	eddin	edyn, ydyn

173

Falx	Korran	corran	
Ferrum	Iaàrn	yiarn	iarn
Filia	Ennien	inneen	iniin
Filius	Mack	mac	mack
Frater	Breyr	braar	braer
Gramen	Pher, Treiach [Hay]	faiyr, traagh	feyr, tragh
Hortus	Gàre	garey	gayr, garr
Ignis	Aul	aile	angil
Infans	Neinfan		
Insula	Alyn	ellan	ellanyn (pl.)
Lacus	Lwch	logh	
Lana	Ylan	ollan	olan
Lapis	Kloχ	clagh	klagh
Lepus	Mu̯yaχ	mwaagh	
Lingua	'Tchania	chiangey	chiange
Linum	Lin	lieen	liyn
Luna	Nèst	eayst	(i)æsk, eask
Luteus	Bwyí	bwee, buigh	
Manus	Law	laue	lau
Mare	Kean	keayn	kien, keyn
Mater	Mymmog	mummig, -og	mummug
Mons	Sliew	slieau	sleu
Mulier	Ban	ben	ben
Murus	Vawl	voalley	ball, ?vall
Nasus	Stroan	stroin	stroanyn (pl.)
Niger	Dw	doo	? dou
Oculus	Swil	sooill	suill
Os, oris	Buel	beeal	beal, beyl
Os, ossis	Kreẏv	craue	knau, (kneefrii)
Ovis	Kẏrri (? pl.)	keyrrey, pl. kirree	kyry, pl. kirri

174

Vervex	Molt	molt	
Aries	Ri	rea	reaghyn (pl.)
Agnus	Yẏn	eayn	eyn, yean
Ovum	Ov	ooh	
Pater	Diseg	jishig	
Pes	Skass	cass	kass
Pileus	Barn	bayrn	
Plumbum	Lur	leoaie	
Potus	Joch, vai	jough vie	jogh vei
Pratum	Leena	lheeannee	
Radix	Rwt		
Rota	Quilyn (pl.)	queeylyn (pl.)	quiil (sg.)
Ruber	Jerg	jiarg	jarg
Rupes	Kreig	creg	kregg
Sanguis	Phụl	fuill	fuill
Sol	Gryen	grian	grian, grien
Soror	Sywr	shuyr	sheur
Stella	Rẏlag	rollage	redlayg
Sus	Mẏckwerin	muck woirrin	muck
Aper	Kallach	collagh	kollagh
Sylva	Magin	maidjyn (pl.)	
Terra	Talụ	thalloo	tallu
Triticum	Kornacht	curnaght	kurnaght
Venter	Bolg	bolg	bolg
Ventus	Geiach, [gèe]	? geayagh (adj.), geay	gyei, gya, gyæ
Vir	Dẏnẏ (? pl.)	deiney, sg. dooinney	dene, sg. duyne
Ursus	Ber		

There is the same large measure of coincidence of form between the Manx and the Irish words entered and omitted as between the Scottish Gaelic and the Irish, so that the principle of selection is just as obscure and apparently random. Two examples (s. v. *cor*, and *ovis-vervex*), the first labelled *Sc.* & *Mon.*, the second *Hib.* & *Mon.*, show that identity of two forms need not exclude one as superfluous. The order of entry is normally Irish-Scottish-Manx when all three are present, as they are in 47 instances, but in 14 of these (s. vv. *amnis, aqua, capra, equa, lingua, luna, niger, pileus, pratum, rota, soror, sus, sylva, venter*) the Manx word occupies the middle place. This may mean that Parry had in front of him three notebooks or similar collections of material, which he did not always take up in the same order, and which he sometimes did not consult, or found defective, or in which he could not find the relevant information.

This Manx material is the earliest collection of vocabulary that we have, and its occurrence in *AB* is probably the first appearance of the language in print. The early seventeenth-century translation of the English Book of Common Prayer (hereafter *PB*) was not printed until 1894; Lhuyd's book received its imprimatur on 9 April 1707, and in a letter before 27 May 1707 he writes of it as having completed printing (*Life and Letters of Edward Lhwyd*, ed. R. T. Gunther (*Early Science in Oxford* XIV) Oxford, 1945); Bishop Wilson wrote on 30 May 1707 'I finished and printed my Manx Catechism', which Keble (*Life of Thomas Wilson*) (Oxford, 1863, p. 251) understood to mean that he sent it to the printers on that date.

The orthography of this vocabulary is mixed: none of it is written in the spelling of *PB*, though there are inevitably some coincidences of form like *korp, bolg*, and it represents in any case a later form of the language; nor is the orthography that of the 1707 Catechism and therefore, with minor modifications, of all subsequent printed Manx, a system exhibiting some similarities to the *PB* spelling, but in many important ways affected by early Modern and perhaps even by late Middle English spelling conventions. In discussing the vocabulary in 1962 (*Journal of the Manx Museum*, VI, 149–51, where the phonological information that can be extracted from these words is also summarized), I drew attention to the mixed nature of the spelling, but the conclusions I then attempted to draw now require some modification in the light of *ELSH*. The words attributed directly to Lhuyd in that article because of their use of some symbols peculiar to his General Alphabet may now be more properly regarded as his or Parry's modifications of forms noted in Welsh spelling; those in Welsh spelling, instead of suggesting a different source of information, as I then supposed, are now to be interpreted in all probability as direct transcriptions from Lhuyd's notes. Thus the two classes are united, and have a common origin but a slightly different history of transmission from the notebook to the printed page of *AB*. The following words are members of this united class: (*a*) with General Alphabet symbols or the circumflex accent—asṡyl, bî, blïen, bụa, dẏnẏ, kloχ, krî, kreẏv, kẏrri, mụyaχ, mẏckwerin, phụl, rẏlag, talụ, yẏn; (*b*) with Welsh values of *u, w, y, i* (consonant), and *ch*—aul, buel, bwyí, drym, dw, geiach, iaàrn, joch vai, kallach, kornacht, law, lwch, rwt, swil, sywr, tarw, treiach, tzeirach, wystèe, ylan.

There are, of course, many other words besides these 35 that may have been recorded by Lhuyd in person. A considerable number of them lack any mark of length in *AB* on the vowel which could have had a circumflex in the notes, though there is also some evidence here for the use of the grave accent as a length-mark, as in *eèr, gàre, lèr, snèd*. The use of final *-e* with the value of a separate syllable, as in *bille* and *gàre* may be Lhuydian. The choice of *e* as the symbol for the Manx reflex of Irish *á* (and sometimes *ó*) where *PB* and later orthography use *a* and digraphs based on *a*, is a clear sign that the notation is independent of ordinary orthography, and testifies to the marked fronting of the sound in Manx; examples occur under *acus, albus, aurum, calceus, equa, frater*. The use of *k* is very common in *ELSH*, and *ph* for [f], though not frequent there, does occur in a few cases like *pheanag* and *phiachgil*. Both these features are found in *PB* as well, the first regularly, the second sporadically (cf. the glossary of early Manx in *ZCP* XXV under *faase, fainney, faaishnaght, feayn, feeyn, flaaoil, foldeyr* and *phadeyr* and its derivatives, in which alone it survives into later spelling).

A handful of words, however, seem to contain instances of sound-values that cannot be attributed to Lhuyd: e.g. *fieigh, gaawr, kean, leena, leigh, magin, mawda, stroan, vawl*, in which silent *gh*, *aw* and *oa* for [ɔː], *ee* for [iː], final *-a* for [ə], and *g* for [dʒ] are all in conflict with other examples of the same sounds or spellings elsewhere in the list.

The evidence from orthography suggests that at some time Lhuyd must have been in contact with a Manx speaker, and taken the opportunity, as he did with Robert Stewart at Oxford in 1704 (*ELSH*, pp. 92–3), of working through his questionnaire, Ray's *Dictionariolum*, with him and noting the responses in his usual Welsh-based orthography. The small number of words the form of which is inconsistent with this interpretation, suggests that in addition Lhuyd must have supplemented this information by correspondence. The absence from the Manx list of any translations of those Latin head-words in the *Appx* which are not represented in the questionnaire tends to support the same conclusion. Unless Lhuyd's notes re-appear it must remain uncertain how much of the questionnaire he was able to get through with his Manx informant, for some sections are not represented in the *Appx* at all. *ELSH* shows that Lhuyd had taken notes of all 32 sections, but only 18 of these are attested by examples in the *Appx*. In the same way only 16 or 17 of the sections are attested by the Manx words in the *Appx*, but it would be rash to assume that no others were translated.

There is, perhaps, a little evidence that Lhuyd may have collected a few Manx phrases, like the Gaelic ones printed in *ELSH*, and that, as with those examples, he may not always have succeeded in analysing them correctly into their constituent words. For example, *chat* and *tzeirach* (the latter probably misprinted or miscopied) both seem to imply a preceding article, though even this will not explain *tchynn* for Gaelic *ceann*; the spelling *skass* for 'foot' seems to be extracted from some phrase such as *laue as cass* 'hand and foot', or *rass as cass* lit. 'seed and stalk', i.e. 'root and branch', 'utterly'.

We have very little direct information about the circumstances in which Lhuyd gathered his Scottish material: for his Manx material there seems to be none at all. There are no details in the *Letters* or in *AB* itself about the genesis of the Appendix to the British Etymologicon beyond the statement in the preface that Parry had compiled Tit. VIII and its appendix. The editor of the *Letters*, R. T. Gunther, believed he had one reference to Parry's work in a letter (p. 460, 20 July 1701) in which Lhuyd refers to a Mr. Parry's *Dictionary* as a source from which he had extracted the meat by copying, apparently during his Welsh tour; but in the context it seems more likely that a MS. Welsh dictionary, or another copy of Davies's *Dictionarium Duplex* with MS. additions, is meant.

Nor does it seem possible to fit a visit to the Isle of Man into Lhuyd's itinerary during his grand tour, for though the details of his timetable are often uncertain, of the two most likely points, the crossing from Wales to Ireland in August 1699 and from Scotland to Ireland in January 1700, the first has no mention of a detour, and the second did not allow time as he was stormbound at Campbeltown for about five weeks.

There are two references to Manx in the letters. The first, from one addressed to the palaeographer Humphrey Wanley on 8 February 1704 (p. 495), in which it appears that Lhuyd knew of Bishop Phillips's activity as a translator, and in which he asked Wanley, if he wrote to Man, to request a copy of Leviticus XI. It is probably in vain to speculate about Wanley's Manx correspondent, for it is not even certain that he ever wrote to Man; he may merely have mentioned to Lhuyd that he thought of writing there to inquire after MSS. No doubt the bishop would be the obvious person to address in the first instance. From Lhuyd's wanting Leviticus XI with its list of animal and bird names, we may deduce with equal plausibility that he wanted these items in order to make a start on sections 7 to 11 of the *Dictionariolum*, or to supplement defective information already received in answers to this part of his questionnaire. If anything, the latter is a little more probable, and would mean that by the end of 1703 at the latest he had already met and interrogated his Manx informant. There may be a parallel here with the Scottish words in *AB*, in that although printing began in October 1703 (*Letters*, p. 492), the copy went to the press piecemeal and additional material for as yet unfinished parts continued to be welcome to the author; thus his northern Scottish Gaelic material was acquired as late as August 1704 (cf. *ELSH* 92–3).

The second relevant letter is dated 18 January 1708 (p. 540), and is rather difficult to interpret. The relevant passage reads:

> The Manks Catechism I miss'd to have a copy of, being out of town when the Bishop was here and enquired for me. Their language is not onely a dialect of the Irish, as the Cornish of the British, but is also (what we cannot say of the Cornish) as intelligible to the people of Ireland as a Scottishman is in South Britain. I hope the Bishop took care to have the Catechism read to 3 or 4 people in manuscript before he put it in the presse, and so to adapt the orthography to their pronunciation with extraordinary care. 'Tis certain that whoever perus'd, never read a page of Irish or Manks, for he uses not onely the English orthography, for which I should never find any fault, but often makes 2 or 3 words of one, and as often unites as many.

The first sentence might mean that Lhuyd was not in Oxford on

3 April when Bishop Wilson received his honorary D.D., but as the book was then not yet printed he could not have been given a copy of it on that occasion; more probably the reference is to an unrecorded visit when Wilson was on his way back to Man in August or September 1707, for it is clear from the fourth sentence that at the time of writing Lhuyd had seen the printed book. The third sentence implies that Lhuyd knew that Manx had no established orthography, and he therefore hoped that Wilson had adapted his spelling to actual pronunciation. This is partly contradicted by the fourth sentence, which, as it stands, implies that Lhuyd was familiar with Manx written differently from the Catechism, not only in respect of spelling but also of word-division. While this may possibly mean that he had seen a specimen of the Phillipsian orthography, it is more likely that 'Manks' here is miswritten (as being the idea uppermost in Lhuyd's mind) for 'Scotch Gaelic', and that the complaint is that the proof-reader ('whoever perus'd'), being unaware of traditional Gaelic orthography, had perpetrated a number of unhistorical word-divisions, though the author's choice of a non-Gaelic spelling is not regarded as a fault. If, as Keble conjectures (*Life*, p. 251), the Rev. William Walker, rector of Ballaugh, accompanied Bishop Wilson to London and read the proofs of the Manx text there, Lhuyd's assumption of the author's and proof-reader's ignorance of traditional Gaelic spelling is no doubt justified.

While William Walker would have made an admirable informant this visit to Oxford in the late summer of 1707 (if visit there was) is, of course, far too late to supply the matter in the *Appx*, which must have been printed by at least August 1706 (*Letters*, p. 510). The date may indeed require to be earlier than this. In Tit. II, which is, in effect, a Latin-Celtic dictionary, there occurs under Cuculus the entry *Man.* kivag. This, as it stands, is most unlikely for Manx since intervocalic [v] had disappeared or been absorbed in a long vowel or diphthong at least a century earlier (cf. *Celtica*, V, 122), and it at first seems likely that *Man.* here is a misprint for *Mun.*, and that this is one of the Munster words collected by Lhuyd in the spring and summer of 1700. *Mun.* occurs, for example, under Folium, glossed *billôg*. The fact of the matter is, however, as Dr. J. L. Campbell kindly informs me, that while *billôg* is certainly in Lhuyd's MS. notebook for Munster, his word for 'cuckoo' in the same place is *kŵach*, so that *Man.* cannot be a misprint, and at least one Manx word seems to have got into Tit. II. The error, in all probability, is of *kivag* for *kŵag*, the sort of spelling we should expect Lhuyd to give for Manx *cooag*. Tit. II was in the press and nearly completed before the end of July 1705 (*Letters*, p. 504), so that this early point in the alphabet must have been printed some weeks or even months previously. It seems probable, therefore, on this evidence, that Lhuyd's Manx words in his own notation must have been collected by at least the end of 1704.

Walker may, however, have supplied in correspondence the words in the English spelling referred to above (p. 177) as untypical of Lhuyd's notation. Bishop Wilson paid a number of visits to England between first entering his diocese in April 1698 and the visit of 1707, but apart from his wife and children we rarely know who accompanied him. One such occasion was the visit from 6 August to 10 September 1703, when he mentions (*Life*, p. 184) being accompanied by one David Christian on a visit to Lord Derby, but this was a very short stay on important business on behalf of his flock, and, as Lord Derby was at Lathom at the time, it is very unlikely that Lhuyd could have met them on that occasion.

The second sentence of the letter quoted above is susceptible of various interpretations. Lhuyd may be repeating a statement made by an Irishman (perhaps during his tour in 1700) or by a Manxman at some unspecified date; neither situation is very helpful for our present purpose. Lhuyd may be speaking from personal observation, implying that on some occasion he had been in company with speakers of the two languages simultaneously. Since the truth of his statement is rather doubtful (the content excludes the possibility that he is using 'Irish' to include Scottish Gaelic, in which case there might have been more truth in it), it is quite possible that he means no more than that he has observed that a very high proportion of the vocabulary is not only cognate but retains a very similar form, and that his assertion of mutual intelligibility is no more than a deduction from this observation.

We may conclude, therefore, that there is sufficient evidence to show that Lhuyd noted a good deal of Manx material, certainly lexical items and possibly some phrases, in his own system, from a Manx speaker, and that it is very likely that this investigation took the form of working through Ray's *Dictionariolum* as a questionnaire with his informant, though he also obtained a small amount of information by correspondence. There is no evidence to show that Lhuyd ever visited Man, though his movements are so inadequately documented that the possibility cannot be excluded. It is not known who his Manx informants were, but his contact with them must have taken place by the end of 1704 on the evidence of the progress of *AB* through the press, and very probably had occurred before the end of 1703 on the evidence of the letter to Wanley.